NCEA in Context

NCEA in Context

Rosemary Hipkins, Michael Johnston, and Mark Sheehan

NZCER PRESS

NZCER PRESS
New Zealand Council for Educational Research
PO Box 3237
Wellington
New Zealand

© The authors 2016

ISBN 978-0-947509-27-9

This book is not a photocopiable master.
No part of the publication may be copied, stored or communicated
in any form by any means (paper or digital), including recording
or storing in an electronic retrieval system, without the written
permission of the publisher. Education institutions that hold a current
licence with Copyright Licensing New Zealand may copy from this
book in strict accordance with the terms of the CLNZ Licence.

A catalogue record for this book is available from the National Library
of New Zealand

Designed by Smartwork Creative Ltd, www.smartworkcreative.co.nz

Distributed by NZCER Distribution Services
PO Box 3237
Wellington
New Zealand
www.nzcer.org.nz

Contents

List of Abbreviations		vi
Acknowledgements		vii

Part 1. The societal context for NCEA

Chapter 1	The context for NCEA: A brief overview	3
Chapter 2	The changing nature of senior secondary schooling	11
Chapter 3	The relationship between curriculum and assessment	21

Part 2. NCEA in the context of known assessment challenges

Chapter 4	Internal assessment	33
Chapter 5	The shift to standards-based assessment	48
Chapter 6	NCEA as a political compromise	67
Chapter 7	The challenges of managing variability in a standards-based environment	81
Chapter 8	The Scholarship crisis and its aftermath	93
Chapter 9	A culture of continuous improvement	108
Chapter 10	Moderation and teachers' professional learning	122
Chapter 11	Assessment in context	134

Part 3. The curriculum as a context for NCEA

Chapter 12	Aligning curriculum and assessment	151
Chapter 13	The washback from NCEA to teaching and learning	164
Chapter 14	The learning experience for students	181

Part 4. (Re)imagining NCEA as a complex system

Chapter 15	Reimagining NCEA	205
References		218
The authors		227
Index		228

List of Abbreviations

ABA	Achievement based assessment
ART	Achievement, Retention, Transition
CICAQ	Committee of Inquiry into Curriculum, Assessment and Qualifications in Forms 5 to 7
ERO	Education Review Office
HPE	Health and Physical Education
NCEA	National Certificate of Educational Achievement
NZC	*The New Zealand Curriculum*
NZQA	New Zealand Qualifications Authority
NZQF	New Zealand Qualifications Framework
NZTA	New Zealand Transport Agency
PEP	Profile of Expected Performance
PPTA	Post Primary Teachers' Association
SPAG	Scholarship Processes Advisory Group
STAG	Scholarship Technical Advisory Group
SOLO	Structured Observations of Learning Outcomes
TEC	Tertiary Education Commission
UE	University Entrance
UEB	University Entrance Board

Acknowledgements

In the early stages of writing this book we interviewed several people who played key roles in the development and critique of NCEA in its early years: Kate Colbert; Jim Strachan; Bali Haque; Cedric Hall; Roger Moses; and Gregor Fountain. We are grateful for their candid insights, which shed valuable light on the complexities of building an innovative national assessment policy within the political and practical constraints of the times.

We owe special thanks to the school leaders and teachers who shared innovative thinking about how to make best use of NCEA, with their students' learning needs in mind. Those whose stories appear in these pages include: Maurie Abrahams; Terry Burrell; Kirsty Farrant; Shelley Gilman; Helen Lowther; and Gerard MacManus. Thank you for being patient as we got these stories right. We are mindful that this group is small in number and many more New Zealand teachers and school leaders are achieving wonderful things on a daily basis. We like to think that the many innovators who have inspired us were all with us in spirit.

Critique is important and our thanks also go to the other researchers whose work we drew on. You didn't do your work specifically for us but our journey was enriched because of your efforts.

Some of Rose's time was supported by NZCER's Government Grant which is agreed with the Ministry of Education.

Bali Haque and Cathy Wylie provided valuable feedback on the final draft. Thank you for your insights and advice.

PART 1. THE SOCIETAL CONTEXT FOR NCEA

This is a book in four parts. Each part explores the National Certificate of Educational Achievement (NCEA) through the lens of a different type of context. We begin in Part 1 with changing aspects of New Zealand society, including the economy and employment patterns, along with changing expectations and pressures on schools in the mid-20th century. In Part 2 we explore NCEA in the context of challenges that need to be addressed within *any* high-stakes assessment system. Then in Part 3 we ask how NCEA does, or could, work in the context of New Zealand's national curriculum, which is a framework on which all schools are expected to build their own local curriculum. Finally, in Part 4 we briefly introduce ideas from the field of complexity theory. We take these ideas as a context within which we review NCEA's potential to be a dynamic, adaptive assessment system for the 21st century.

Chapter 1 The context for NCEA: A brief overview

In the first decade of the 21st century New Zealand introduced a new standards-based qualification system for secondary schools. One important component of this system was a new school-exit qualification called the National Certificate of Educational Achievement (NCEA). NCEA has now been in place for just over a decade. The time seems right to look back over its chequered introduction and the subsequent trajectory of its development. We initially called this book *NCEA in Context* because we could not examine NCEA itself in isolation from its many social and educational influences.

The book explores many key questions about NCEA. We discuss why it was introduced, how it was implemented, and the challenges and opportunities that have emerged as this qualification system has evolved since implementation began in 2002. NCEA saw a seismic shift in assessment for qualifications. This shift took us away from the norm-referenced assessment model that shaped the way secondary schools operated during the second half of the 20th century, under which predetermined proportions of students passed and failed. We moved to a standards-referenced model, under which students are assessed against specific criteria. Students are now required to demonstrate competence against specific learning goals, in units of assessment called *standards*. These standards can be assessed either internally (by schools) or externally (usually by public examination).

Alongside the change to assessment, a new school curriculum was introduced—*The New Zealand Curriculum* (*NZC*) (Ministry of Education, 2007). *NZC* complements NCEA in many respects, including its framing of achievement objectives. However it was not published until several years after the full implementation of NCEA had been completed. Enacting the sweeping changes called for by NCEA and *NZC* has required a significant shift in thinking about the purpose of secondary school assessment and a major reorientation for students, teachers, parents, and other stakeholders involved in secondary school qualifications.

In the second section of the book we develop the argument that, contrary to what is implied by many NCEA critics, there was no golden age before NCEA, when all was well with assessment and learning in the senior secondary school. In any case, NCEA was not a brand-new concept. Rather, it was a compromise that combined elements of previous assessment models (e.g., external examinations) with more innovative approaches (e.g., the splitting of assessment into small components). It was an outcome of many a number of attempts to introduce alternative assessment models during the previous 40 years, with the aim of accommodating the changing nature of secondary schooling. Thus the time before NCEA, with all its growing pressures for change, is an important contextual element that we have woven into our analysis throughout the subsequent chapters.

NCEA was welcomed by many in the education sector when it was introduced, but those familiar with its development will be aware that there were initial implementation problems. We include a frank discussion of these—they too, are part of the NCEA context. While many of these problems have now been addressed, NCEA regularly continues to generate new controversies as it continues to evolve. In part this is because innovation in any field has a tendency to generate controversy. This is especially true of innovation that explicitly seeks to overturn entrenched practices and hierarchies, as NCEA does. A related consideration is that secondary school qualifications carry high stakes for students, parents, and teachers. All these groups are sensitive to (and concerned about) any changes to assessment in the schooling sector that they perceive to be potentially detrimental, either to students' learning or to schools' reputations.

We think there is also another really important, but less obvious, dimension to the NCEA question that we would like to see attain greater prominence in the public debate. For us, curriculum thinking is a key contextual frame for critique of NCEA. It is an educational truism that assessment drives curriculum. In this book we explore the manner in which NCEA has impacted on students' and their teachers' approaches to, and experiences of, the senior secondary curriculum, for better and for worse. Towards the end of the book we make some suggestions about ways in which sophisticated approaches to the use of NCEA can support the existing potential of the curriculum to develop rich learning experiences that motivate students and deepen their educational experience. Our examples are drawn from current practice—some teachers and schools are already using NCEA in innovative ways that bring real benefit for their students' learning.

NCEA was set up as a flexible standards-based model that aimed to be inclusive of all students. This included those who have previously been excluded from gaining qualifications simply on the basis of their position in a rank-ordering of assessment results, and for whom the schooling process was typically an alienating, negative experience. Judged superficially on the twin bases of improvement in the proportions of young people achieving qualifications, and of senior secondary school retention, NCEA appears to have been highly successful. Young people are motivated to stay at school for longer than they ever have before, and the proportions of them who achieve qualifications are increasing. The increase includes students who would typically have left school without any qualifications under the previous assessment system. On closer inspection, however, it is not altogether clear whether the increase in qualifications attainment always represents an improvement in the learning of what we might call "knowledge that matters" or "powerful knowledge". One of the important questions that we address in this book is posed by a book edited by British educationalists Michael Young and David Lambert: what do increasing qualifications mean if they don't result in a more well informed and knowledgeable population? (Young & Lambert, 2014).

Just to be clear, we think that NCEA is producing many well-educated young scholars, across a range of domains of study, who are well-prepared for either tertiary or vocational pathways. However, some students appear to be gaining their NCEA qualifications by accumulating credits in a more haphazard manner. They may be gaining NCEA qualifications, but they are not necessarily gaining knowledge that provides them with either a clear vocational direction, or with sound understanding of established fields of inquiry. Beyond the somewhat facile and anachronistic divide between "vocational" and "academic" learning, we believe that a capacity for *critical thinking* is an essential component of education in a healthy democracy. However, despite claims to the contrary, it is not clear to us that all students participating in NCEA are experiencing the kinds of rich learning that develops the capacity to think critically and to make reasoned and evidence-based judgements. We agree with theorists who claim that these qualities lie at the heart of what it means to be educated. They are "as important for the brain surgeon and the Airbus pilot they are for the beauty therapist and the car mechanic" (Biesta, 2014, p. 32). To return to our point about there never having been a golden age in education, we hasten to add that students who are not being well served by NCEA would probably not have been successful under the previous assessment regime either. But NCEA is still a work in progress, and we think we can all do better.

What is NCEA and how does it work?

The following is a brief introduction for those unfamiliar with the structure of NCEA awards and the processes that allow students to achieve these qualifications. Readers who are familiar with NCEA may want to skip straight to the next chapter at this point. This is a bare bones outline. Many of the points are discussed in more detail in the various chapters of Section 2.

NCEA is one of the most complicated school qualification systems in the world. Since its initial implementation in 2002 it has evolved formally, through the introduction of initiatives such as endorsements, and informally, in terms of the way in which it is used by teachers and schools. In this initial overview of NCEA, we will focus on its present state. The ways in which it has evolved are described in detail in the chapters that follow.

The qualification comprises three levels, with one level typically approached in each of the final 3 years of secondary school: in Year 11, students usually work towards a Level 1 certificate; in Year 12, towards a Level 2 certificate; and in Year 13, a Level 3 certificate. However, students can and do vary from this pattern, with some students attaining a level of NCEA ahead of the typical year and many taking more than one year to gain a given level.

To gain NCEA, students accumulate credits from assessment units called *standards*. These units are much finer-grained than the subject level at which most formal assessment took place under the previous assessment system. The assessment programme for a typical year-long secondary course might carry around 18–20 credits of assessment across about five or six standards. Thus most standards carry 3–5 credits, although a few carry substantially more than this. A typical secondary student (if there is any such person) enters for between about 90 and 110 credits in a given year.

The standards used for NCEA, as well as the qualifications themselves, are all registered at one of ten levels of the New Zealand Qualifications Framework (NZQF), which comprises a great many tertiary-level qualifications as well as NCEA. Most (but not all) of the standards that are typically used to contribute to NCEA come from the first three levels of the NZQF.

Standards come in two broad kinds. Achievement standards, of which there are some 800, and which are linked to *NZC*, almost solely contribute to NCEA. Very few, if any, achievement standards can contribute to other qualifications. Unit standards, which are not curriculum linked, mostly contribute to tertiary qualifications. There are thousands of unit standards registered on the NZQF and only a relatively small subset are typically used by secondary school students working towards NCEA, although in theory all could be. There are externally and internally assessed achievement standards, but unit standards are always internally assessed (i.e., close to the point of the learning). Moderation processes are used to manage variability between assessors of internally assessed achievements. Depending on each school's policy, students might be granted one further opportunity[1] to be reassessed for, or resubmit revised work for, some internally assessed standards.

To attain the credits for a standard, a student must meet achievement criteria, as specified in the documentation for that standard. Unit standards specify a single set of criteria, and when they are all met, a student receives the credits for that standard with a grade of Achieved. A few unit standards carry higher grades, but this is atypical. Achievement standards specify three-graded criteria, all of which carry the same number of credits, but which designate increasing levels of quality-of-attainment. Meeting the most straightforward of these criteria results in a grade of Achieved, the next, a grade of Merit, and the most advanced achievement is awarded a grade of Excellence. Both unit and achievement standards, when used to assess school students, result in grades of Not Achieved being recorded if assessment for a standard is attempted but the criteria are not met.

NCEA certificates are gained by accumulating a requisite numbers of credits at each level. To attain NCEA Level 1, a student must gain at least 80 credits registered at NZQF Level 1 or higher. To attain NCEA Level 2, at least 60 credits must be attained at Level 2 or higher, with an additional 20 credits from any level (including Level 1). Similarly, NCEA Level 3 requires 60 credits at Level 3 or higher, and an additional 20 at Level 2 or higher. The only additional requirements include specific literacy and numeracy requirements, which are the same for all three levels: 10 credits must be attained from approved literacy-related standards, and 10 from approved numeracy-related standards.

Credits can be counted towards multiple NCEA levels, so that a student attaining NCEA Level 3 automatically attains Levels 1 and 2 as well, if they have not already done so. Certificates attained with at least 50 Merit credits at or above the level of the certificate attract an endorsement of the certificate at Merit level. Similarly, 50 Excellence credits at or above the level of the certificate attract an Excellence endorsement. Any mix of standards at all, provided it meets the level requirements described above, results in the award of a level of NCEA. This means

---

1 http://www.nzqa.govt.nz/providers-partners/assessment-and-moderation/assessment-of-standards/generic-resources/gathering-evidence-of-achievement/assessment-opportunities-in-schools/

that the concept of a course or subject is in no way captured by the certificate itself. However, schools can use a course code that allows NZQA to recognise which combination of standards is being used to assess that particular course. If a student is attested by the school as participating in a course and attains at least 14 credits declared against that course with Merit or Excellence, they receive a course endorsement at the appropriate level.[2]

We should mention two adjuncts to NCEA which are not formally part of the qualification. One is University Entrance (UE), which entitles a student to enrol in any New Zealand university (although not necessarily in any specific degree programme). To attain UE, a student must gain NCEA Level 3 with at least 42 credits coming from three approved subjects, with at least 14 credits from each, and a literacy requirement that is somewhat more stringent than basic NCEA literacy. The other adjunct is New Zealand Scholarship, which is examined entirely at the subject level, with a largely traditional assessment approach; most Scholarship subjects are assessed by 3-hour examination, although a few—all arts subjects—are assessed by portfolio. Scholarship is undertaken by relatively few students and is designed to recognise high achievement, with a successful result being awarded to just 3 percent of the NCEA Level 3 cohort in each subject.

A note about our use of terminology

Researchers in the field of knowledge use the term *powerful knowledge* to describe knowledge that can help us explain and understand the world (Young 2008; Muller, 2012). Such knowledge is typically generated in subjects that are informed by academic disciplines. These, in turn, are shaped by distinctive methods of inquiry, methodological approaches, theoretical perspectives, and core concepts. It is this sort of knowledge that we have in mind when we use the word *knowledge*. It is important to be clear that we do not simply mean curriculum content. Disciplinary thinking requires a comprehensive understanding of the observational and cognitive procedures that lead to knowledge production and, more than this, experience and practice in the use of

---

[2] At least one standard contributing to a course endorsement must be internally assessed, and at least one, externally assessed.

these procedures. For example, concepts of historical thinking and of scientific practices used for theory testing are powerful because they provide insights into the processes of knowledge production in these disciplines. The field of philosophical inquiry into how disciplinary knowledge is created is called *epistemology*. We debated long and hard about whether to use this more technical term in the book (and the associated adjective, *epistemological*). In the end we decided we should because we saw a risk that what we hoped to convey might be misinterpreted if a specific aspect of the discussion was understood as being about curriculum content per se.

Chapter 2 The changing nature of senior secondary schooling

Policies and practices to do with education, including qualifications and assessment, do not occur in a vacuum. They reflect the values and aspirations of the wider community and the economic and social pressures that a society faces at a particular time. To understand the development of NCEA we need to begin by considering wider questions than those to do with secondary school qualifications. NCEA was introduced as one of several educational initiatives to address the challenges New Zealand faced in the early 21st century. These included the pressures of engaging successfully in a rapidly changing and competitive global marketplace, the increasingly diverse nature of New Zealand society and the changing nature of work. These challenges were not new. They had been apparent since the 1970s when, after 30 years of relative prosperity, stability, and social cohesion, New Zealand found itself facing economic uncertainty and growing unemployment.

Secondary schooling in the post-war years

New Zealand looks very different in the early 21st century than it did in the decades following World War Two. Many of our secondary schools were built in the 1950s and 60s when increasing numbers of young people began to attend secondary school and to stay at school for longer. Until the 1960s most young people attended secondary school for only 2–3 years and the qualifications system reflected the social and economic ethos of these years. New Zealand was a prosperous, socially conservative, largely monocultural society with one of the highest standards of living in the world and a centrally controlled economy that was primarily based on exporting a narrow range of agricultural products for the British market. Most people either worked in the areas related to farming, fishing, and forestry or in small-scale manufacturing enterprises that catered for the local market. There was little manufacturing for the export market and almost all manufactured commodities (such as cars) were imported directly from Britain.

Secondary school assessment was structured to reflect the priorities of New Zealand at the time. Classes were typically streamed, with a majority of students studying academic subjects (e.g., mathematics, English, history, science). The major exit examination was School Certificate, sat at the end of the 5th Form (or Year 11 as it is now known). School Certificate had been introduced in 1945 for those who did not plan to attend university, and it served as an entry qualification for positions in the public service or the business sector (e.g., insurance or banking). Very few young people attained university qualifications and a considerable number left school without any qualifications at all—some, as soon as they turned 15. Only around half of those who stayed at schools for long enough to sit "School C" gained the qualification. This was deliberate—School Certificate examinations were scaled under a norm-referenced model, to produce predetermined distributions of results, with around half of the candidates (the precise percentages varied between subjects) destined to fail. Thus, School Certificate was an explicit social sorting mechanism, as were its contemporaries, the UE and Bursary examinations. The prevailing view of secondary school education was that, for a majority of young people, achieving academic school qualifications was not a priority. Until the oil shock in the early 1970s, unemployment was almost non-existent. Many young people actively continued employment-based learning in the immediate post-school years (e.g., in structured apprenticeships) and there were a many unskilled and semiskilled employment opportunities available, some of which were lucrative and had good prospects.

Economic change as a context for educational change

In the 1970s the national context began to change. The New Zealand economy experienced a number of major blows. These included the loss of the United Kingdom as a major trading partner when it joined what we now call the European Union, and increasing prices for oil and imported manufactured commodities. It became increasingly difficult for New Zealand to maintain the levels of prosperity it had enjoyed in the years after World War Two. Successive governments addressed this crisis by borrowing and the 1970s and 80s were characterised by spiralling inflation, growing unemployment, social unrest, and financial insecurity for many. The areas of the economy that were hardest hit were the agricultural and manufacturing sectors. Unemployment increased dramatically for those who were unskilled and unqualified and many secondary students stayed longer at school. Schools for their part were slow to make provision for the learning needs of these students, continuing instead to focus on the final years of schooling as a preparation for tertiary study (Wylie, 2012, documents commentary to this effect from a 1983 OECD report on New Zealand's schooling system at the end of the 1970s).

While New Zealand was not alone in facing these pressures (the economic problems were an international phenomenon) this country addressed these problems by adopting a market-orientated economic approach when the fourth Labour government came to power in 1984. This was a major shift from the centralised and controlled economic policies of both Labour and National governments since 1945 who largely shared a commitment to government-funded education, health care, and social welfare provisions. Influenced by the ideas of neoliberalism, which was also dominant in the United Kingdom and the United States at the time, the solution to New Zealand's economic problems, it was argued, was to reduce the role of the centralised government and let what was popularly called "market forces" shape responses to the challenges that were faced. The Labour government instigated a radical shift in the political, economic, and social features of society. The centralised economic model of the previous 40 years was dismantled and the size and responsibilities of government departments was reduced. These changes intensified under the National government of the 1990s.

During this period, New Zealand was coming to terms with operating as a small trading nation in an increasingly competitive global environment. The response was a major shift from being one of the most centralised, regulated economies in the western world to one of the most deregulated. On the positive side, this shift contributed to an increasing diversification of the New Zealand economy. High-quality products began to be made and exported, and many New Zealand-made products now have excellent profiles in international markets. The creative industries (such as the film industry) began to flourish and there was substantial growth in service industries such as tourism. In the cultural and social arena the 1990s also saw a growing commitment to address the legacy of New Zealand's colonial past. A number of significant Treaty of Waitangi settlements were made between the government and major iwi. There was a growing awareness of the importance of conservation and the environment. During this period, New Zealand society became more open in other respects as well, with the passage of the homosexual law reform bill in 1986, significant waves of migration from non-European countries, and ever-greater numbers of women participating in the paid workforce all contributing to an increasingly diverse social environment.

It could be argued that aligning the economy with market forces contributed to New Zealand becoming more economically successful by the early 21st century (and most of the changes made in the 1980s and 90s have remained intact). However, the consequences of these policies had an adverse impact on many young people. Opportunities for unskilled and semiskilled labour declined and youth unemployment increased. The most prominent impact of these changes on the secondary schooling sector was that even more young people who would have previously left school with no qualifications (and entered the labour market) stayed on into senior secondary school. The flow-on effect was a growing demand for young people to gain qualifications even if they did not intend to go on to tertiary study. Tertiary study itself became very expensive, and although the numbers of young people participating in tertiary study increased, it became the norm for graduates to be burdened with significant education-related debt.

Inevitably, this changed the way in which many young people oriented to tertiary education; university study in particular began to be seen as a commodity rather than as a cultural experience.

By the turn of the century commentators were calling for New Zealand to become a "knowledge society" (Gilbert, 2005). Internationally, a well-educated society was increasingly seen as the basis of a successful economy (Beare & Slaughter, 1993). As the National Minister of Education, Dr Lockwood Smith, noted:

> If we in New Zealand wish to progress as a nation, and to enjoy a healthy prosperity in today's and tomorrow's competitive world economy, our education system must adapt … We need a learning environment which enables all our students to attain high standards and develop appropriate personal qualities. As we move towards the twenty-first century, with all the rapid technological change which that entails, we need a work-force which is more highly skilled and adaptable and which has an international and multicultural perspective. (Ministry of Education, 1993a, p. 1)

On several fronts, then, pressures were mounting for young people to stay at school longer, and to recognise the achievements of a much greater range of students with qualifications. The radical changes in policy thinking about curriculum and assessment during the 1980s and 90s were largely a response to these pressures and to the rapid social, cultural, and economic changes that had created them.

The last 25 years have also seen an increase in the qualifications needed to access employment that had previously required only minimal qualifications or none at all. For example, in the 1960s the minimum qualification to become a primary school teacher was School Certificate (equivalent to today's Level 1 NCEA). In the second decade of the 21st century it is a 3-year bachelor's degree, and increasingly primary teachers are being encouraged to complete postgraduate qualifications. While market-orientated reforms have had their most adverse impact on young people who have typically not been successful in the schooling sector, even students who were academically successful have found themselves required to attain ever-higher grades to enter particular university courses, and, to borrow substantial sums to fund their tertiary study.

How education policy responded to the challenges

The challenges to the education system posed by the economic and social changes of the 1980s and 90s saw increasing dissatisfaction with the structure of schooling. The existing assessment and curriculum models came under increasing critical scrutiny. Until this time students who were not academically inclined were not a high priority for secondary schools. As we have seen, it was assumed they would leave school with no formal qualifications and enter a labour market that could accommodate them. However, as this assumption began to prove unjustified, pressure came to bear for more students to be retained into the senior school. The normative assessment system, which was built on the assumption that a more-or-less fixed proportion of students would not be retained, was manifestly inadequate in this new environment. Furthermore, a diverse range of interest groups, including Māori and Pasifika activists, feminists, and social conservatives, all claimed that the education system was failing their constituencies. The idea of a centralised school system that catered in the same way for the needs of all students was no longer seen as either possible or desirable given the increasingly diverse nature of the student cohort, and of New Zealand society generally.

Critics had little in common philosophically, but they all agreed that the secondary schooling system needed to become more autonomous and flexible (Openshaw, 2009). Reflecting the wider suspicion of government intervention that was prevalent, they were especially critical of the Department of Education. This institution was characterised as an over-centralised bureaucracy which was slow to respond to challenges, and was a barrier to community involvement in schools and to the achievement of disadvantaged students.

Questioning of the relevance of the externally assessed UE qualification had been growing since the 1970s and now became harder to ignore. UE was based on a narrow range of academic subjects, which did not cater for the increasing number of students at this level who did not intend to study at university. Critics argued for a qualification framework that allowed for more flexible models of teaching and learning, and met the learning needs of all young people. Much of the momentum for this change came from the Post Primary Teachers' Association (PPTA) who had been calling for alternative models of assessment since the late 1960s (Alison, 2008). Although the PPTA's position on internal assessment largely reflected the views of a radicalised leadership rather than those of the wider membership (Openshaw, 2003), these ideas were very influential when the qualification structure was changed in the late 1980s.

In its first term (1984–87) the fourth Labour government responded to these criticisms by instigating widespread curriculum and assessment reform in senior secondary schooling. Russell Marshall (Minister of Education in that government) set up a Committee of Inquiry into Curriculum, Assessment and Qualifications in Forms 5 to 7 (CICAQ) with the objective of introducing alternative methods of assessment. In its report the CICAQ recommended that UE be shifted to Form 7 and that Sixth Form Certificate become the sole national qualification for Form 6. Both recommendations were implemented in 1986. Significantly for the development of NCEA, the CICAQ proposed a shift to a standards-based achievement model. Notwithstanding flaws that were already evident in existing quality assurance systems for managing high-stakes internal assessment, it came to be a central strand of the ongoing impetus for change that finally evolved into NCEA.

A far-reaching curriculum review planned for 1987 would have reshaped secondary school assessment even further. However this was shelved when David Lange replaced Marshall as Minister of Education in 1988. In the wake of the shattering impact of the 1987 sharemarket crash, the Labour government scaled up the sense of urgency around more radical changes in the economy and in education. The government shifted focus during its second term to the administration of schools. Reflecting a distrust of centralised bureaucracy, and a prevailing view that market forces were the best way to address the shortcomings of education, the government introduced a model that made schools more autonomous and self-managing. The introduction of Tomorrow's Schools in 1989 abolished the education boards and their centralised bureaucracy (Minister of Education, 1988). Ironically, schools did actually have considerable autonomy in educational matters—the bureaucracy against which they chaffed concerned matters such as regulations to do with staffing and property. What they did lose in the sweeping policy changes was the advisory network that had kept professional knowledge circulating. This new gap was exacerbated by the intention that schools would now compete rather than cooperate (Wylie, 2012).

Each school was now run by an elected board of trustees made up of parents and community representatives, the principal, and teacher and student representatives. The Department of Education was replaced by a smaller Ministry and an autonomous New Zealand Qualifications Authority (NZQA) replaced the Department's Examination Division. Curriculum and assessment were now seen as separate entities, to be administered by separate organisations. As we will see in the later sections of the book, this separation of responsibilities for assessment and for curriculum would pose a number of challenges with the implementation of NCEA.

The National government (1990–99) had an even greater zeal for market economics than the previous Labour government, and this impacted on their thinking about assessment policies and structures. They moved towards developing a flexible qualifications system that was aligned with a new curriculum framework. This prioritised "the diverse educational and training needs of students" (Ministry of Education, 1993a, p. 8). Education was to be more closely aligned with the economy and business. In this context, NCEA emerged as a flexible, portable assessment model to cater for the needs of all young people, not only those who were university bound. The ground was prepared to adopt a new approach to secondary qualifications, designed to support a curriculum that would equip them to engage in a diverse, rapidly changing world.

Assessment pressures in the lead-up to NCEA

By the 1980s the status of School Certificate had diminished. The increasing retention of students in New Zealand secondary schools meant its scarcity value was significantly reduced (Openshaw, 2009, p. 26). Under the leadership of Bill Renwick the Department of Education had begun to question the relevance of the external examinations used to award School Certificate. A number of principals and teachers, and the Post Primary Teachers' Association (PPTA), called for School Certificate to be internally assessed. This, they argued, would allow for a wider range of skills to be assessed and provide teachers with the opportunity to develop programmes of learning which were more relevant to their students (Fountain, 2012).

Meanwhile a different type of tension was becoming harder to ignore. School Certificate was managed by the Department of Education, but 6th and 7th Form examinations were run by the University Entrance Board (UEB). The UEB was independent of the Department of Education and dominated by university academics who were specialists in the parent disciplines of particular school subjects. Given the composition and interests of this group, UE was primarily focused on ensuring that students who gained the qualification were academically prepared for tertiary education. The UEB saw calls to introduce alternative models of assessment as undermining the status of examinations. They believed there would be serious implications for maintaining academic standards in the universities. This was somewhat ironic given that UE was actually determined by an unusual mix of internal and external assessment: many students were accredited UE on the basis of their school examination results. But at least 5 percent of the students from each school were required to sit the external examination (Fountain, 2012).

This divergence of interests led to a compromise. A two-tier system of qualifications was developed for the 6th Form year, with students studying for both UE and Sixth Form Certificate. The latter allowed the Department of Education to follow through on its commitment to introduce alternative models of assessment. Students staying on into the 6th Form could gain an award for their year's work, even if they had no interest in attending university. Meanwhile, UE would continue to be controlled by the UEB. Compared with its big cousin, UE, Sixth Form Certificate had little status in the hierarchy of qualifications. Nevertheless it would go on to have a significant impact on the impetus to develop NCEA after 1986, particularly as a result of the manner in which quality assurance was managed.

Although Sixth Form Certificate allowed for a wide range of innovative, internally assessed courses, the grading system used (see Chapter 4) was seen by teachers as being unfair and having little credibility. The system was not especially contentious while UE remained the major qualification in Form 6. However, as we've already noted, in 1986 UE was shifted up a year level to become a 7th Form qualification, and the internally assessed Sixth Form Certificate became the stand-alone qualification of the 6th Form year. Once this move had taken place, the rather arbitrary process of allocating grades became more contentious and contributed to growing dissatisfaction with the existing qualification system. In some quarters (especially among elite boys' schools) the unfair process reinforced opposition to internal assessment and saw calls for a return to norm-referenced examinations at the 6th-Form level. Others looked towards alternative models of assessment. As we will soon see, many advocates of NCEA believed that this new qualification would successfully address the serious inadequacies of Sixth Form Certificate.

In the lead-up to NCEA the pace of change in secondary assessment became increasingly rapid. Opponents and critics were often dismissed as simply not understanding the context, or as being nostalgic for a world that had now passed. The focus was on improving pass rates and increasing the number of students gaining qualifications rather than addressing the complex question of what students were actually learning, and why.

Chapter 3 The relationship between curriculum and assessment

Core aims of NCEA were for the majority of young people to experience success at school by gaining qualifications, and to take a much more egalitarian approach to valuing different kinds of learning than had been the case in the past. Traditional school subjects with a more academic orientation were not to be valued any more (or less) highly than practical subjects that led more directly to employment opportunities. This so-called *parity of esteem* was to be achieved by enumerating credits on the basis of the (nominal) time needed to achieve specified learning. This was a major departure from judging the relative value of learning on the basis of its intellectual challenge, as the previous assessment system had done. Despite this radical departure from traditional assumptions and practices, careful debate about this aspect of NCEA was not encouraged by the agencies charged with implementing it. This has proved to be a real missed opportunity. In our view, the very idea of parity of esteem continues to be problematic for NCEA and needs to be proactively addressed.

NCEA was implemented in stages between 2002 and 2004, before the development of *NZC*, which was implemented between 2007 and 2010. This might, at least in part, explain why addressing the comparative status of different types of knowledge was not seen as a high priority during the development and implementation of NCEA. Ideally, assessment reform would follow curriculum reform rather than precede it. The curriculum should set the direction for learning by specifying the skills and knowledge that are seen as valuable in society. But what sort of directions for learning, and how might these relate, or not, to traditional assessment practices? With these questions in mind, we now outline challenges for the senior secondary school curriculum during the years in which assessment pressures were also mounting. We begin with a brief overview of the messy state of the senior secondary curriculum up until the development of *NZC*, which was published in its final form in 2007, half a decade after the work of shaping NCEA. These two major policy platforms were belatedly aligned several years after *NZC* came on the scene. Our overall aim is to demonstrate the complexities of curriculum-building for the final years of schooling, when gaining qualifications is still the only game in town for many students, teachers, and parents.

The senior secondary curriculum before NZC

There was no golden age in which curriculum led the way and examinations simply followed along. For most of the 20th century examination prescriptions *were* the senior secondary curriculum. Form 5/Year 11 courses prepared students for School Certificate examinations. Form 7/Year 13 courses prepared them for Scholarship, and later, for Bursary examinations. There was some wiggle room to build a more local curriculum in Form 6/Year 12 once Sixth Form Certificate had been introduced. In practice, however, anticipation of a connected-up learning trajectory between Year 11 and Year 13 still dictated teachers' choices of what they must address during Year 12.

The situation began to change in the 1990s when far-reaching curriculum reform was initiated under Minister of Education Lockwood Smith's leadership. The sweeping changes that took place led to the development of outcomes-based curriculum documents in seven learning areas.[1] Bringing this model into being generated many

---

1 These were: English; Mathematics; Science; Social Science; Technology; Health/Physical Education; and The Arts. The next round of curriculum work in the early 2000s saw the addition of Learning Languages as an eighth learning area (it was subsumed under English in the first model).

challenges for the people creating the new curricula. These challenges included the forced integration of subjects that had previously been treated as quite separate. For example physical education (PE), health, and home economics had to find common ground, and so did visual arts, music, drama, and dance. Technology was a totally new subject that brought many practical employment-oriented subjects under a more intellectual and conceptual umbrella. This was intended to be a seamless curriculum, which meant that it would cover all years of schooling from entry at age 5 until school exit. However, this so-called seamlessness created a challenging set of issues in the senior secondary school because the seven learning areas were too generic in their scope to provide the specificity of curriculum content that teachers sought to guide their work in preparing students for school-exit assessments.

During all this curriculum-building activity in the 1990s, the level of attention paid to different senior subjects was very uneven. For example, the sciences seemed to receive comparatively more attention than other learning areas. The traditional senior science subjects of biology, chemistry, and physics gained their own separate curriculum documents several years after a generic science curriculum was published (Ministry of Education, 1993b). A new, integrated science subject, with its own Bursary examination, melded together selected aspects of the traditional sciences and the newer areas of earth science and astronomy. No other learning areas received this same special treatment. The social sciences could have argued for separate senior curriculum documents because they brought together the traditional subjects of history, geography, art history, and economics, while also accommodating the new subject of social studies. Arguably there are greater differences between the knowledge-building practices of the various social science disciplines than there are between the physical sciences. We can see no evident epistemological justification for the different treatment these two learning areas received.

On a more positive note, the learning areas developed towards the end of the 1990s were able to benefit from lessons learned by the curriculum teams that had broken the new ground earlier in the decade.[2]

---

[2] Curriculum documents for the Mathematics, Science, and English learning areas were the first to be developed. PE/Health and The Arts were the last to be developed.

Their curriculum teams worked hard to achieve greater coherence in their underpinning philosophical structures. We've already noted that health, PE, and home economics were melded into one learning area. Rose was a member of the team that did this development work and she recalls the comprehensive debates that took place as common ground was gradually forged. An explicit sociocritical orientation to knowledge provided one unifying factor. The Māori metaphor of a whare tapa whā (four-sided house) was used to describe the holistic nature of wellbeing. This metaphor provided another type of common ground for the subjects being brought together. These were important developments because they provided new ways of thinking about purposes for learning in these subject areas as the first tranche of achievement standards was being developed in the following decade.

Entirely new subjects such as media studies could only be developed in an ad hoc manner. Media studies includes elements of English, but aspects of the social sciences are also critically important. Depending on the context of the phenomenon being investigated, other learning areas could also be implicated—for example, when examining how science issues are treated by different media. A curriculum structure with discrete learning areas cannot readily accommodate such a subject. Environmental education (now more likely to be called education for sustainability) and design and visual communication are two more examples of subjects that straddle the learning-area structure.

A result of the manifestly uneven curriculum treatment of different subjects during the 1990s was a somewhat ramshackle overall senior secondary curriculum (see Part 2 of Bolstad and Gilbert, 2008, for a more detailed account). Detailed examination prescriptions continued to serve as the de facto curriculum for those subjects that did not find a natural home, or a sufficiently specific home, under the learning area structure of the new outcomes-based curriculum documents.

This was also the decade during which standards-based assessment was being explored and developed. Some teachers had opportunities to expand their curriculum thinking as a consequence of that work, but many more did not. For most teachers the purpose of learning in the senior secondary school continued as before. Gaining qualifications was seen as a sufficient end in itself, and the very word *curriculum* mostly cued thinking about examination prescriptions and content. An important opportunity was lost to support teachers to think differently about what a curriculum could be and do. Yet this was the challenge that was about to confront all secondary teachers head-on.

The senior secondary curriculum in NZC

The development of *NZC* in the early 2000s consolidated the outcomes-based developments of the 1990s by bringing all the learning areas together in one slim framework document. It only partially addressed the uneven curriculum support for different subjects in the senior secondary school.

- Substantive differences between learning English and learning other languages were acknowledged by the creation of an eighth learning area for the latter.
- The three traditional sciences lost the special privilege of separate curriculum documents, although in practice many teachers continued to use these to supplement the pared-back and integrated science learning area.
- The Social Sciences learning area continued to provide a home for a range of subjects with related but different underpinning theoretical commitments (history, geography, economics, social studies). A structure of separate curriculum strands was developed to accommodate this range in the senior secondary curriculum levels, but this structure is at odds with the more integrated approach taken to social studies at lower curriculum levels (Abbiss, 2011).
- Some subjects continued to lack a logical home in any of the eight learning areas (e.g., accounting was, for a time, placed with the Mathematics learning area, presumably because of its number aspects).
- Some non-traditional subjects could have found a home in one of the eight learning areas but were not included (e.g., psychology could, in theory, have come under the Science learning area umbrella).
- As outlined above, some non-traditional subjects still crossed several of the traditional learning areas (e.g., environmental education/sustainability, design and visual communication, and media studies).

The overall trend in the development of *NZC* was to pare back and streamline the specification of important learning to a brief framework of achievement objectives. As in the decade before, many teachers continued to look to assessment to flesh out and guide their thinking about what they should teach. By now, NCEA and its achievement standards were already in place. However, the achievement standards developed for the assessment of many traditional subjects had been derived by chunking up former examination prescriptions and so they did not reflect the shifts in curriculum thinking that were rapidly gaining pace. In particular, achievement standards for those subjects whose curriculum documents had been developed in the first half of the 1990s did not necessarily reflect new curriculum thinking. Yet when we consider the development of *NZC* as a whole framework, there was a clear need for all senior secondary teachers to be supported to think more strategically and critically about the *purposes* for which they taught their subjects. To expand on this point we need to briefly outline the ways in which *NZC* represented a break from traditional practice, signalling a need to shift important aspects of curriculum thinking in response to wider societal changes that are often short-handed as 21st century imperatives.

Building a curriculum for new times

When it was released in 2007, *NZC* was explicitly described by Minister of Education Steve Maharey as a curriculum that responded to contemporary social challenges:

> As a nation, we face new issues and new opportunities. The pace of social and economic change is faster than ever before. We live in a world of globalisation, cultural diversity, and rapidly changing technologies. There is increased specialisation in the workplace; there are new social roles and forms of self-expression. (Minister of Education, 2007)

In stark contrast to the collection of individual curriculum documents in the 1990s, the whole of *NZC* fits into one slim volume. It is presented as a framework whose "principal function is to set the direction for student learning and to provide guidance for schools as they design and review their curriculum" (p. 6). Even in this brief introductory phrase there were several critically important signals to schools and to teachers; the *NZC* does not hand them ready-made curriculum thinking.

Every school is expected to use the framework to build their own curriculum design. This comment begs important questions for anyone who thinks about curriculum as primarily being the specification of content that needs to be taught and learned. What exactly are schools and teachers supposed to think about and why should they do this now when school-by-school curriculum design was not necessarily seen as so important in the past? Answering this question requires a brief detour to describe the overall structure of *NZC*'s framework, and the stated aim of creating a curriculum for the 21st century.

NZC is a document of two halves. The "front half" of *NZC* provides what could be described as a curriculum-thinking framework. It is a collection of pieces that collectively convey various facets of a vision for what schools should help students be and become as a result of their education:

- A vision statement elucidates "what we want for our young people", namely "confident, connected, actively involved lifelong learners" (*NZC*, p. 8).
- Five key competencies, based on a set developed by the Organisation for Economic Co-operation and Development (OECD, 2005), are described in *NZC* as "capabilities for living and lifelong learning" (*NZC*, p. 12). They highlight the importance of: self-management and development of greater autonomy; the ability to relate to a wide range of other people; developing strong critical and creative thinking skills; learning about how meaning is created and conveyed by different cultural tools and texts; and making a contribution, including working collaboratively with others (pp. 12–13).
- A set of values is described. These were determined by a national consultation process (Keown, Parker, & Tiakiwai, 2005) and are expected to be "encouraged, modelled and explored" (*NZC*, p. 10).
- A series of pithy statements, one for each learning area, identify overarching purposes for learning. Some statements point to capabilities that students are expected to develop for their lives well beyond school. For example, the Science and Social Sciences statements both allude to responsible citizenship, and the Technology statement talks about "discerning consumers who will make a difference in the world" (*NZC*, p. 17).

- A set of principles provides the "foundations of curriculum decision-making" (*NZC*, p. 9). These principles highlight important matters for schools to take into consideration in the 21st century context: curriculum concepts (*learning to learn, future focus, coherence*); social commitments (*Treaty of Waitangi, inclusion*); meeting the needs of all learners (*high expectations, cultural diversity*); and a more participatory ethos to more strongly locate each school within its own community (*community engagement*).

There are also sections that discuss effective pedagogy and school-based curriculum planning. Collectively these features point to purposes for learning that have value in addition to, and beyond, content and skills acquisition. There is a focus on what 21st century learners need to know and be able to do, along with some guidance about how to shape a local curriculum that demonstrably meets the learning needs of every student in the school.

What the framework does *not* do is show how to weave these fine-sounding aspirations in and through the day-to-day stuff of learning. The "back half" of *NZC* specifies content as sets of achievement objectives for the eight learning areas. Each learning area is in turn differentiated into eight curriculum levels that broadly indicate progress across all the years of school from age 5 to around age 17 or 18. The achievement objectives in this part of the *NZC* essentially represent a continuity of traditional curriculum outcomes from the 1990s and before. Schools are expected to keep in mind the front-end elements of *NZC* as they weave together the various achievement objectives within and between learning areas. They should be able to articulate how their overall curriculum design will help achieve the *NZC* vision for all their students to experience learning success, as relevant to their local community, and as articulated by the front-half elements of *NZC*.

It should be evident that there are multiple possible design solutions to the curriculum-building challenge we have just sketched. There is no one right way to create a local curriculum that will satisfy *NZC*'s vision. The high-level purposes articulated for learning potentially transcend a narrow view of learning in the senior secondary school. But expansive curriculum design thinking can be quite alien for teachers who are used to thinking about curriculum as content.

Mixed messages about knowledge in NZC

The curriculum developments we have just outlined were arguably dominated by two main ideas about knowledge. Constructivist, learner-centred pedagogies place a high value on students' everyday or prior knowledge, and specific outcomes-based achievement objectives emphasise bite-sized knowledge gains that can be easily measured. Neither of these ways of thinking about knowledge necessarily raises the question of what knowledge matters most for young people to acquire. *NZC* does address this challenge via high-level statements about the contribution each learning area might make to its overall vision. But as we have already noted, the two-halves structure of the framework has contributed to the neglect of the more visionary aspects of *NZC* at the expense of what is assessed. In this context, knowledge, concepts, and processes that shape powerful ways of thinking about the world can be seen as either elitist or irrelevant (Wood & Sheehan, 2012).

Young people need to acquire a wide range of knowledge and skills in their education but we need to think carefully about when and how they should do so. The principle of parity-of-esteem, which informed the design of NCEA, treats all knowledge as being of equal worth. But the sort of knowledge required to complete food preparation tasks or make coffee is very different from the sort of knowledge that is required to solve algebraic equations, explain the causes of international conflicts, or adjudicate the case for and against climate change. It is the latter sort of knowledge that is emancipatory and lies at the heart of what it means to be educated. This is the sort of knowledge that should be at the centre of a school curriculum because it equips young people to think critically and participate effectively in a democratic society on their own terms. Regardless of how they decide to use this knowledge, young people are entitled to have access to this way of learning and thinking if they are be educated and not simply qualified. Of course, in an ideal system the two would be synonymous.

The respected international educator David Perkins calls the sort of knowledge we have in mind "lifeworthy" (Perkins, 2014). He identifies four features that make it powerful. Such knowledge should: generate insights into how the world works; empower the taking of action in appropriate ways; support the development of ethical and more humane mind-sets; and be likely to come up in a range of circumstances (i.e., it is knowledge that can transfer to different contexts). Perkins notes that traditional content learning per se will not necessarily fulfil these criteria. It is how the knowledge is framed and used that determines its lifeworthiness. This is a very important qualification given the seemingly common assumption that learning the traditional content of a subject will inevitably confer the high-level benefits spelled out in the front part of *NZC*. We will come back to this dilemma multiple times as we explore the evolution of NCEA and discuss the opportunities realised, as well as those that seem to have been missed.

PART 2. NCEA IN THE CONTEXT OF KNOWN ASSESSMENT CHALLENGES

It seems to be human nature to look back fondly on a better past when the going is tough in the present and the future looks uncertain. In this vein, we think that some critique of NCEA tacitly or explicitly harks back to a mythical golden age in which learning held more meaning for students (i.e., was not just undertaken on the promise of gaining more credits), and high-stakes assessment was fair, easily understood, and generally seen as unproblematic. Others have recognised the same dynamic at work. For example, in her doctoral studies Judie Alison investigated why it seemed that teachers had forgotten the hard struggle for assessment reform once NCEA was fully in place. She concluded that spiralling workloads associated with NCEA had caused teachers to look back more kindly on the very assessment systems that had once seemed so problematic to the profession (Alison, 2007).

In this second part of the book each chapter addresses one assessment challenge to which NCEA either could have responded, or actually did respond. Most chapters begin by casting a critical eye back to the pre-NCEA years, explaining the nature of the challenge at that time. As we introduce the highlighted challenge we draw on personal experiences—our own and those of others—in ways that we hope will bring more theoretical aspects of the argument to life for a wider readership. We have tried to write these pieces that recall our personal experiences in a way that will resonate with the experiences of others who have lived through the same pressures and changes. Of course it is easy to be wise after the fact. Things that are much clearer to us now were not necessarily so when the recounted events unfolded. With this meaning-making challenge in mind, we have tried to ensure that any retrospective meaning-making on our own part is clearly visible.

Towards the end of this second part of the book the weighting within each chapter shifts. We start to look more towards the future than back to the past, drawing on examples of innovative thinking and practice that are already occurring despite the current limitations of the assessment system. We draw encouragement from the evolving changes that have already been used to address issues and strengthen NCEA-related assessment practice. Our aim overall is to pinpoint areas where further improvement gains await.

Chapter 4 Internal assessment

The use of internal assessment has generated considerable debate since it began to contribute to senior school qualifications in the 1980s.

Internal assessment provides a degree of flexibility in assessment processes that is not possible under an external assessment regime which, by its nature, usually requires uniformity of assessment conditions and timing. Under NCEA, for example, students at different schools are often assessed for a given internally assessed achievement standard using different tasks, and at different times of the year. This flexibility is a strength of internal assessment because, if used appropriately, it affords the possibility to assess in contexts that are relevant and accessible to specific groups of students. It also allows assessment to be integrated into a course. This integration can improve the coherence of the course and maximise both the opportunity for teachers and students to use assessment results formatively, and the opportunity for students to learn from working on the assessment.

Nonetheless, this flexibility necessarily creates challenges for assessment reliability, in particular, the national consistency of the standard required for each grade. Quality assurance processes, in the form of a moderation system, are therefore needed to ensure a measure of comparability between schools in their internal assessment judgements. However, it is not easy to find a moderation model that encourages the innovative exploitation of the opportunities afforded by internal assessment, and also invests the system with sufficient reliability to maintain a high level of public confidence; these purposes tend to be in tension with one another. The difficulty of managing a large-scale, high-stakes internal assessment regime is exacerbated by the fact that evidence generated by the more innovative tasks that are possible in such an environment can unsettle traditional assumptions about what actually constitutes achievement, and who can be seen to be a successful learner. In the case of NCEA, this has led a degree of hostility towards internal assessment from quarters that have historically benefitted from those assumptions. We explore the challenges of large-scale moderation in detail in Chapter 10.

As we recall ...

Two of us were early to mid-career teachers during the turbulent pre-NCEA years of change. We begin by recounting personal experiences of both the highs and lows of working in an internal assessment environment. Although internal assessment conferred advantages for teaching and learning, we both felt the allocation of grades was manifestly unfair, and we felt this unfairness keenly. Both of us can still recount the details, all these years later. But, embroiled as we were in the unfolding changes, we did not have a clear sense of *why* we got caught as we did—nor were we able to do anything to address the root cause of the challenges. Indeed one of us (Rose) coped with the dilemma recounted by reverting to the traditional assessment system. The remaining author (Michael) has never been a school teacher, but like almost every other New Zealander, he has been a school student. Michael contrasts his experience of 6th Form in 1984, during which all of his assessment was internal, with his entirely externally assessed School Certificate experience a year earlier.

Rose: When students in an alternative course cannot be rewarded for hard work
Coming back into teaching early in the 1980s, after a break to care for my young family, I was asked to teach a 5th Form biology class that was to be fully internally assessed. Students were placed in this class because they were considered unable to pass the School Certificate science course, which was assessed by the traditional 3-hour examination. The alternative course, carefully prepared by another teacher the previous year, looked wonderful.

I'd never thought about doing anything like it. I enjoyed teaching the topics set out and my students responded well. They worked hard and turned in very good evidence of their learning gains, or so I thought. Unfortunately for them, I did not appreciate the full import of the reference test they were required to sit quite early in the year. As I later found out, other teachers coached students to do as well as possible in this multiple-choice test, which covered all areas of science, not just biology. My students did not do well, and with that their grades for the year were sealed.

That year, just one student passed School Certificate in my alternative biology class. All the others in the class failed, notwithstanding the wonderful work they had done during a year of sustained effort. The following year I refused to be party to such a travesty again. I took the equivalent class but switched them to the fully externally examined subject of human biology. Now we were back to playing by rules I knew well, my students enjoyed much more success. One got an A grade in the examination and almost all got at least 50 percent and hence passed. All these years later, I can still conjure up images and names for many of those students who were let down so badly by the system, and inadvertently by me.

Mark: Assigning grades for an internally assessed Sixth Form Certificate course

Teaching Sixth Form Certificate in the 1990s was the "best and worst of all possible worlds" for me as a history teacher. The teaching and learning was perhaps the most satisfying and enjoyable of my secondary teaching career. My classes were invariably made up of highly motivated, interested, and intelligent students, and I was able to structure an internally assessed programme that was innovative and provided my students with a historical background to current issues that dominated the news. These young people were learning to think for themselves about questions that mattered. We looked at the historical context of the break-up of former Yugoslavia, the actions of the Taliban in Afghanistan and the genocide in Rwanda. We made extensive use of guest speakers, critiqued the historical interpretations that informed popular feature films, and visited historical sites. The opportunity to shape the teaching and learning around what was significant to young people at the time was enormously satisfying. So was being able to employ a range of assessment approaches that evaluated a wide range of abilities: presenting seminars; film studies; newspaper research and so on.

This flexibility of the teaching and learning was at odds with the rigid and unreliable way that grades were allocated. Every teacher of a 6th Form course was allocated a series of grades for that particular class. One year I remember I had twelve "1" grades to give out (the grade allocated to the top 4 percent of the national cohort). The rest of the grades were 2s, 3s, or 4s (a pass was a 5 grade). This was a very academically able group of 32 students and these high grades were generated by their School Certificate marks the previous year. To work out how to allocate the grades in the pool, I had to add the marks for my various assessments during the year (about 8) and then rank the students. The top 12 would receive a 1, the second group a 2 and so on. I recall that the marks for a 1 went from 96 (1st) to 89.1 (12th).The top "2" was 88.2—in all cases the differences between the grades allocated on either side of the cut-off was less than 1 mark. Although this happened almost 20 years ago the unreliability and unfairness of this process has stayed with me. It seemed to have no validity from an assessment viewpoint and was primarily driven by administrative convenience.[1]

Michael: Internal and external assessment from a student's perspective

When I attended secondary school in the early 1980s, School Certificate remained both a rite of passage and a moment of reckoning for young New Zealanders. It was the gateway to the final 2 years of secondary school for those who achieved the requisite number of passing grades and the end of the line for those who did not, unless they chose to repeat the entire 5th Form year. On the evidence of my previous academic performance, I had little reason to be nervous as the exam season approached; I came from a family with plenty of intellectual capital and had been described by my teachers as an able, if not always an attentive, student. But I *was* nervous—indeed terrified—when I fronted up to my first examination, for my best subject, English. Although I was confident that I had done well after that exam, my nervousness was undiminished as I undertook the exams for my other five subjects. I am not a nervous person by nature—I have given confident lectures, public addresses, and musical performances to audiences numbered in the hundreds, and I have given radio interviews that have been broadcast nationally. But even as an adult, a formal examination setting still causes in me a panic reaction which is

---

1 Bear in mind that this is Mark's recall and how he experienced the process of grade allocation as a young teacher. Different schools used different methods to allocate the pool of grades they were given (based on the school's results in School Certificate the previous year). Some methods were fairer than others. No process could eliminate the inherent unfairness of very similar scores going into different grades on other side of cut-off points (as Mark has described).

not only very unpleasant to experience, but which, I have no doubt, materially affects my performance.

Despite my terror, I came through School Certificate with six subject passes, three of them in the A-grade range, and duly went on to the 6th Form in 1984. I was quite confident of being accredited UE (see Chapter 3), so I approached the year's study without the spectre of formal examinations that had dogged me in my School Certificate year. As a result I enjoyed the 6th Form more than any other year of high school. In English, my teacher could see that I was not challenged by the reading and assignments, so she gave me work from the 7th Form Scholarship syllabus, which, because of the internal assessment regime, counted as evidence both to my Sixth Form Certificate and UE accreditation. I finished the year with good enough results to leave school and attend university with a bursary. I was, in large part, blissfully unaware of the unfairness inherent in the allocation of grades to Sixth Form Certificate described above by Mark, until I found that I had been awarded a grade of "3" for classical studies on the basis of a performance that I thought to be at least on a par with my performance in English, for which I was awarded a "1". When I queried the teacher, she informed me, somewhat apologetically, that she had been allocated nothing better than a "3" to give to her highest-achieving students.

Although I was in the category of student typically assumed to thrive in an examination environment (I was thought to be academically able, I was highly competitive, and I am male), there is no question that, from an educational perspective, the relatively flexible and informal nature of the internal assessment environment suited me far better than the high pressure of the end-of-year formal examination system. Not only did the lack of pressure allow me to perform better in the assessments themselves, but the lack of worry about a looming day-of-reckoning allowed me to focus my attention on the epistemological character of the disciplines I was studying, rather than on the cramming of content that had characterised my preparation for School Certificate.

Internal assessment as an opportunity for equity

It could be argued that the stories of unfairness we recounted arose because traditional assessment thinking was used to manage the results of the more innovative internal assessment processes. In particular, in Rose and Mark's accounts, formal test- or examination-based assessments were used to moderate the internally assessed results. This moderation constrained the extent to which the more flexible internal assessment environment could be used to recognise the achievement of those who did not thrive in traditional examination conditions, or who changed their achievement trajectory from one year to the next, or both.[2] This was a conundrum that was acknowledged among educators at the time, and could be seen as one pressure that kept the momentum of change on track towards NCEA.

Debates over the merits and flaws of internal assessment have been part of the secondary school landscape since the 1960s. Many progressive educators had called for alternative models of assessment that were inclusive of disadvantaged students and evaluated a wider range of abilities than was possible in a 3-hour examination. They were largely informed by critical theorists who highlighted the ways in which traditional curriculum structures and assessment practices reinforce existing inequities in society (for example, Apple, 1979). Secondary schools of the time largely operated on the basis that only a minority of students would be expected to enjoy any sort of academic success. A substantial proportion of students left school as soon as they turned 15 and around half the students who sat School Certificate at the end of the 5th Form were destined to fail under the norm-referenced scaling model (to be discussed Chapter 5). As we have already noted, School Certificate was the major school-exit examination for 30 years after World War Two, and in the 1970s only a minority of young people went on to the 6th and 7th Forms, with the attendant opportunity to sit UE and qualify to go to on to university.

For progressive educators internal assessment was seen as one way in which schools could become more inclusive of students who were marginalised and disadvantaged. However, these were radical views. They were not part of the mainstream ethos and did not reflect tacit assumptions about learning and learners held by most teachers and by the general public. Echoing the criticisms of NCEA almost two decades later, some schools (especially high-decile boys'

---

2 When one year's examination results are used to moderate the next year's grade allocations, students who improve markedly, in effect, push other students further down the allocation list. The reverse dynamic also applies of course—students whose performance deteriorates markedly will have added grades to the pool that end up generating higher grades for others.

schools such as Auckland Grammar)[3] were vehemently opposed to the introduction of internal assessment for Sixth Form Certificate. They argued that internal assessment was contributing to a dumbing down of educational standards and it lacked the rigour and competitive aspect required to bring out the best in their students and teachers (Fountain, 2012). These critics largely shared the view of Merv Wellington (National government Minister of Education, 1981–84) who said that the external examination system was "the first guarantor of excellence" ("Statement of Hon M L Wellington for the New Zealand Times," 1984) and a mechanism for holding teachers accountable:

> [The] philosophy of the examination system is to reward hard work, accuracy of knowledge, logic and clarity of thought … Moreover external exams are a test of the individual teacher. It is against his or her pupils' results that the most accurate guide is given. Without such a 'frame of reference' pupil and teacher, parent and employer would be left to wander without rudder or guiding ("Statement of Hon M L Wellington for the New Zealand Times", 1984, quoted in Fountain, 2012, p. 34)

One tension between traditional and progressive thinking concerns assumptions about the purposes for learning in the senior secondary school. This is primarily a curriculum question, although its overt expression concerns assessment. If the primary purpose of assessment in the senior secondary school is seen to be the identification of suitable candidates for tertiary study, any deliberately abstract and difficult curriculum might be seen as suitable. As noted in Chapter 2, university thinking had a strong influence on the shape of the traditional curriculum, via the examination prescriptions determined by the University Entrance Board. If, however, learning is expected to help students build lifeworthy knowledge, of the sort we discussed in Chapter 3, a wider spectrum of curriculum possibilities opens up and new types of questions need to be addressed. What learning is of worth for whom, when, and why? Such questions are universal

---

3 Decile 10 schools are located in the most socioeconomically advantaged communities, while decile 1 schools are located in the communities with the highest proportions of low income households.

curriculum concerns, but they gain a new acuity when multiple different answers to these questions are acceptable and actionable.

A related tension between traditional and progressive assessment thinking concerns which types of students can be seen as successful learners. As we have seen, traditionalists expect high-stakes assessment to sort the most academically able students from the rest. From this perspective internal assessment carries a whiff of cheating—it allows students to demonstrate learning success when they don't really deserve to be thought of as successful (as learning success is traditionally defined). The derogatory phrase "all must have prizes", which emerged in the early NCEA years, echoes this assumption that assessment is a sort of competition, used primarily to identify the most academically able. This point remains valid, notwithstanding the absence of normative scaling. Scaling provided an explicit sorting mechanism, but even in its absence the implicit barriers to achievement inherent in the conditions of time-limited formal examinations tend to work to the relative advantage of students with higher levels of cultural capital. Under NCEA, with no normative criteria for the award of qualifications, the achievement differential between students at high- and low-decile schools is much greater in external assessment than in internal assessment, as Table 4.2 makes clear.

The three recollections at the start of this chapter expose mirror-image flaws in the related assumptions that an assessment system is suspect if it affords success to students who do not thrive in traditional examinations, and that external assessment is ipso facto more rigorous than internal assessment. Rose's first group of students were denied formal recognition of learning success by an unfair quality assurance process. Yet her next, very similar, cohort showed that with the right coaching to play the assessment game— that is, learning a lot of content off by heart combined with some simple logics of strategic question-answering—they could demonstrate the sort of learning success constructed by the School Certificate examination. Conversely, Michael was a highly successful student, as traditionally defined. Yet he experienced the internally assessed courses as more intellectually demanding and accordingly valued these learning gains more highly. Rose would also argue that her first cohort, who mostly worked on assignments and essays, actually thought more deeply about the content of the learning and its relevance to their lives, despite their poorer showing in the final assessment.

Internal assessment as a controversial component of NCEA

Internal assessment is a core feature of NCEA; at least half of the standards offered in each subject are internally assessed and many students achieve a majority of their credits from internally assessed standards. Table 4.1 shows the percentages of students' NCEA results from 2009 to 2014 for each standard type—externally assessed achievement standards, internally assessed achievement standards, and unit standards, which are also internally assessed. The most striking change over time is the decline in the percentages of results that come from unit standards and the concomitant rise in the percentages for internally assessed achievement standards. This reflects the phasing-out of curriculum-linked unit standards that took place between 2011 and 2013.

The overall percentages of externally assessed results also fell during this period, albeit much less dramatically than the changes for the other standard types. Again, this is largely a result of changes that took place between 2011 and 2013, in this case, the implementation of a reviewed set of (curriculum-linked) achievement standards. One of the principles informing this review was that each externally assessed standard must have at least one hour of examination time, to ensure adequate reliability. However, some subjects had had more than three externally assessed standards, which would have necessitated more than 3 hours of examination time. Yet the timeframe for the annual examination round is such that no more than a single 3-hour time slot can be scheduled for each subject at each level. Thus, the number of externally assessed standards attempted by any one student needed to be reduced in these subjects. In any event, in 2014 about one-quarter of all results were externally assessed, down from slightly more than 30 percent in 2009.

Advocates of internal assessment laud the flexibility that it offers. They argue that it allows for innovative teaching and learning and evaluates a broader range of students' skills and abilities than examinations. Critics, however, have continued to claim that internal assessment is an unreliable measure of students' academic achievement compared to examinations. A 2011 article in the *North and South* magazine alleged that NZQA "fudged the figures" to make it appear that moderators and teachers agreed on the internal assessment mark for students' work (Coddington, 2011). Such claims are not atypical. The *New Zealand Listener* has claimed that because teachers are involved in marking their students' internal assessment assignments, the system is less than "robust" and "open to rorting" ("Editorial: Performance pay for teachers has caveats", 2012).

Table 4.1. Percentages of results by standard type (2009–2014)

Year	Externally assessed achievement standards (%)	Internally assessed achievement standards (%)	Unit standards (%)
2009	30.4	31.5	38.1
2010	31.0	32.9	36.1
2011	28.4	40.4	31.2
2012	27.8	48.7	23.5
2013	26.5	53.2	20.3
2014	26.1	54.8	19.1

Source: NZQA (2010–2015)

The well-publicised concerns about the unreliability of internal assessment in the early years of NCEA were not entirely unjustified, even if the public reporting of these problems was not always carried out with a high degree of journalistic integrity. When moderator and teacher assessment judgements were analysed for the first time in 2008, agreement between them was less than 70 percent. Since then, improved resourcing of the moderation system has resulted in a substantial improvement in these figures. Agreement rates are now above 85 percent, which, from a psychometric viewpoint, is probably as high as can be expected without sacrificing assessment validity. *Reliability* (i.e., the consistency with which teachers across the country make assessment judgements against a standard) is always a challenge for internal assessment, but if it is used well then the educational benefits that it affords are worth the trouble of the technical and political work required to address this challenge. In this regard, the continued existence of an external assessment system actually provides an important protection for internal assessment. Because it is much more uniform in its processes, it invests a greater degree of reliability into assessment for qualifications than would be possible in a purely internally assessed system. Furthermore, it acts as a political pressure valve for those who mistrust internal assessment and, as we will see in Chapter 10, it affords a statistical mechanism to check the consistency of internal assessment judgements at different schools, although not, under NCEA, to modify them.

Sorting teachers and schools, as well as students

The tenor of early NCEA controversy about internal assessment entails more than just the concern with sorting students that characterised much of the criticism of internal assessment in the pre-NCEA years. One new dimension relates to assumptions of self-interest on the part of teachers and schools; that is, that they will cheat the system given half a chance. The second added dimension is an intensified media focus on assessment results as an indicator of school quality. In fact the latter dimension is related to the former, because the use of qualifications achievement rates to compare schools provides a prima facie motivation to exploit the internal assessment system in order to achieve higher achievement rates. While both of these issues were present under the previous examination system, they have become more acute under NCEA, partly because there are indeed more opportunities for the unscrupulous to manipulate results. One infamous case early in the implementation period received widespread publicity. In 2005, the principal of Cambridge High School was forced to resign on the back of the revelation that students had been receiving NCEA credits for activities such as picking up litter around the school. The worst excesses of this kind of exploitation of internal assessment have been dealt with through a combination of policy change and oversight by NZQA and ERO. However, there remains the practice of "credit-farming", whereby some schools find ways to get students across the line for qualifications outside the context of rigorous courses. The learning behind the credits gained under this kind of practice is sometimes questionable. We discuss this challenge more fully in Part 3 of the book.

Public confidence in any internal assessment system is certainly essential if is to withstand (inevitable) criticism from schools that have benefitted in reputation and prestige from traditional, external-examination-based assessment systems. The reputational advantage that high-decile schools would stand to gain from an abolition of internal assessment for NCEA is made very clear by a comparison of the comparative pass[4] rates for internally and externally assessed achievement standards between high- and low-decile schools (NZQA, 2014). A snapshot of this data is shown in Table 4.2.

Table 4.2. Comparative success rates in higher and lower decile schools (2013)

Overall achievement rate for externally assessed achievement standards	%
Decile 8–10 schools	80.6
Decile 1–3 schools	59.8
Overall achievement rate for internally assessed achievement standards	**%**
Decile 8–10 schools	85.4
Decile 1–3 schools	75.8

The differential for externally assessed standards is 21 percentage points, compared to a differential of 10 percentage points for internally assessed standards. Clearly, in a purely externally assessed system, high-decile schools would enjoy an even more marked advantage over low-decile schools in qualifications achievement than is the case at present.

What explains the much greater differential across school deciles in achievement for externally assessed standards than for internally assessed standards? There are no publicly reported data that can be used to adjudicate between various plausible explanations for this phenomenon, and the possibilities we discuss here are speculative. Nonetheless, these speculations are worth making because they expose some of the political tensions that make a nuanced public discussion about internal assessment difficult.

One possibility, which could be taken as support for the accusations of inconsistency made by the *Listener* ("Editorial: Performance pay for teachers has caveats", 2012), is that assessment judgements at low-decile schools are simply more generous than those made at high-decile schools. However, it is not necessary to resort to accusations of widespread dishonesty to support an argument that there might be systematic differences in the application of internally assessed standards across the decile range. Rather, the smaller differential for internal

---

4 Students who entered the standard gained at least an Achieved level and were awarded the attached credits.

assessment might be explained, in part, by a tendency for teachers to think normatively about their students; to see the best of them as being at Excellence level, and the poorest at the Not Achieved level. This kind of thinking could plausibly result in students at low-decile schools being awarded credits on the basis of performance that would not attract credits at a high-decile school.[5]

There are at least two other possible explanations for the much smaller differential between high- and low-decile schools for internal assessment than for external assessment. Neither explanation involves any systematic difference in the application of assessment criteria. One is simply that students at high-decile schools are much more practiced in external assessment than they are in internal assessment. Compared with low-decile schools, a considerably higher overall proportion of NCEA results from students in high-decile schools come from external assessments. For example, in 2014 some 42 percent of achievement standard results for students at decile 10 schools were externally assessed, compared with about 28 percent at decile 1 schools.

Another contributor to the differential might be that low-decile schools are deliberately choosing internally assessed standards that they think will be easier for their students to achieve. (Chapter 14 discusses this challenge in more detail.)

Yet another, related, explanation is that students at low-decile schools might struggle to perform in an examination environment to a much greater degree than those at high-decile schools. They might, for example, be more likely to be intimidated by the formality of the setting, or to have difficulty with literacy-related aspects of these assessments. In an internal-assessment environment, these factors can be mitigated by a lack of time pressure and a much greater range of available assessment formats.

---

5 Moderation processes should be able to address this challenge of course. But to do that effectively the moderation system would need to be geared towards opportunities for teacher professional learning. (Teachers would have the chance to critique work of a wide range of quality, not just from their own school, building towards a widely shared understanding of where the standard actually resides.) As we will show in Chapter 10, the moderation process is actually geared more towards system accountability.

Looking to the future: The liberating potential of internal assessments

If the greatest potential weakness of an internal assessment system is its *reliability*, its greatest potential strength is its *validity*. The flexibility afforded by internal assessment can be used to tailor assessments to particular courses, and to the needs and proclivities of particular students. Internal assessment tasks can potentially be used as learning experiences to a much greater degree than time-limited examinations. Furthermore, the skilled usage of internal assessment could go a very long way towards mitigating one of the great outstanding problems dogging the NCEA system: what Cedric Hall and others have described as the *fragmentation problem*.

The fragmentation problem arises largely because of a mistaken identification of standards as units of curriculum. Under this misunderstanding, teachers typically treat standards as units to be taught for a period of time, and then assessed. A typical NCEA course, then, comprises a series of such units, taught and assessed, with a single assessment event following each unit. While an opportunity for reassessment of a standard is allowable, there typically remains a one-to-one mapping between the teaching relating to a particular standard and the task used to assess it. A result of this approach is precisely the fragmentation problem; a subject or discipline becomes cut up into chunks relating to standards, and they are not typically put together again.

Standards are not units of curriculum but units of assessment. They are not, therefore, designed to be treated as a basis for time-bounded, sequential teaching units. They do not, and will never, comprise a comprehensive compilation of all that is worth learning in a subject or discipline. They obviate neither the need for careful course design, nor for careful thinking about the relationship between teaching, learning, and assessment. When they become the design template for a course, as they do in many cases at present, the fragmentation problem is an inevitable consequence.

It is highly likely that the overall design of NCEA has inadvertently contributed to this problem. As we saw in Section 1, examination prescriptions were, in effect, the senior secondary curriculum—at least up until the curriculum reforms initiated in the 1990s. Designing a three-level assessment structure that broadly equated with the 3 years of senior secondary schooling did nothing to disrupt the close association teachers habitually made between curriculum and assessment at any one year level. As the next two chapters will outline, the manner in which previous examination prescriptions and subject syllabi were used as the basis for chunking potential learning into NCEA standards constituted another lost opportunity to use assessment reform as an opportunity for rethinking the relationship between curriculum and assessment.

Chapter 5 The shift to standards-based assessment

Gaining greater consistency in teachers' assessment decision-making posed a significant set of challenges to the further development of internal assessment in the pre-NCEA years. As we saw in Chapter 4 this problem was largely managed by quality assurance processes that made only indirect reference to the *actual learning* being judged. In some cases reference tests of variable relevance to the actual learning were used to set a range of grades. In other cases the imposed range of grades was based on broad assumptions about the ability levels of a class of students. There was no systemic support for the sort of widespread professional sharing that might have allowed teachers in different schools to be involved in more actively aligning the types of judgements they were making.[1] Widespread dissatisfaction with these processes provided an important impetus for a system-wide shift to standards-based methods of assessment.

In this chapter we explore two different early efforts at making assessment decisions in a manner that did not rely on a comparative

---

1 Recall that the Tomorrow's Schools administrative reforms effectively dismantled the processes by which professional learning insights had flowed between schools in the days of the Department of Education—see Wylie, 2012.

ranking of students to determine how well they had achieved. While the first attempts were located in internal assessment contexts, the potential to use standards-based methods in external assessments was also explored. The developments outlined in this chapter, with their mix of successes and challenges, laid the foundations for NCEA's development in the following decade.

As we recall...

There are multiple recall narratives in this chapter, to support the distinct but sequentially related initiatives that are discussed. We begin with achievement based assessment (ABA). This was the first model of standards-based assessment to be systematically explored in New Zealand. First we share an insider account of this development from one of the key players. This is followed by Rose's recollections of her first encounters with ABA. Like other biology teachers all over New Zealand, she was not involved in the pre-development of the ABA initiative and hence met it cold via a series of professional learning workshops to which all biology teachers were invited.

Kate Colbert: Development and trialling of ABA

In the second half of the 1980s Kate Colbert was a science and biology teacher with a passionate interest in educational reform. In 1986 the Committee of Inquiry into Curriculum, Assessment and Qualifications in Forms 5 to 7 published a report of its findings with the title *Learning and Achieving*. Kate recalls that this manifesto for change resonated strongly with her personal experiences and concerns about meaningful learning and assessment for *all* students, not just those who were more academically able. Kate began to experiment with different forms of assessment in her classes. These efforts came to the attention of Jim Strachan, who was leading the assessment policy team in the Department of Education. He seconded Kate into his team to work on the development of a practical model of standards-based assessment.

Jim recruited a team of strong science teachers from around New Zealand to work on the development of a model of ABA. Recalling those heady times, Kate noted that those were the days of week-long development meetings, when there was time and space to debate ideas vigorously and to work on innovation as a strong collective. A whole year was spent on developing the approach. Kate led the development of supporting professional learning materials and the training of the facilitators who were recruited to help with the roll-out. Biology, geography, and physical education teachers were chosen to take part in early trials of ABA. They were introduced to the key ideas and resources in a series of full-day meetings, held regionally in each subject. Kate said the approach provided a united front for change, with experienced teachers working side by side with academics and policy-makers. She placed a high value on this collaborative development process.

One clear objective of ABA was to enhance the ability of teachers to make strong assessment judgements about the achievements of their own students, supported by new moderation processes. Kate recalls that teachers who understood this intent "went for it", but others were less comfortable making judgements that were "not black and white". The latter group were reluctant to engage and take up the responsibility for making their own judgements about their students' achievement in higher-stakes contexts. One sticking point concerned the deliberate philosophy to acknowledge positive learning gains, as opposed to the strongly established practice of "marking by error". The latter approach gives students the impression that not making mistakes is more important than taking learning risks. Kate noted that her driver then—and in the following NCEA years—was that "assessment shouldn't get in the way of excellent teaching and learning".

Rose: Early encounters with standards-based assessment

The mid 1980s brought my first encounter with standards-based assessment. All the biology teachers in the region were gathered together to be introduced to a new method of assessing student work called achievement-based assessment (ABA). For a specific task four or five levels of possible performance were identified. Each level was intended to add a *qualitative* difference to the level below (examples follow in Figure 5.1).

During an early professional learning session we (the gathered biology teachers) soon found ourselves assessing actual examples of student work that had been developed for a sample task and its accompanying criteria. Challenges were immediately apparent. Even though we all had the same ABA criteria in front of us, different teachers arrived at different judgements of these samples. Debates were heated! In a subsequent workshop we were challenged to design task or criteria sets of our own. It was clear to me that some teachers still did not understand ABA and would not be able to apply standards-based assessment principles to their work. For me, as for some other teachers, the whole experience was transformative. I began to think more critically about multiple potential *purposes* for doing specific types of tasks, and to design and refine sets of ABA criteria according to the purpose I wished to foreground. The impact on my *curriculum* thinking, not just my assessment thinking, was profound.

The desirability of sharing the sets of criteria with students before they were assessed was one of the hotly contested features of the whole ABA initiative. Many of my colleagues could not get past the feeling that this was somehow cheating and so was particularly inappropriate for formal assessments. I also had to think my way through this challenge but my expanded view of purposes for learning helped me understand and get past my initial unease. In an intuitive move that anticipated today's learning-to-learn pedagogies, I began to build negotiated sets of criteria in collaboration with my students. These were then displayed prominently in my classroom where students could check them at will. The set I most readily recall described five levels of quality for drawing biological diagrams, following appropriate scientific conventions. Some of my senior students later came back to tell me how useful these criteria had been after they transitioned to university studies, where they were seemingly expected to intuit the features of quality biological drawing with no specific guidance.

ABA as a learning foray into standards-based assessment

Figure 5.1 provides two examples of ABA assessment schedules. Tracking these down highlighted the ephemeral nature of pedagogical initiatives that flare and die. We had to cast a wide net to find surviving examples, written as they were in an era of WordPerfect for DOS and floppy discs. These examples were transcribed from an acetate sheet intended for display on an overhead projector—the very latest technology at the time. The first example describes achievement at five different levels. The second example describes achievement at four levels. Whether four or five levels constituted an ideal number was being debated at the time.

Looking back at these examples with the benefit of hindsight, several things stand out. It will be evident that using a schedule such as this required careful judgement on the part of the teacher. No matter how carefully the developers thought they had constructed the criteria, these were still subject to interpretation. What, for example, are "appropriate" time intervals? This challenge of semantics has continued on to bedevil NCEA to this day. Interpreting the intended meaning of terms that are key to understanding "where the standard resides in a standard" generates considerable work and anxiety for teachers. It is now recognised that verbal descriptions alone are a woefully inadequate means of achieving consistency in teachers' judgements. Exemplars are also required. To increase the chances that these exemplars will be interpreted as intended, they must be carefully annotated. Preferably, a range of exemplars should be available for any one set of criteria, annotated to cast light on the features that might be observed at different levels of achievement, with particular attention given to borderline cases that sit very close to grade boundaries.

Figure 5.1. Examples of ABA criteria developed for specific tasks

A practical investigation of material properties of socks

1. Presents some relevant ideas about heat and types of fabrics.
2. Attempts to link relevant ideas in a logical way.
3. Presents relevant ideas and a logical plan that is clear and sequential.
4. Presents relevant ideas and a logical plan that is clear and sequential and has only ONE [dependent] variable. One or more observation(s) made at irregular intervals.
5. Presents relevant ideas and a logical plan that is clear and sequential and has only ONE [dependent] variable. More than TWO measurements made at appropriate time intervals.

Observing and drawing a plant (for younger children)

1. Attempts to draw plant. Drawing shows at least three parts.
2. Draws plant. Correctly labels three parts (e.g. flower, leaf, root, stalk).
3. Draws plant. Correctly labels four parts. Gives functions for two parts.
4. Draws and labels plant. Correct functions for four parts given.

Again with the benefit of hindsight, the criteria in the ABA example have a *quantitative* sensibility that also proved to be problematic in the early NCEA years. Students achieve a higher level if they do *more* of something. Yet the differences between levels were actually intended to denote *qualitative* differences in achievement of a specific task. Such differences could obviously be hard to describe, especially if a task was insufficiently rich to clearly differentiate levels of performance. Consider, for example, two variants of a task that draws on a specific body of knowledge from a course of learning. Task 1 asks students to recall and briefly outline several ideas from the course. Assessing successful completion can be achieved by adding the number of correct answers. Task 2 draws on the same content, but asks students to use the ideas for a purpose that requires them to think more critically—perhaps they have to compare and contrast the ideas in some way, or say how they do or don't support a given argument. Task 2 can be completed in a superficial way, or in a manner that demonstrates insight into the interconnections between the ideas. These are indications of qualitative differences in performance of the task.

The need to design tasks and criteria that differentiate between superficial and deeper levels of understanding could help account for the rapidly increasing popularity of the structured observations of learning outcomes (SOLO) taxonomy in recent years. This taxonomy provides a framework for task and criterion design by differentiating levels of interconnection of ideas, along the lines just sketched.[2]

Looking back at these early examples, it is no wonder teachers have continued to struggle to identify qualitatively different demonstrations of learning in NCEA achievement standards. As will become clear in the discussion of unit standards later in this chapter, the type of learning to be certified is an important consideration when addressing this problem.

Yet another challenge is evident in the dual nature of the tasks being assessed by these criteria. In one task students design a plan for an investigation *and* then they carry it out. What if they do one part well and not the other? They could, for example, develop a good plan then muck around, or conversely not develop a good plan but fix up any shortcomings as they try to enact the plan they do have. Trading off different aspects of achievement within one standard is another challenge that has caused problems when making judgements about achievement for NCEA.

---

2 One of the original developers of this taxonomy explains it here: http://www.johnbiggs.com.au/academic/solo-taxonomy/

Shortcomings of the type just outlined certainly created practical changes that have been controversial. However they are symptoms of a deeper challenge. What might making progress actually look like when framed in terms of qualitatively different demonstrations of achievement? While this might seem like an obvious question to ask, traditional practice has tended to see knowing more about topics, or learning about more difficult topics, as a proxy for making progress. This is a curriculum question that needs to be taken seriously if new and more apt standards-based learning progress is to be described.

It should be evident by now that actually designing these schedules was not an easy matter. They were task-specific and so needed to be designed afresh for each new assessment task. No wonder many teachers resisted their adoption, despite the fact that they did have the potential to open up a wider range of tasks to standards-based assessment decision-making by teachers themselves.

A different type of challenge relates to the types of task that might be assessed using ABA. Both these examples were for practical tasks. However it was not at all clear that the method would be appropriate for assessing demonstrations of knowledge. Rose experimented once—and only once—with the use of ABA to assess mock examinations at Year 12. It simply did not feel right to award a level from 1 to 5 for a whole examination. All the challenges outlined above were amplified when applied across multiple knowledge questions. In Part 3 of this book we return to the challenge of how knowledge is treated in NCEA.

The move to unit standards

Notwithstanding the exploratory foray into ABA, the recommendations of the Committee of Inquiry for Curriculum and Assessment Change were largely ignored. In the late 1980s the Labour government's focus in education moved away from curriculum and assessment to the widespread administrative reforms known as Tomorrow's Schools (see Wylie, 2012, for an extended discussion of these changes). The Department of Education was replaced by a smaller Ministry of Education. An autonomous qualifications authority (NZQA) was established to pick up the work of the former Department's examination division. The election of the National government (1990–99) saw the focus of assessment and curriculum shift to developing a flexible qualifications system aligned with a new curriculum framework. This was intended to prioritise "the diverse educational and training needs of students" (Ministry of Education, 1993a, p. 8). Education was to be more closely aligned with the economy and business.

During the administrative turmoil that prevailed in the 1990s, School Certificate, Sixth Form Certificate and UE (Bursary and Scholarship) continued as before. At the same time NZQA developed and trialled a series of standards-based assessments at all three levels of the senior secondary school, for which judgements were made on the basis of unit standards. These standards functioned on a pass/fail (or Achieved/Not Achieved)[3] basis which meant that there was just one *overall* judgement for a teacher to make (but also no way to differentiate between different levels of achievement, as had been modelled in ABA). However multiple smaller judgements had to precede the overall one in cases where a unit standard was made up of a series of discrete elements, all of which must be judged separately to come to the overall result. The examples of unit standards in Figures 5.2 and 5.3 provide an indication of what these standards looked like.

Even though the unit standards gave teachers a degree of curriculum and assessment flexibility in principle, the model was not well received. Teachers did not like the way these standards broke up the assessment of each particular subject into a number of separate components, each assessed by a different unit standard (Fountain, 2012).

As Kate recalls

Kate Colbert was on maternity leave in 1990. Recalling the sweeping changes outlined above she described this as "a good year to have off". She returned to work as an employee of the newly created NZQA and was soon hard at work transferring learning from the ABA trials to the newly proposed unit standards. Kate had observed at first-hand that many teachers struggled to make sound judgements using the ABA criteria. She believed that the finer-grained unit standards would provide better support for teachers in this regard. However

---

3 Until 2008, Not Achieved was not a formal result category for unit standards, and was not consistently reported to NZQA, making it impossible to determine overall achievement rates for these standards.

she also saw that these potential gains also came at a cost. Whereas ABA had been driven by a *conceptual* framework that addressed different *purposes* for learning, Kate saw unit standards as being *content*-driven. Setting aside these early reservations, she invested a number of years in supporting this next stage in the shift to standards-based assessment, which she saw as preferable to returning to previous assessment practice.

As Rose recalls
I was invited to be part of the development of unit standards for senior secondary biology. With *Biology in the New Zealand Curriculum* (Ministry of Education, 1996) as our guide we developed titles and assessment criteria that reflected the established content of our subject. This felt really hard. I recall struggling with the Achieved/Not Achieved distinction as the only basis for judgement. Getting to grips with the technicalities of elements within a standard and the accompanying range notes also felt like an unnaturally hard struggle, especially for someone like me who was a very intuitive curriculum thinker. Even though I was involved in developing them, I never did adopt unit standards as enthusiastically as I had taken to ABA.

In one week-long residential retreat at Lincoln University we created illustrative tasks to support the newly minted unit standards. I was assigned to work on the team developing exemplars for human biology. Between us all the science learning areas were being addressed at the same time. Again this felt hard and I recall strong ideological debates between some team members slowing our progress. Perhaps I was just too tired. It was late in the year and I was getting up very early to complete my day's quota of marking for Bursary biology before the working party's day began. I include this detail only as a reminder that it is not easy for busy teachers to deal with multiple assessment systems running in parallel, yet this was the reality for many of us during those years (and indeed continues in other guises to this day).

How unit standards work

Unit Standard 1100 (Level 4) in Figure 5.2 is from the Plumbing, Gas-fitting and Drain-laying domain of the New Zealand Qualifications Framework. It has six outcome statements, each with a number of very concrete criteria indicating the elements required for the outcome to be judged successful. Collectively the outcomes and criteria describe the entire process of drain-laying in some detail.

Clearly this approach is appropriate and desirable when the subject matter of a standard can be described and assessed in this sequential manner. It is also appropriate when the purpose of the qualification to which the standard contributes requires confidence that all elements of the standard have been mastered. More specifically, the unit standard model is appropriate for the certification of skills and of process-oriented knowledge. These things lend themselves to a mastery assessment approach, under which individual elements can be assessed on the basis of a required level of competence. Furthermore, most of the qualifications to which these standards continue to contribute are professional and vocational in nature. They require the certification of all elements of the standards in order to ensure professional competence and, in many cases, individual or public safety. Note that a relevant industry training organisation (ITO) owns and manages the processes for making judgements about each student's success achieving the various elements, and hence the overall standard. This is a timely reminder that NZQA was set up to administer assessment in the tertiary sector as well as in the school sector (although as we will soon see, universities made a deliberate decision to opt out of the unit-standard approach to assessment).

Figure 5.2. An example of a unit standard owned by an ITO

Unit Standard: Install surface water intake and outfall structures

Outcome 1: Determine the position of surface water intake and outfall structures.

1.1 Line and gradient are positioned to measurements in accordance with job specifications.

1.2 Other services are located, avoided, and protected in accordance with the owning utility operator's working practice.

1.3 Other services are identified by label and/or colour in accordance with job specifications and relevant standards and codes.

1.4 Any obstructions are avoided or removed.

Outcome 2: Prepare for installation.

2.1 Stable sub-base is identified in accordance with visual assessment and job specifications.

2.2 Base material is selected, placed, and levelled in accordance with site conditions and job specifications.

2.3 Surface water intake and outfall structures are positioned to measurements in accordance with job specifications and relevant legislation and codes.

Outcome 3: Complete the installation of surface water intake and outfall structures.

3.1 Surface water intake and outfall structures are installed in accordance with job specifications.

3.2 Surface water intake and outfall structures are completed in accordance with job specifications.

3.3 The installation meets requirements of the Building Act 2004.

Outcome 4: Carry out backfilling and clear the site.

4.1 Site is backfilled, and compacted as necessary, in accordance with job specifications.

4.2 Site is cleared of construction debris and working equipment.

Outcome 5: Work safely and with care.

5.1 Practical activities are carried out avoiding harm to people and damage to property, other services, materials, tools, and equipment.

Outcome 6: Demonstrate knowledge of concepts and principles underpinning the installation of surface water intake and outfall structures.

6.1 Underpinning concepts and principles are explained in terms of their application to the installation of surface water intake and outfall structures.

Unit standards are more problematic in traditional (disciplinary) curriculum subjects

The plumbing example illustrates a key design feature of unit standards: each one specifies a range of elements, all of which must be attained before the standard is awarded. As in the example here, unit standard assessment can be readily adapted for specific multidimensional vocational skills. The application of the unit standard design to traditional academic disciplines is more problematic. To illustrate the nature of these problems, Figure 5.3 introduces Unit Standard 18982 (Level 1). We chose this example more or less by default, as one of a very few surviving examples of its kind. We've already noted the challenge we faced in tracking down surviving ABA criteria. Most of the curriculum-linked unit standards have now been withdrawn and removed from NZQA's website. This survivor may well also have disappeared by the time this book appears in print.

Figure 5.3. An example of an academic unit standard

Unit standard: Demonstrate knowledge of Earth science

Outcome 1: Describe the structure of the Earth.

1.1 The description outlines features of the Earth's structure. Features include—mantle, core, crust, plates; evidence of three features is required.

Outcome 2: Describe the formation of rocks.

2.1 The description outlines the process of rock formation. Processes include—sedimentary, igneous, metamorphic; evidence of two processes is required.

Outcome 3: Describe the breakdown of rocks.

3.1 The description outlines natural processes that break down rocks. Natural processes include—rain, wind, ice, temperature changes, mechanical weathering, chemical weathering, biological weathering; evidence of three natural processes is required.

Outcome 4: Identify rocks in a local area.

4.1 Rocks in a local area are identified by name and type. Types of rock include—sedimentary, igneous, metamorphic; evidence of two named rocks, of any type is required.

This standard was developed as part of a set that could be used either in a polytechnic or in a secondary school to assess earth science components of the school science curriculum.[4] All such academic unit standards were scheduled to be withdrawn from use in 2012. However many teachers objected and the withdrawal of this and several other similar science unit standards has been deferred several times. In Part 3 we'll come back to debates about the place (or not) for these unit

---

4 A Planet Earth strand was added to the overall science curriculum mix in the 1990s move to standards-based curriculum documents. It would be fair to say that this addition was enthusiastically received by some groups of teachers, but shunned as a disciplinary imposter by those who held a strong view that the traditional subjects of biology, chemistry and physics had more status and therefore should receive more emphasis (see also Chapter 12).

standards when we discuss course design to meet the needs of different groups of students.

Do the various parts add up to the indicated result? The title indicates that standard is intended to certify knowledge of earth science. What is actually assessed is knowledge of a collection of facts arising from earth science. An alternative understanding of the title could be that it assesses students' understanding of the way in which theories in earth science are constructed and validated (i.e., the "nature of earth science"). Clearly the actual standard does not do this because no epistemic knowledge of the discipline itself is required to satisfy the criteria. In fairness this problem was not new to unit standards. Collections of examination questions, and for that matter of achievement standards, are also often assumed to add up to an understanding of a discipline. This is an assumption that we think bears careful critical scrutiny and we discuss it in greater depth in Chapter 12.

Notice that US 18982 has four outcome statements but, unlike the plumbing standard described above, there is no logical sequential connection between them. In effect this standard is assessing whether students can recall and perhaps apply of a set of facts about the structure of the earth, the formation and breakdown of rocks, and the identification of rocks. (We say "perhaps apply" because the types of tasks that could generate the evidence are not specified.) Notice also that achievement is defined in mix of qualitative and quantitative terms: a set number of examples must be provided to satisfy each outcome statement. The challenge of making an overall judgement in this circumstance has been discussed above as a problematic aspect of ABA criteria. Here that same challenge has been carried through into unit standard criteria.

There is another problem in the design of the unit standard in Figure 5.3 (and indeed all other academic unit standards that followed this same design pattern). Whereas there was a clear justification for requiring all outcome statements to be met for the plumbing unit standard—the elements were parts of a whole task, such that the task could not be successfully completed without being able to do all the parts in an appropriate order—no such justification is evident when a unit standard specifies a collection of facts to be recalled. Suppose for example that one student describes three features for Outcome 1, two processes for Outcome 2, three processes for Outcome 3 and identifies two rocks for Outcome 4; the minimum requirements for each outcome. This student therefore attains credits for the standard. A second student describes two features for Outcome 1, all three processes for Outcome 2, all seven processes for Outcome 3 and identifies five different rocks for Outcome 4. This student does not achieve the standard despite demonstrating a greater breadth of recall than the first student, because they fell slightly short on the first outcome. In the absence of a coherent connection between the four outcome statements, and of a clear rationale requiring all four to be met, a better approach might be to allow an on-balance judgement; in other words, to allow superior performance on some outcomes to compensate for weaker performance on others. We'll come back to the challenge of making on-balance judgements in Chapter 10.

All these issues eventually led to the development of achievement standards and, following the alignment of the achievement standards with the curriculum implemented between 2011 and 2013, the demise of unit standards as means of assessing curriculum-related learning.

Resistance to unit standards in the university sector

The specification of a range of elements under the unit-standard model, all of which must be attained, probably reflects the early influence of the Scottish Vocational Educational Council on New Zealand's approach to developing unit standards (NZQA, 2004). As we have seen, this approach can work well for the certification of vocational skills such as sanitary plumbing and piloting aircraft. However when it came to the application of the unit-standard mode to disciplines with more powerful epistemological processes for the discovery and construction of knowledge, problems were quickly identified.

Cedric Hall: Rejection of unit standards by the universities

Cedric Hall, an assessment expert with a deep knowledge of the New Zealand qualifications system, recalls that in the mid-1990s unit standards came close to being the mandated approach for assessment at degree level. At the time Professor Hall was director of Victoria University's Teaching and Development Centre. He became involved in a project in which faculty representatives attempted to envisage how they might examine courses using unit standards.

The approach was unanimously rejected as being unsuitable for the kind of disciplinary knowledge that is the staple of university degrees, for the kinds of reasons we noted in relation to our case study of an earth science standard. The only application for which unit standards were deemed suitable was for certifying specific skills tangentially associated with disciplinary knowledge-building; for example the use of scientific apparatus.

Having written about this project, Professor Hall was asked to be part of a panel set up by the New Zealand Vice Chancellor's Committee. This group was asked to develop an official position on the implications of the proposed changes to the national assessment regime for universities. In the event they persuaded Cabinet to set up a second tier of qualifications separate from the National Qualifications Framework. These were called *provider qualifications* and they included university qualifications. Because provider qualifications need not be assessed using standards registered on the qualifications framework, universities could, and did, opt out of the unit-standard approach.

The unit-standard model faced similar objections from the school sector as those that led to its rejection by the universities. It was not clear to secondary teachers that the elements-based design of unit standards could work in the school curriculum disciplines. Experience with those unit standards that were used in curriculum areas between 2002 and 2013 vindicates these reservations.

The politics of unit standards

There were a number of different motivations in play as unit standards were developed. Being internally assessed, they fulfilled the aims of the PPTA and educators who wanted to shift the focus of teaching and learning away from externally set examinations designed to rank students. David Hood, the chief executive of NZQA in its founding years, strongly supported and endorsed the vision of progressive educators for an assessment system that could acknowledge the learning gains made by all students. The alternative, as he saw it, was a cost that society could no longer afford:

> If "rights" to education include the right to achieve success, then once again schooling has failed to reach the expectations of our forebears. Many of our people of all ages carry the stigma of learning failure, a stigma carried throughout their lives. In an age in which lifelong education is a must, learning is seen by too many as irrelevant, inappropriate and unattainable. (Hood, 1998, pp. 17–18)

Unit standards also aligned with an emerging agenda for education that sought to provide a set of prescribed outcomes that served the interests of business and the economy (see O'Neill, Clark, & Openshaw, 2004). Thus the introduction of unit standards gave a superficial appearance of reconciling the interests of "progressive" educators and those with a narrower, economically focused agenda for the education system.

Unit standards were initially developed as part of Lockwood Smith's vision for a national qualifications framework. This framework was intended to create a seamless education system that brought together secondary education, industry training, and tertiary education within a unified structure. However, far from being seamless, the unit-standard approach arguably had a *fragmenting* effect on curriculum-based learning. It was understandable that teaching and learning tended to become focused on specific minutiae when teachers were required to assess whether all the elements of each unit standard had been met. Learning about disciplinary thinking, including the nature of theory construction and the role of evidence in different disciplines (i.e., epistemic practices), can be seen as integral to the way discipline-based subjects are presented in *NZC*. Yet this type of learning could never be adequately represented or assessed using a fragmented, content-focused unit standard model.

In addition to these epistemological concerns, unit standards signalled a major shift from the norm-referenced, prescription-based framework for assessment that had dominated secondary schooling for decades. There was vocal opposition to the lack of grading, the absence of external assessment, and the anticipated impact of internal assessment on teachers' workloads (see for example Alison, 2008). Given the PPTA's ongoing support for alternative models of assessment, it was somewhat ironic that the union instigated a moratorium on unit standards in the mid-1990s as a response to the perceived impact of internal assessment on teachers' workload.

Another difficulty threatened the implementation of the new qualifications system: The technical demands of running such a system on a national scale, based entirely on internally assessed unit standards, were not well understood by the public agencies and politicians charged with overseeing the transition. This was not for want of technical experts providing criticism and advice in relation to the new policy.

Academics such as Warwick Elley (then a professor of education at Canterbury University) did provide critical feedback, but they were largely ignored. For example, as early as 1987, Elley warned the then Minister of Education, Russell Marshall, of the tensions between internal assessment and criterion-based assessment:

> The main problem I see with the current proposal… is that it is attempting to move in two contrary directions at the same time. The movement towards internal assessment is a decentralizing movement. Each of 500 [6th Form] English and Science teachers will soon be evolving different courses and setting different tests and assignments, which is fine. But any move towards describing accurately what students *know* and *can do* requires a careful standardization of tasks and conditions which is easiest to bring about under a uniform examination and hardest under school-based systems … (Elley, cited in Fountain, 2012, p. 37)

Elley also wrote a letter on the same theme to Jim Ross, chair of the CICAQ and Assistant Director General of Education. The letter outlined the difficulties which would confront content-based subjects in the standards-based assessment environment:

> Whatever else the Liberal rhetoric has achieved, it is clear that it has raised an unrealistic expectation about what is possible in the matter of establishing standards of achievement, independent of any norm referencing … Subjects like English, Science, History, Geography and Economics are multi-dimensional in their objectives, they have no homogenous knowledge domain that can be neatly carved up and they defy any accurate attempt to describe achievement in concise summary terms. (Elley, cited in Fountain, 2012, pp. 37–38)

Some of Elley's criticisms and warnings were certainly vindicated as events unfolded. In particular, the variability crisis that plagued the early NCEA years was largely attributable to an "unrealistic expectation about what is possible in the matter of establishing standards of achievement, independent of any norm referencing" (Fountain, 2012, p. 37). The way out of this crisis was to develop quasi-norms for external assessments. These quasi-norms—the profiles of expected performance (PEPs)—are described in detail in Chapter 7.

On the other hand, Elley's comment to Marshall, to the effect that "a careful standardization of [assessment] tasks and conditions" is required "to describe accurately what students know and can do" is a claim we would challenge. What the NCEA system affords via its internally assessed component is a national expectation of skills and knowledge embodied in a standard, with local freedom to assess those skills and knowledge in a context that is best suited to a particular course or to particular students. While achieving acceptable consistency under this system has certainly been challenging, expensive, and remains a work in progress, great gains were made in the decade following the 2005 crisis (see Chapter 8). Furthermore, the as-yet-unrealised potential for developing a wider range of internally assessed courses in the NCEA system (see Part 3) benefits from the "contrary directions" described by Elley. It also provides a means of allowing decentralised course design and creating more standardised means for judging how well these courses have achieved their stated objectives. If even an approximation of this potential can be realised, the challenge and expense will have been well worthwhile.

Drawing this account of early experimentation with standards-based assessment to a close, it is important to note that unit standards continue to play an integral role in assessment of employment-based (vocational) learning. Assessment developers have continued to refine them over time. Some of the ITOs who own these unit standards have worked hard to develop robust new assessment systems that provide strong support for those being assessed (see for example Vaughan & Cameron, 2011). Given the political imperative to support all young people to see themselves as successful learners, and to go on learning in their post-school years, these are important gains to celebrate.

Taking stock, moving on

As the experiment with standards-based assessment in the 1990s moved towards the full implementation of a new qualifications system in the early 2000s, it became clear that, for all the epistemological, political, and technical reasons discussed above, a pure internally assessed approach based entirely on unit standards would not work. The schools could not be allowed to go the same way as the universities; if they had, standards-based assessment for qualifications would have been dead in the water. At the proverbial eleventh hour, the achievement standard model was developed to keep schools on board with the process of reform. In the next decade NCEA would progressively replace the School Certificate, Sixth-Form Certificate and Bursary qualifications in the senior secondary school.

Chapter 6 NCEA as a political compromise

As we saw in Chapter 5, controversy over unit standards was motivated by three specific concerns: the unsuitability of unit standards for the assessment of curriculum disciplines; discomfort with the notion of a qualifications system entirely based on internal assessment; and the lack of differentiation between levels of performance (grades). It was clear that the fractious political environment engendered by this controversy was not going to be conducive to the introduction of the new qualifications system. Recognising this, Wyatt Creech (Minister of Education from 1996 to 1999) made significant compromises to establish sufficient consensus amongst the various interested parties. Many, but not all, of Creech's compromises were embodied in the development of the achievement standard model for the assessment of the school curriculum.

In contrast to unit standards that provided only one passing grade, achievement standards were designed to denote four levels of performance, with three passing grades: Achieved; Merit; and Excellence. New Zealand Scholarship was conceived as an adjunct to the incipient NCEA to recognise elite performance at curriculum Level 8—in effect the final year of schooling. In most subjects it was based on a traditional 3-hour examination format.

The differences between unit and achievement standards are important from a knowledge perspective. As illustrated by the plumbing and earth science examples in Chapter 5, unit standards typically comprise a number of highly specific criteria, all of which must be fulfilled to achieve credit for the standard. In contrast, achievement standards typically comprise a single criterion for each grade level, with a progression of conceptual sophistication distinguishing the criteria for the successive Achieved, Merit, and Excellence grades. In consequence, achievement-standard criteria tend to be much more abstract than unit-standard criteria, with some explanatory notes to guide the judgement of assessors.

Achievement standards also made provision for external assessment. Half of the inaugural set in each subject were designed to be externally assessed. (However, by 2014 well over half were assessed internally.) Concerns of progressive educators were to be addressed via policies and processes that would allow flexibility in pacing assessments and in combining credits from both unit and assessment standards to reach the overall targets specified for NCEA Levels 1, 2 and 3.

Following the election of the Labour government in 1999, the new Minister of Education Trevor Mallard implemented the NCEA assessment model incrementally between 2002 and 2004 with no significant changes to Creech's revisions. However, the implementation was delayed by one year to placate criticism that it was being rushed.

- Level 1 NCEA (broadly corresponding to Year 11 of schooling) was awarded for the first time in 2002.
- In 2003 NCEA was mostly implemented at Level 2/Year 12.
- In 2004 Level 3 NCEA was awarded for the first time, with Level 4 an optional scholarship award for the most able students.

Recollections related to NCEA's development

As we have just noted, achievement standards had a controversial and turbulent birth. Many innovating teachers had invested time and energy in the unit-standards model and now they were being asked to try something different again. Inside NZQA similar pressures were being felt by those committed to assessment reform. We asked two key players to look back on this time, and Rose does the same. These recollections illustrate how goodwill was stretched thin, creating less than ideal conditions for dispassionately thinking through all the ramifications and implications of the changes being made.

Jim Strachan: New Zealand's doyen of assessment

Jim Strachan, now semi-retired, has spent much of his working life in public education agencies, first at the Department of Education (the precursor to the current Ministry) before becoming a founding employee of NZQA. As such, he has a near-encyclopaedic knowledge of the assessment reform movement in New Zealand that began in the 1970s and culminated in the implementation of NCEA.

Our conversation with Jim afforded us many insights. One of these addresses the seemingly inexplicable failure of NZQA to see the Scholarship crisis of 2005 coming (see Chapter 8): Jim noted that NZQA was not established specifically to reform secondary assessment, but rather, to build a new national qualifications system, of which secondary assessment was but one part. The desire to found the new system, including school qualifications, on a unified approach to assessment—that of unit standards—is understandable. NCEA is just one of some hundreds of qualifications registered on the qualifications framework and this explains, to some extent at least, the initial reluctance of NZQA to develop an approach specifically for schools, and their later failure to heed the advice of technical experts warning them of the looming crisis. Indeed, as Jim also noted, a now-defunct qualification based entirely on unit standards, also called NCEA, was registered in the mid-1990s, well before achievement standards had been conceived of. He pointed out that political decisions in 1997 confirmed the reformist policy path, but also established an intention to replace the original NCEA with the system of qualifications that was eventually introduced between 2002 and 2004, and led to the development of achievement standards to support this qualification.

For Jim, the development of the achievement standards in the late 1990s, and the structure of NCEA itself, were pragmatic compromises. He explained that schools that had done well under the previous regime—mainly, but not entirely, high-decile boys' schools—were trying to keep hold of examinations as the primary assessment mechanism. Their mechanism for doing this was to exert influence within the Principal's Lead Group, which, Jim informed us, was broadly supportive of a new qualification based entirely on unit standards and, therefore, entirely internally assessed. While the group seeking to retain external examinations was a minority within the Principal's Lead Group, they were a powerful minority, and their discontent resulted in sufficient political pressure to depart from the purely unit-standards approach. Achievement standards, based on the conventional curriculum, with graded achievement and a strong component of external assessment, were developed. At the behest of (Minister) Lockwood Smith, the unit standards linked to the school curriculum, which had been developed earlier, were retained in parallel. These were intended for students who would struggle with mainstream academic work and their retention had the unfortunate effect of tainting all unit standards as being easy.

Jim commented that it is debateable whether the remodelling of school qualifications to bring on board the group of schools that wanted to retain external assessment was worth the compromise, noting that many are now running alternative qualifications systems anyway. Furthermore, the requirement under the initial achievement-standard model that half of the suite of standards in each subject were to be externally assessed meant the sacrifice of a core principle of assessment validity: that each standard ought to be assessed using the most appropriate assessment mechanism for the skills or knowledge to be certified.

As an experienced assessment expert with his eyes nonetheless firmly set on the curriculum, Jim expressed some disappointment in the rather pedestrian way in which internal assessment is typically deployed under NCEA. While internal assessment for qualifications can be used formatively, there is little evidence that this opportunity has been taken up to any great degree. Another under-exploited opportunity is for the use of *naturally occurring evidence*—that is, students' everyday class work, with few formal assessment events, or none at all. While "multi-levelling'—students undertaking standards at more than one framework level in the same year—is taking place, it usually takes the form of students undertaking standards at a lower level than is typical for their year level. Jim believes that schools haven't taken up these opportunities to the extent that they might largely because of a concern with safety, that is, as a defence against the expectations of parents.

Gregor Fountain: A gradual awakening to the potential of NCEA
Gregor Fountain was a history teacher who was closely involved in the early unit standard trials. He recalls initially being resistant to the introduction of achievement standards because he wasn't comfortable with their potential to be used to rank students. On reflection, he came

to see achievement standards as a politically necessary move to attain acceptance of NCEA by schools. But more importantly, he could also see their potential to address a tricky curriculum challenge. Gregor noted that history teachers' courses were typically shaped around their favourite topics. The 1980s history curriculum had introduced many elements of the discipline of historical thinking, but these were initially ignored in favour of tried and true topics that teachers liked to teach. When the achievement standards were developed the disciplinary (epistemic) elements of the curriculum were built into the achievement criteria of the new standards. The curriculum then started to gain greater currency because these disciplinary elements were being explicitly assessed for the first time. This shift spread across the 3 years of senior secondary as the new achievement standards were progressively rolled out. The new emphasis on disciplinary thinking has gradually strengthened history teaching pedagogy in a way that Gregor believes teachers would have resisted if it had been introduced as a radical and more abrupt change to a discipline-based approach. Gregor now sees the development of achievement standards as more than an expedient compromise to win the acquiescence of schools to the new system.

Rose: Developing prototype Level 1 achievement standards for science

I was invited to be part of the team that developed the very first suite of Level 1 science achievement standards. *Science in the New Zealand Curriculum* (Ministry of Education, 1993b) had been published earlier in the decade and I had been strongly attracted to its change sensibilities, in particular the idea of more holistic and contextualised learning experiences, and the fledgling Nature of Science strand. However the development of the achievement standards began before these new pedagogical ideas had had time to consolidate. I walked into the very first meeting of the achievement standards writing group to be told, "You're a biologist. Your group is over there." I recall thinking "there goes the curriculum" as I walked across the room to pick up my pre-prepared, colour-coded folder of development materials. Sure enough it quickly became clear that our task was to divide up four content strands of science into chunks that would become separate achievement standards. We were repeatedly assured that only the method of assessment was changing—the "curriculum" was to be the same as before. I've put curriculum in quotation marks here because, even though we did have the 1993 curriculum available, people's experience and expectations of School Certificate science largely drove the coverage thinking that prevailed as the division into discrete standards was carried out. I, for one, was not reassured because I was looking for change and saw an opportunity about to be squandered.

Some years later I spoke with one of the Ministry of Education staff who helped with achievement standard development across a range of learning areas. Comparing the working conditions in different curriculum groups he described science as a case of "blood on the floor". Every tiniest shift from traditional practice was hotly disputed by some members of that initial development team. For example, some of us argued that the number of credits assigned to achievement standards for earth science/astronomy should reflect the status of this area of knowledge as one of four contextual strands in the new curriculum (the other three being biology, chemistry, and physics). We lost and this strand remained the poor relation in the Level 1 mix until the whole suite was revised and updated some years later. The debate got stuck at this coverage level so we never even attempted a more radical transformation of the learning area to reflect greater clarity around purposes for learning, as was done in history for example.

The development of achievement standards and the birth of NCEA

The different perspectives outlined above go some way to explaining how and why the development of achievement standards looked and felt different in different learning areas. Some teams were able to develop suites of standards that reflected new curriculum thinking but others remained firmly wedded to a traditional content coverage foundation. Because the learning area teams largely worked in isolation from each other there was no formal process for addressing these discrepancies. It did not help that the Ministry of Education held the curriculum mandate while the work was carried out but NZQA was responsible for ensuring that the new achievement standards were technically correct in their structure and specifications.

Like the expired unit standards it is not easy to find intact examples of the very first sets of achievement standards. They have undergone considerable revision in the intervening years. However old examination papers are still readily available. Figure 6.1 shows the criteria for one of the original Level 1 achievement standards in biology (NZQA, 2002).

Figure 6.1. Achievement standard 1.6 (4 credits): Describe the functioning of human digestive and skeletomuscular systems

Achievement Criteria		
Achievement	Achievement with Merit	Achievement with Excellence
Describe biological ideas and process relating to the functioning of human digestive and skeletomuscular systems.	Explain biological ideas and processes relating to the functioning of human digestive and skeletomuscular systems.	Apply biological ideas and processes relating to the functioning of human digestive and skeletomuscular systems.
	Overall Level of Performance	

Notice the taxonomy of "describe, explain, apply" used to differentiate the three levels of achievement. This type of taxonomy was commonly, but not universally, used as the different subject suites were developed. In essence, this set of specifications continues the content coverage emphasis of School Certificate. Indeed, the questions inside this examination paper would not have looked out of place in a School Certificate examination, except that this NCEA paper would have been expected to take just an hour to complete because several such papers would typically be aggregated into one 3-hour examination.

If used as a set of School Certificate questions, marks would have been awarded for the various components of the answers and tallied to arrive at an overall score. Using the above criteria to arrive at a grade judgement was much less straightforward. Table 6.1 shows the type of evidence being sought for Question 3b—just one of six questions in the paper overall.

Multiply this set of decisions by six (the number of questions in the paper) and it will be evident that marking involved a number of fine judgement calls. Furthermore, once all the questions had been assessed there remained the issue of how to combine the various judgements to arrive at the overall grade. The judgement statement developed for this purpose is shown in Table 6.2. Here another complication becomes evident. There are in effect two topics in this one achievement standard. They are differentiated as A1, M1, E1 and A2, M2, E2 in the judgement statement. There is a decidedly quantitative feel to the formula to be applied to arrive at an overall judgement when melding achievement evidence for two topics and three levels each.

Table 6.1. An excerpt of the evidence statement for the 2002 examination for Biology AS 1.6

Question	Evidence contributing to Achievement	Evidence contributing to Achievement with Merit	Evidence contributing to Achievement with Excellence
Three (b)	A1 Describes effects of ulcers on normal functioning of the stomach. Normal functioning / abnormal function / changes caused by ulcer / effects on person. eg mucous protects the stomach from digestion by enzymes / lining of stomach gets eaten away.	M1 Explains effects of ulcers on normal functioning of the stomach. Normal functioning: abnormal function / changes caused by ulcer. eg in the ulcer, the stomach wall has been damaged by enzymes. This part of the stomach can no longer work / inflammation / swells so the stomach cannot digest as much food.	E1 Applies biological ideas to the effects of ulcers on the normal functioning of the stomach. Normal functioning: abnormal functioning / changes caused: elaboration, eg effects on person. eg usually the mucous lining protects the stomach from digestion by enzymes / this part of the stomach produces secretions to assist protein digestion (normal functioning). A person with ulcers will feel pain / because their stomach wall is damaged due to digestion by enzymes (abnormal function) / causes muscle contractions to slow so cannot digest as much food (elaboration).

Table 6.2. The judgement statement for Biology AS 1.6

Achievement	Achievement with Merit	Achievement with Excellence
Describe biological ideas and processes relating to the functioning of human digestive and skeletomuscular systems.	Explain biological ideas and processes relating to the functioning of human digestive and skeletomuscular systems.	Apply biological ideas and processes relating to the functioning of human digestive and skeletomuscular systems.
The student can DESCRIBE the functioning of the digestive system (A1) and functioning of the skeletomuscular system (A2).	The student can EXPLAIN the functioning of the digestive system (M1) and functioning of the skeletomuscular system (M2).	The student can APPLY the functioning of the digestive system (E1) and functioning of the skeletomuscular system (E2).
Three A1 and three A2 required	Two M1 and two M2 required	One E1 and one A2 required

This process created problems when the judgement statement was followed to the letter of the law. Occasionally a student would write brilliant Excellence answers but overlook the precise content specified at the Achieved level. Some assessors judged such work to be at the Not Achieved level—a nonsensical state of affairs which brought the prototypical assessment process into disrepute. This problem did eventually get sorted out, but it would not have happened in the first place if the assessment questions had been reshaped to afford more clear-cut opportunities for students to demonstrate achievement at different levels. The continuing emphasis on demonstrating recall and understanding of a wide range of content (carried over from the era of examination prescriptions of content) contributed in no small part to these early teething problems, and arguably still lingers in some subject areas.

How achievement standards responded to curriculum concerns

The biology example above illustrates the tensions of a system undergoing a radical shift. As we've already noted, some other subjects such as history did manage to build a different emphasis into their achievement standard specifications. A more up-to-date example of an achievement standard will help to illustrate the potential to bring a strong disciplinary focus to the fore. Achievement Standard 91435 is one of the current internally assessed standards for Level 3 history. As in the biology example above, there is a single outcome statement for each grade, with the only difference between the criteria for successive grades being a modifier of the same verb (in this case *analyse, analyse in depth,* or *comprehensively analyse*). Note that there are brief explanatory notes clarifying what must be assessed as having met the outcome for each grade. Furthermore, the focus is on conceptual aspects of historical analysis, rather than any particular historical event or period (although it is specified that the material analysed must be of significance to New Zealanders). It is worth comparing this structure and emphasis with the strong content-knowledge focus of the earth science unit standard example in Chapter 5 (pp. 58–61) and the prototype achievement standard in biology above.

Figure 6.4. An example of an achievement standard

> **Achievement standard: Analyse an historical event, or place, of significance to New Zealanders**
>
> **Achievement: Analyse an historical event, or place, of significance to New Zealanders.** *Analyse* involves using historical evidence to communicate key historical ideas with supporting evidence and establishing the significance of the historical event or place to New Zealanders. Merely describing what happened in an historical event is not by itself an analysis.
>
> **Achievement with Merit: Analyse, in depth, an historical event, or place, of significance to New Zealanders.** *Analyse, in depth,* involves explaining key historical ideas using in-depth supporting evidence.
>
> **Achievement with Excellence: Comprehensively analyse an historical event, or place, of significance to New Zealanders.** *Comprehensively analyse* involves presenting sound understanding, well-considered judgements of the evidence, and conclusions from an historian's perspective. The analysis is presented through key historical ideas that are supported by comprehensive evidence drawn from primary and secondary sources.

For a number of reasons, the achievement-standard model is arguably more appropriate than the unit-standard model for the assessment of disciplinary knowledge:

- Because there are no elements, and because the outcome statements are broad and abstract, different students can bring different specific content to the task of historical analysis, emphasising for them (as well as for teachers) that the most important thing in history (as in other disciplines) is bringing together the epistemology of the discipline and knowledge of the *particular* content being discussed.

- The complexity of the process of historical analysis, as illustrated by the explanatory notes for each grade, inherently allows for a degree of flexibility in balancing judgements about the various elements of a student's overall performance. One student might be better at communicating ideas, and another, at evaluating evidence. This distinguishes it from the unit-standard approach under which all elements must be met before any achievement is acknowledged.

- While the higher grades are attained by demonstrating more sophisticated analysis, the broad requirement—analysis—is the same. (It is worth nothing, however, that in this specific example the explanatory note for Merit actually does nothing more than reiterate the verb modifier, *in depth*.)

In summary, achievement standards were designed to certify broad conceptual and communicative achievement in the cognitive disciplines. An NCEA qualification based on achievement standards should mean that the qualified person can use a range of powerful epistemological techniques, with some degree of sophistication, in a way that will serve not only in the workplace, but also in a range of civic and political activities, and which will also enrich life aesthetically and intellectually. By contrast, unit standards are most suitable for the domain of human knowledge for which they were first designed to assess; that is, skills and processes often associated with vocations and trades. Here, the imperative is to ensure that professionals and tradespeople have mastered all of the skills and processes required to ensure that they practise their vocations in a thorough and safe manner. The meaning of a qualification based on such standards is that the qualified person can be relied upon to carry out work that meets professional standards.

This summary of the differences in the kinds of knowledge and skills that can be assessed using unit and achievement standards should not be taken to imply that we see one as more valuable than the other. Indeed, as we make clear in Chapter 14, *all* students need an overall learning programme that balances more intellectual and more practical learning.

How the structure of the qualification responded to the concerns of progressive educators

The achievement-standard model went some way towards alleviating the concerns of assessment traditionalists who favoured external examinations and who argued that grade differentiation is an important motivator for students, as well as those who foresaw difficulties with assessing curriculum disciplines using the highly disaggregated elements approach inherent in the unit-standard model. Nonetheless, for many involved in the early development of the unit-standard approach, the advent of achievement standards was seen as an undesirable compromise. Some people saw achievement standards as pandering to the "elite" schools lobby, most especially high-decile boys' schools. Two aspects of the achievement standards were behind this specific discomfort: the differentiation of grades (i.e., the inclusion of Merit and Excellence); and the strong component of external assessment.

Notwithstanding these concerns, the design of the qualification was intended to provide greater flexibility to meet different learning needs. Towards the end of the implementation period the Minister of Education, Trevor Mallard, described NCEA as providing "a range of new tools to customise programmes to meet individual learner needs" [for career pathways that do not necessarily include university study] (Mallard, 2004). This flexibility to customise programmes rested on the modular structure of NCEA, in combination with the retention of industry-owned and curriculum-based unit standards alongside achievement standards. All three types of standards were included in the overall assessment toolkit, ostensibly with parity of esteem. Credits generated by achievement standards could, at least in theory, be mixed and matched with credits generated by industry-owned unit standards, or curriculum unit standards, or both. So long as the specified total number of credits was reached, and literacy and numeracy requirements were satisfied, the relevant level of certificate could be awarded.

Teachers were quick to understand the potential to design more customised courses. The Learning Curves research project tracked NCEA implementation in six medium-sized secondary schools between 2002 and 2004. All six schools immediately began to design a range of alternative courses in core subjects. Typically there would be three different versions of Year 11 mathematics, differentiated and paced by the assessments, that is, which achievement and unit standards were used, and the way in which they were combined (Hipkins et al., 2004). However, by the end of the third year of the Learning Curves project, the researchers concluded that these changes had effectively consolidated existing tensions between academic and vocational learning pathways (Hipkins et al., 2005). Unit standards were widely seen as having a lower status than achievement standards, and students taking courses with a more practical orientation were well aware that their learning was not as highly valued in schools as the more conceptually oriented learning of their "bright" peers. Parity of esteem cannot be legislated into being.

There is an important tension here that is well worth making explicit. On one hand, it was epistemologically naïve to insist that all knowledge could be assessed using a unit-standard model. On the other hand, the greater valuing of conceptual or abstract learning over practical learning is often accompanied by an underlying belief that the former is for students with high cultural capital, and the latter for those who struggled to attain qualifications under the old and highly competitive School Certificate and Bursary system (i.e., Māori and Pasifika students, and students at low-decile schools). Those who sought to establish parity of esteem for different kinds of learning by treating all learning equally in the assessment process were largely motivated by a concern for social justice. However, the failure to recognise the epistemological issue led, unfortunately, to the entrenchment of existing disparities. Achievement standards, especially those that were externally assessed, were heavily used at high-decile schools, while low-decile schools were more inclined to rely on internally assessed achievement standards and unit standards.

The potential for double dipping

Some unit standards were used heavily after the introduction of NCEA because they addressed learning that was highly valued by teachers, but which was not addressed by achievement standards. A unit standard, now long defunct, that assessed students' wide reading was a case in point (Hipkins et al., 2004). More often, some double dipping took place. Curriculum unit standards often duplicated achievement standards in their content, although not their assessment approach. Some teachers assessed much the same thing with both unit standards and achievement standards, with students attaining credits for both. This problem was quickly addressed by the use of exclusion rules which prevented students from attaining credits for an achievement standard and a unit standard that largely overlapped in their content. There was, however, a cost to NCEA's credibility while the issue was sorted out.

Designing two-tier pathways through school

Predictably enough, curriculum-focused unit standards quickly acquired a reputation as being easy options. It became clear that, from the point of view of establishing parity of esteem between skills-based and discipline-based qualifications, the retention of curriculum-based unit standards had been a mistake. The poor reputation of this comparatively small subset of unit standards had the effect of tainting all unit standards (recall that most of them were used to assess practical skills related to specific employment pathways). All came to be seen as being of low educational worth, even though, as we outlined in Chapter 5, they work very well to assess practical skills and knowledge. This development effectively established two tiers within NCEA. The first was the achievement standard tier, being populated largely by students representing demographics that had done well under the previous qualifications system; and the other, the unit standard tier, populated by Māori and Pasifika students, and students at low-decile schools (Hipkins et al., 2005). This, needless to say, was precisely the opposite of what those championing parity of esteem had hoped for. For this reason, and also because of the sheer absurdity and waste involved in running two sets of standards that substantially duplicated one another, the curriculum-linked unit standards were progressively phased out between 2011 and 2013.

Chapter 7 The challenges of managing variability in a standards-based environment

As NCEA was progressively rolled out from 2002 to 2004 it became evident that there were large shifts in the proportions of students gaining credit, merit and excellence in the same externally assessed achievement standards from one year to the next. Experts in assessment and psychometrics, critical of the approach taken to standards-based assessment under the NCEA system, had predicted that these kinds of anomalies would arise. They sought evidence to investigate the extent to which their warnings had been warranted as soon as the data became available to make year-to-year comparisons.

Elley, Hall, and Marsh (2004) presented a range of examples of statistically unexpected variations in grade distributions for specific Level 1 externally assessed achievement standards after the 2003 examination round—the second round for Level 1. They also noted a general trend for an increase in performance in Level 1 internally assessed achievement standards in 2003 compared with 2002, whereas for Level 1 externally assessed standards in the same year there was a decline. Clearly, if students' performance had improved in one type of standard, a decline in the other raised serious questions about the moderation of internally assessed standards, the setting and marking of external assessments, or both. The problem, as they saw it, had several possible explanations:

> The significance of these results is threefold. First, movements of the kind demonstrated here should have triggered alarm bells in NZQA that something was seriously wrong. Secondly, that no action was taken is highly indicative of two interpretations—that [standards-based assessment] has become an ideological position rather than just the application of an assessment approach to school qualifications, and/or that NZQA did not have the expertise amongst its staff to understand the implications of these results. (Elley et al., 2004, pp. 11–12)

In this chapter we explore the challenges of managing variability in a standards-based environment. We begin with a brief exploration of how this challenge was managed in the pre-NCEA years. We then expand on the ways in which the challenge became more visible as NCEA was rolled out, and then address the management strategies that eventually evolved.

Managing year-on-year variability before NCEA

Before the mid-1990s, all assessment for qualifications run in New Zealand schools was norm-referenced. This included not only the examination-based systems for School Certificate, UE, and Bursary, but also the internally assessed Sixth Form Certificate. The practice of norm-referencing is designed to ensure that a set proportion of candidates attain each grade available for a particular assessment.

In the case of the examination-based systems, the mechanism of norm referencing was a scaling procedure. Once all the papers had been marked, candidates were placed in a rank order on the basis of their raw score. The highest available grade was allocated to the highest scoring candidates, working down the distribution from the top, until the normatively defined quota for that grade had been filled. Then the quota for next highest grade was similarly filled, and so on. Finally, percentage marks were adjusted to sit within the range defined for the grade actually received for each candidate. For example, if the lowest passing raw score was 38 percent, then all results of 38 percent would be adjusted (scaled up) to 50 percent, because this was the bottom of the passing range.

An effect of normative scaling is to mask a number of potential flaws in the assessment process. For example, if examinations were consistently set to be too difficult (or too easy) for the cohort, this would have been masked by the scaling procedure because the lowest passing mark, and the approximate middle of the overall distribution was always set to 50 percent. Thus there was little incentive for examiners to pitch an examination such that the middle-ranking candidate could actually be expected to attain half of the available marks in the paper. From a psychometric point of view this is unfortunate because an examination set so that the middle-performing students perform in the middle of the range yields the best information at the critical grade boundary separating passing candidates from failing ones.

It is important to note that normative scaling masked year-on-year variability, because the reported distributions of results were forced to be the same every year. Knowledge of these procedures was largely hidden from public view until New Zealand became the first country in the world to adopt the practice of returning marked examination scripts to students. Once that happened the discrepancy between raw and scaled marks became more visible. However post-hoc scaling of marks was abandoned soon after the change that saw scripts returned to students.

The norm referencing of (internally assessed) Sixth Form Certificate grades worked slightly differently. It was accomplished by the proxy of the previous year's School Certificate results. Schools were allotted numbers of each available grade for Sixth Form Certificate (from 1 to 9), based on the performance of their students in School Certificate. Because until the mid-1990s School Certificate was itself normatively scaled, the national distribution of School Certificate results was always the same, and thus, the national distribution of allotted Sixth Form Certificate results was also always the same (see Mark's recall narrative in Chapter 4, pp. 35–36).

While much of the criticism of the reliability of the early NCEA was well-founded and justified, this same criticism could equally have been levelled at its predecessors. That said, the smaller grain size of NCEA assessments did exacerbate pre-existing reliability problems. Furthermore, the high variability in NCEA results, when it became evident in 2005, was politically more damaging than it might have been, because the masking of reliability problems under the previous systems had engendered a false public conception that assessment for qualifications could be carried out with essentially perfect reliability.

There was no management plan in the early years of NCEA

After normative scaling was abandoned for external examinations, tacit norm referencing remained in place through adjustments to the marking process, to ensure that there were no radical shifts in the year-on-year proportions of candidates gaining the various grades. For example, the leader of a marking panel would monitor the distribution of results during marking based on an early sample of marked papers. If it looked as if there would be a substantial deviation from the previous year's distribution, adjustments to marking criteria would be made to bring the spread of marks into line. However, practices like this clearly were not carried through when NCEA was introduced; if they had been, the variability crisis might have been averted. As it was, NZQA had no plan, and seemingly no intention, to manage variability under the new system.

Exactly why that was so can only be guessed at. It seems probable, however, that NZQA held the view that the description of the criteria for Achieved, Merit, and Excellence grades, and the accompanying explanatory notes in the standards specifications, would be sufficient to calibrate teachers' and markers' judgements on their own. It may also be that NZQA did not understand the extent to which variability would prove to be as politically damaging as it was. This seems naïve, especially given that assessment experts had warned about both possibilities.

As we were writing this book, one of the key players we interviewed was Professor Cedric Hall. He believes that the failure of NZQA to avert the political crisis that unfolded following the 2004 examination round was attributable to an over-zealous and psychometrically ignorant stance taken by NZQA before the inception of NCEA. The crisis was precipitated by egregious variability in assessment results over time and between standards. Hall warned NZQA of the likelihood of such problems arising, but his warnings were not heeded. His sense of the NZQA line was that, under a standards-based approach, no provision need be taken to ensure the reliability of assessment. The lack of any such provision before 2005 suggests that his sense was correct. In Professor Hall's opinion, measurement issues were ignored simply because NZQA didn't have the skill base to cover them, and acquiring such expertise would have resulted in an unacceptable delay in the implementation of the system.

As we recall

We now outline some of our own experiences with variability. Rose gives a first-hand account of processes used to manage variability in the final pre-NCEA years, and Michael recalls his turbulent arrival at NZQA just as the variability crisis was unfolding.

Rose: The experience of being on a Bursary marking panel

Marking Bursary biology examination scripts in the last decade pre-NCEA gave me first-hand experience of how year-to-year variability was managed. The action took place behind the scenes. Each marking round began with a day-long meeting of the panel, led by the chief examiner and their moderator. During this day the range of acceptable answers for each question was thrashed out. Then each marker was sent away to apply the agreed schedule to a sample of papers—20 of them as I recall. Once this first batch had been marked we sent them in for check marking by the panel leaders, after which the panel reconvened for another long and tedious session of building a shared understanding of acceptable evidence of learning. If necessary, individuals who were out of line were given feedback to that effect. (The ultimate feedback to persistent renegades was to be dropped from a panel.) If an issue had come up for several markers it was discussed by everyone. If there was early evidence that the schedule was going to be too harsh or too lenient for the desired distribution of grades, it was adjusted as needed. Random check marking continued throughout the whole marking period. If an adjustment was made later in the process, all markers would then be required to go back and adjust every script to reflect the new decision.

One of the challenges each panel faced in those last pre-NCEA years was that examination scripts were returned to candidates once the whole marking process had been completed. At that point a student could apply for reassessment if they (or their teacher) thought a decision was not justified. We had to draw a line across any part of an answer booklet left blank (so that nothing could be added to it later). If we found an answer outside the agreed range, which we nevertheless thought was legitimate, we wrote PJ beside it (to signal we had used our professional judgement). If an answer was borderline, or not clearly expressed but along the right lines, we could use BOD (benefit of the doubt) and mark it correct. On one level then, the process was transparent and decisions were out in the open. But behind the scenes the range of marks was just as tightly managed within an agreed range as it had been when scaling was directly applied.

Michael: An eventful arrival at NZQA (1)

I commenced work as a research analyst at NZQA in early April 2005. I joined the NZQA research team, which had until then concerned itself entirely with qualitative, largely interview-based, canvassing of the views of stakeholders on the new NCEA system. When I was hired, I was the only member of the team with specific statistical training, although Jim Strachan, who was already semi-retired, was certainly capable of conducting statistical analysis. Jim acted as a valuable mentor for me, schooling me in the philosophy of assessment and in well-established effects of assessment on teaching and learning in schools. Nonetheless, the research team was not at all focused on understanding the technical functioning of the new assessment regime, and this surprised and disappointed me. I had no interest in the kind of research that the team seemed to be engaged in; I wanted to use my research skills to investigate and evaluate the new qualifications system, to provide evidence as a basis for improving it.

I spent the first couple of weeks in the job reading about the new system; its development from the early 1990s unit standards trials, the legislation underpinning it, and its internationally unique approach to assessment and reporting of students' achievement. As I read, I become curious about its various elements—the examinations for externally assessed standards, moderation, and the consistency of teachers' assessment judgements in relation to internal assessment. I began to search the organisation for data that might be used to evaluate the functioning of these systems, but was stymied at every turn. I found that NZQA kept almost no data on external assessment at the level of individual questions, making an analysis of the quality of the examinations impossible. Neither were moderation data readily available, and I found that, not only was there no appetite for examining the consistency with which teachers made judgements on internally assessed standards, there was active opposition to doing so. When I raised ideas for evaluating the quality of the new system the attitude that I encountered from NZQA management (with the notable exception of Andrew Kear, the Manager of Schools Liaison Monitoring and Reporting) was one of suspicion, and in some cases, strong opposition.

Why NCEA created predictable variability challenges

What led assessment experts such as Elley et al. (2004) to predict an escalation in problems with variability in NCEA external assessments with such certainty? One answer concerns what they already knew about the *grain size* of assessments.

As a general rule of thumb, the reliability of tests and examinations tends to decrease with the time available to complete them. During examinations for School Certificate and Bursary, students effectively had 3 hours for each assessment. Although these exams were divided into discrete questions that assessed different parts of the course of learning, the result (in the form of a percentage mark) was in effect a summative accumulation of the pieces into one whole.

The grain size changed when NCEA was introduced. A 3-hour external assessment session in the early NCEA years usually comprised at least three standards, and in some subjects, as many as five. The results for each standard were to be judged and reported individually, not accumulated as questions had been in the former examinations. Thus, in most subjects, students undertaking all external assessment opportunities for a specific level of a subject had no more than an hour to complete each standard, and frequently less. The small grain-size of assessments and the relatively brief examination time for each externally assessed standard, in conjunction with the lack of any mechanism to control variability in the first 3 years of NCEA, made problems with reliability a virtual certainty.

Variability is inherent in many stages of an examination process. It is exceedingly difficult, no matter the skill of an examiner, to write questions that are matched to the difficulty of those used in previous years. Apparently small details of a question, such as the context for a problem or concept, can have substantial effects on its accessibility to students. The marking schedule—that is, the plan for the allocation of marks during marking—and the vagaries of the markers themselves are further sources of variability.

Elley and his colleagues took NZQA to task, but they also criticised a range of other agencies and groups for allowing a foreseeable crisis to unfold by not taking action to avert it. They held the Ministry of Education partly culpable, as the body responsible for the design of the system. They also criticised the New Zealand Vice Chancellors'

Committee, the Post-Primary Teachers Association and the Secondary Principals Association of New Zealand. All of the groups were seen as stakeholders who were aware of the warnings of assessment experts, but failed to apply political pressure to ensure that there was at least some mechanism to manage the inevitable variability. More than a decade later, Bali Haque, the deputy chief executive of NZQA who oversaw the reforms that followed the variability crisis, largely echoed these criticisms. His critique focused specifically on the lack of research basis behind the new system, and an over-hasty timetable for implementation (Haque, 2015).

Evolving processes for managing variability

The State Services Commission recommended that NZQA enact measures to ensure that "the extent of variability in the results of the external assessment of NCEA ... is within acceptable professional and public tolerances" (Martin, 2005, p. 7). This recommendation forced change on NZQA, and actions intended to control variability in the distribution of results were finally taken. A number of new measures were introduced to better manage variability. These measures included: undertaking closer scrutiny of examination-setting processes; the adoption of statistical analysis of examination results to inform future examination rounds; and eventually, a new marking system for NCEA examinations, implemented progressively between 2011 and 2013.

The most immediately effective action, and probably the most controversial, was the development of profiles of expected performance based on statistical analysis of assessment results from previous years. The process is now briefly outlined.

A closer look at PEPs

Profiles of expected performance (PEPs) are established individually for each standard. A PEP comprises four percentage ranges. These signify the percentage of results that are expected to fall into each of the four grade categories, Not Achieved, Achieved, Merit, and Excellence. For example, the PEP for a given standard might comprise four ranges as follows: Not Achieved (20%–28%), Achieved (40%–46%), Merit (17%–25%), and Excellence (8%–16%).

In the first few years following the variability crisis, PEPs were developed by a small group of NZQA staff. Some members of this group already had psychometric expertise, while others had a critical sense of the political implications of results distributions. This group spent many hours perusing historical results and discussing the ways in which various distributions might be received by the public. Later, the PEP-setting process was devolved to the national assessment facilitator for each subject, with the original group providing oversight and review.

The exercise was first conducted in the lead-up to the 2005 examination round. By this time the available historical results spanned 3 years for Level 1, 2 years for Level 2, and just one year for Level 3. Where there was relative consistency over more than one year for Levels 1 and 2, the profiles were set in a way that reflected these result patterns. Other statistical information, such as the extent of variability that might be expected on the basis of various cohort sizes, was also taken into account. It was used to calculate bands of tolerance for each PEP in any one year. However, the primary motivation for creating the profiles, as Nash (2005) astutely alludes, was "political rather than educational" (p. 106). That is, the primary consideration in the adoption of PEP was the extent to which to it would yield a distribution of results that was politically and publicly acceptable, rather than whether it was a true reflection of the achievement of students against a standard. Fortunately, far more often than not, these two considerations were well-enough aligned.

Do PEPs constitute a return to scaling?

The implementation of the profiles attracted immediate criticism from NCEA supporters and scorn from its detractors. The main thrust of both the criticism and the scorn was that the PEPs signalled a return to scaling (see Nash, 2005, for a cogent discussion). This practice had been discontinued for School Certificate under the ministership of Lockwood Smith in 1993. Indeed, as we have outlined above, the injustice of scaling to yield set proportions of students attaining each grade was one of the primary motivating ideas behind the shift to a standards-based philosophy. Gregor Fountain, for example, cited this injustice as one of the primary reasons that he became an enthusiast for a move to standards-based assessment. Even so, from a pragmatic perspective, he accepted the adoption of the PEPs as a necessary mechanism to shore up public confidence in the nascent and beleaguered NCEA system.

Is the criticism that PEPs constitute a return to scaling warranted? What lies beneath the superficial similarities? Do PEPs constitute a victory for conservative forces, privileged by normative assessment practices, or are they a fundamentally different, and even indispensable, practice in a large-scale standards-based assessment system? To answer these questions it is necessary to carefully tease out similarities and differences between the two sets of processes.

As Cedric Hall pointed out when we spoke with him, there is no necessary conflict between standards-based and norm-referenced assessment when the cohorts being assessed are sufficiently large. With a large cohort, if the same standard applies from year to year, it is statistically very improbable that there will be substantial shifts in the proportions of candidates falling into the various grade categories, unless the shift is commensurate with a substantial change in students' performance. Furthermore, Jim Strachan noted that abandoning the formal scaling of School Certificate in the mid-1990s was understood at the time as a politically risky move. The assessment experts understood that any radical shifts in the proportions of students attaining the various grades would have an extremely deleterious effect on public trust in the assessment process. As outlined above, measures were put in place to avoid such variations, including adjustment of marking schedules during the marking process.

One clear point of difference concerns the ability of a process to respond to variability that reflects a meaningful shift in achievement patterns. Normative requirements for Bursary examinations, and for School Certificate before 1993, were fixed over time. In other words they were the same from year to year, and were not responsive to shifts in students' knowledge and understanding. Scaling was applied in a mechanistic fashion after marking had been completed, without any consultation with senior markers or examiners. The results of the process were designed to deliver fixed proportions of students in each grade category, and that is just what they delivered.

By contrast, PEPs do not act as a normative prescription. They are not used to scale post-hoc to produce a predetermined distribution of results. Instead PEP distribution patterns are used as a monitoring tool during marking. When an actual distribution of results begins to fall outside the PEP bands, the convener of the marking panel is asked to check the extent to which this is justified by students' actual performance. If an observed shift in distribution can be well justified it is allowed to stand. If, however, the observed distribution cannot be justified, then adjustments are made to the marking schedule to bring the results into line with expectations.

At its best, the PEPs system strengthens the standards-based approach, because it helps to ensure that any variability in results for a standard from year to year is attributable to differences in the performance of the cohort, rather than in the difficulty of examinations. To reiterate Cedric Hall's point, on any reasonably large cohort, there is little inherent conflict between normative and standards-based assessment, because unless there is a change in the knowledge or understanding of students, very little difference between the results profiles of successive cohorts is expected. When there is a change in their knowledge or understanding, the profiles, unlike the previous norm-referenced approach, need not be mechanically applied. Furthermore, the new results distribution, which might well fall outside the profile, becomes part of the historical data on which the next year's profiles are based; thus profiles can change to reflect changes in students' knowledge and understanding.

Despite a more-than-superficial similarity between the PEPs and norm-referenced assessment, the argument that the profiles constitute a return to normative assessment philosophy or, for that matter, a norm-referenced result, does not stand close scrutiny. Rather, the *lack* of any such mechanism at the outset of NCEA, to ensure that any variation from one year to the next was warranted by students' performance against a standard, reveals naïve radicalism on the part of those who introduced it.

Legitimate concerns about PEPs

While the PEPs mechanism is not inherently in conflict with standards-based assessment, and in fact is necessary to prevent unjustified variability, there are aspects of its application in practice that *can* undermine consistency with standards.

Statistical information can only be used in a limited way in the setting of PEPs. Ideally, statistical analysis would be used to determine the relative difficulty of all grades for all achievement standards, and PEPs would be set on the basis of this analysis. However, any such analysis would rest on the false assumption that there is some grand achievement scale upon which all school-based achievement can be positioned. On the contrary, the correlations in performance between different subjects and courses, even between standards in the same subject, while almost always positive, are typically quite modest in magnitude. To clarify by using an intuitively appealing example, there are many students who perform much better in visual arts than in mathematics, and many others for whom the reverse is true. The point here is that a statistical basis for PEPs would be founded on the unverifiable, and usually false, epistemological assumption that it is possible to compare the difficulty of one subject with that of another.

The lack of any sound statistical mechanism to compare the relative difficulty of standards, and the fact that the cohorts of students undertaking standards in different subjects are vastly different, limits the role of statistics in setting PEPs largely to the analysis of historical results, and to providing information regarding the desirable breadth of the bands of tolerance. If the PEP process is properly applied, it does not lock standards into historical distributions, because, as noted above, the actual performance of candidates, when it is justifiably and consistently above or below the expected performance, will result in distributions of results falling outside the PEP range. These distributions then become part of the historical information on which future years' PEPs will be based. Because more recent distributions are weighted more strongly than older ones, this will result in concomitant movement in the expected bands.

The comparative weakness of statistical influence on PEP setting means that they are necessarily an imperfect mechanism for ensuring the consistency of standards over time. Nonetheless, they are much better than nothing; without their inception for the 2005 examination round, the variability problems would have persisted, and it is most unlikely that NCEA would have survived at all.

Chapter 8 The Scholarship crisis and its aftermath

Early in January 2005 a scandal began to brew once critics had digested patterns in the results of the first round of the Scholarship examinations. This additional examination had been put in place as a compromise solution in response to perceptions that NCEA did not sufficiently test and extend the most able students in their final year of schooling. While not strictly part of NCEA, the same standards-based assumptions were applied to the processing of these additional examinations and this resulted in anomalies that quickly became controversial. In some subjects few students were successful in gaining Scholarship awards in proportion to the numbers participating. In others, more students than expected were successful. The variability seemed inherently unfair, especially given that there were financial rewards at stake. Yet there were no processes in place to mitigate the variability that inevitably arises in any set of examinations that compares multiple, very different subjects, and involves many different examiners and markers. This section discusses these developments, and explains why this scandal brought many of the simmering tensions around NCEA out into the open.

As we recall ...

The personal experiences with which we begin this section shed light on the Scholarship scandal from three quite different insider perspectives. Rose made sense of what happened in her main teaching subject (biology) by reflecting back on contentious practices during the marking of Bursary examinations in the preceding decade. Mark brought a historian's critical eye to the wider political climate and its impact on the Scholarship examination in history, adding an extra edge of controversy in that subject to that which surrounded the examination as a whole. Michael recalls the Scholarship crisis coming to public attention, and NZQA's response.

Rose: Assessment for a coherent biology curriculum

Biology was one of the subjects where too few students were successful in the first round of Scholarship examinations. I had a hunch that there could be good reasons for this. During the final decade of Bursary examinations I was involved in the assessment of biology in several different roles. The 3-hour examination mostly consisted of short-answer questions, each restricted to a specific prescribed area of biological knowledge (e.g., Mendelian genetics, animal behaviour). However, there was one extended essay question. Here students wrote about a selected biological issue, either in genetics or ecology. The bursary prescription specified that they should study an issue in both areas, although only one essay would be required. This situation provided a modest opportunity, taken up in different ways by two different examiners, to assess aspects students' ability to draw links between different areas of biology, or between biology and life beyond school. What happened in each of these experiments is salutary, given the subsequent Scholarship scandal.

One year the examiner shaped the essay question to be written as a letter to a local council, outlining the chosen issue and making a specific request of an action to be taken in response. The *substance* of the prescription was addressed, but the *format* was unfamiliar. I was on the marking panel that year. Even amongst this leading group there were a few teachers who said their students would be disadvantaged by not being able to reproduce an essay learned by heart. Among the wider collective of biology teachers it would be fair to say there was outrage, for essentially the same reason.

Another year the examiner decided to address a widely held concern that students were only investigating one issue, even though the examination prescription (which stood as a proxy curriculum) clearly specified that they study two issues. The essay question that year was shaped in such a way that students had to draw broad links between the issue they wrote about and the second issue they had studied. I was more closely involved in this development. As I recall, my role was to be the moderator, with responsibility to ensure the examination did not stray beyond the bounds of the prescription. I knew we were pushing the boundaries but thought the curriculum signal was important, and the essay subsection in question clearly indicated that only 4 marks out of the 20 percent allocated for the essay were at stake. Again there was outrage from the wider community of biology teachers. Those who objected said it was unreasonable to expect students to draw unrehearsed links between different parts of their course. (They could hardly argue that students who only studied one issue were disadvantaged, but of course that was true—to the extent of 4 marks out of 100.)

What links these two episodes is the treatment of essay writing as an opportunity to demonstrate *knowledge recall* rather than the ability to link ideas and build a coherent argument in the spaces between them. Students who prepared for essay writing by rote learning of discrete topics could be expected to flounder when required to demonstrate their grasp of the underpinning coherence of the big ideas of biological disciplines. This, I suspected, was why so few students gained Scholarship in biology in that first year. I correctly guessed the identity of the examiner, who soon confirmed my hunch. Students had not been able build links between topics, as any demonstration of actual scholarship would, and should, demand. No doubt weaving coherent links is now firmly established as part of able students' preparation for the Scholarship examination. However I think that all biology students should get opportunities to practise building such links, not just the top scholars.

Mark: The contentious nature of history as a subject

For me the crisis over Scholarship was enmeshed with the 2005 Education and Science Select Committee investigation into the history curriculum. It highlighted the political nature of curriculum and assessment matters. The Select Committee investigation was sparked off by a National opposition complaint that the 2004 history examination had unfairly portrayed a National Party politician (who bore a strong resemblance to party leader Don Brash) as unsympathetic to Māori. In short the complaint was that the examination was biased. In 2005 Treaty-related questions were highly sensitive in light of the seabed and foreshore issue (the Foreshore and Seabed Act, passed in 2004, had elicited widespread Māori protest), and Don Brash's "Orewa speech" that explicitly criticised the Treaty of Waitangi as an outmoded historical artefact. The debate, however, spilled over into questions about NCEA. The government was fielding continuing criticism of NCEA from high-profile academic schools who were outraged by the variability of the 2004 Scholarship results. In response, a Scholarship reference group was set up to overhaul the Scholarship examination process. Allegations of bias in the history examination were drawn into the work of this group.

The Education and Science Select Committee went beyond a focus on one particular examination question to include the history curriculum in its entirety. While the Select Committee found no evidence of deliberate political bias it was highly critical of NZQA, especially in relation to the setting and checking of the examination paper. NZQA were unused to this level of public scrutiny. They insisted the examination was not designed to be offensive and assured the committee that there was no intention to satirise any individual. For NZQA the robust nature of the investigation process was seen as threatening and appeared to send them the message that school history examinations should avoid controversy in future. Soon after the report was released to the public in August 2005 an external reviewer was appointed by NZQA to ensure future examination questions did not cause offence. The evaluator (whose identity was not made public) was charged with the responsibility of alerting the authority to any material that could be perceived as stereotyping or inappropriate in areas such as gender, ethnicity, religion, or politics. In the following year the NZQA group manager assured the public that the authority did not "want anybody being offended by national exams or to be given any messages that undermine in any way any group of people" (see Sheehan, 2011, for more detail).

Michael: An eventful arrival at NZQA (2)

I had been an employee of NZQA for under a month when the Scholarship crisis broke in the press. On the back of the crisis came a series of criticisms of NCEA, mostly based on data showing large variation in the proportions of students achieving credits for specific standards between 2004 and 2005. Within a few weeks, the chief executive had resigned. Karen Sewell, who was chief executive of ERO at the time, took over as acting chief executive at NZQA. The State Services Commission investigated the performance of NZQA and produced two reports, one in relation to Scholarship and the other in relation to NCEA. The reports were not complimentary and made a range of recommendations for changes NZQA's processes for managing NCEA and Scholarship. The first of these to be implemented was the development of the profiles of expected performance (PEPs). I developed the process for the profiles with Jim Strachan and Andrew Kear. This marked the beginning of my involvement in the reform of NCEA.

Karen Sewell oversaw a restructure of NZQA. Most of the senior management departed and this laid the way for a new management regime. In 2006 Karen Poutasi was appointed as the new chief executive, and Bali Haque as one of three deputy chief executives. Bali set about a programme of sweeping reform, partly based on the recommendations of the State Services Commission's reports. He quickly identified me as having a skill set that could assist him in his endeavours, and I spent the next 5 years working closely with him to deliver his reforms.

The rationale for adding Scholarship to the qualifications mix

In many ways Scholarship was more politically important than NCEA, although it involved far fewer students and was not associated with a formal qualification. The government was vulnerable over the implementation of NCEA in 2005 (NZQA, 2007). Despite growing support for the standards-based model among teachers (Alison, 2005), NCEA was still attracting criticism. NZQA hoped that the Scholarship examination would allay ongoing criticism from high-profile academic schools such as Auckland Grammar (Morris, 2008), who were not convinced of the academic credibility of the achievement-based assessment framework.

The academic status of high-profile, affluent schools such as Auckland Grammar rested on their students' achievement record. Notable success in clearly defined, public examination results was seen as reinforcing their academic character. By 2005 a number of affluent schools were offering the international Cambridge examination. They said they had little confidence that NCEA was robust enough to cater for their high-achieving students. NZQA hoped that the Scholarship examination would allay such fears and demonstrate that the standards-based framework was academically rigorous. Thus Scholarship was, and is, an assessment for the highest-performing students, and a source of prestige for successful students and their schools. Importantly for those with traditional views about assessment, it remains primarily a traditional 3-hour examination system.

History educator Gregor Fountain was deeply involved in trying to make NCEA work. He regarded the re-implementation of a specific Scholarship examination process as a compromise to the anti-ranking philosophy of standards-based assessment. For him, Scholarship was initiated to satisfy the conservatism of high-decile schools and high-decile Auckland boys' schools in particular. When we spoke to Roger Moses, principal of Wellington College (a high-decile boys' school), he agreed that the introduction of Scholarship examinations in 2004 was designed by the government to mitigate the move of some schools to alternative qualifications systems such as Cambridge International Examinations and the International Baccalaureate. But for him, Scholarship was not a compromise. He saw this development as a necessary element of the new system, allowing it to recognise high performance and motivate the most able students.

How the Scholarship variability challenge played out

When the first round of Scholarship results was published early in 2005 the crisis that broke had very similar causes to the one that led to the establishment of profiles of expected performance for externally assessed achievement standards. In late January 2005 reports began to emerge about the extreme variability in the results of the standards-based Scholarship examination, which had been examined for the first time in 2004.

This crisis centred on substantial discrepancies between the proportions of candidates receiving awards in different subjects. The standards-based examination model did not allow for examiners to scale the raw marks if there were variations in the pass rates of candidates. And in some of the 2004 examinations there were extreme variations. For example although 51 percent of accounting candidates were awarded Scholarship, in biology and physics only 2 percent and 4 percent respectively were successful. None of the 152 physical education candidates who sat the Scholarship examination passed (NZQA, 2006).

Like the variability in achievement-standard results distributions, these discrepancies ought to have come as no surprise. There were no guidelines in place to place limits on the acceptable variability between subjects. Indeed, it is unlikely that any such guidelines would have been acceptable to the pure standards-based orthodoxy that prevailed at NZQA, who appeared to be blind-sided by the public outcry that ensued. Cedric Hall commented that NZQA's fervour for the new system caused them to lose sight of what would be politically or publically acceptable.

The political fallout

Both the assessment issue and its political implications are evident in a parliamentary question to the Education Minister, asked by a member for the ACT party, Deborah Coddington, in the weeks after the crisis unfolded in the media:

> Does the Minister realise that 30 out of 50 students who sat NCEA level 4 Māori got scholarship, but only nine out of 1,000 students who sat biology got scholarship; if so, was that not an unexpected result, either? (Coddington, 2005, p. 18,575)

The substantive issue is straightforward enough; whereas 60 percent of the candidates in one subject attained Scholarship, less than one percent in another attained a successful result. Irrespective of which two subjects these were, this contrast called into question the natural justice of the system, as well as the reliability of the examinations themselves.

The political dimension to the question is more subtly manifest in the specific subjects compared by Coddington. Within the hierarchy of competing subjects, the link to public examinations is a key factor as to whether a subject is perceived as having "academic" status (Goodson, 1987). From the point of view of progressive ideology, the fact that the best scholars in te reo Māori were apparently far more successful than those in a traditional, high-status subject such as biology might have been seen as a victory for ethnic and cultural equity. However the constituency represented by Coddington included the high-decile Auckland schools leaning towards alternative qualifications systems. For them the success of students in non-traditional subjects such as te reo Māori was more likely to be seen as a threat to their dominance of the elite awards.

The variability crisis dealt a serious blow to the credibility of NCEA. The greatest impact of this was on affluent, academic schools who had considerable social capital in the educational arena. It generated heated criticism from articulate, high-profile, well-connected educators such as Roger Moses, principal of Wellington College, who described the situation as a "shambles" (Moses, 2005). The Scholarship crisis provided an opportunity for the National opposition to attack the government's secondary assessment policy, despite having themselves initiated NCEA in the years prior to this series of crises.

The measurement problems with Scholarship were indeed substantive, and their political consequences threatened to haemorrhage the entire NCEA system. It was the Scholarship crisis more than anything else that prompted the resignation of Karen Van Rooyen, the chief executive of NZQA at the time. It was this crisis that constituted the pivotal point for the NCEA system. After this, NCEA was in survival mode; it had to adapt or perish. Its purist proponents were, from that moment, on the back foot.

Rethinking the management of variability in Scholarship

The Labour government was firmly committed to NCEA, even though it was initially a National government initiative. Fearing that the variability of Scholarship results could damage their political standing in the educational community, they established two advisory groups to oversee the reform of the Scholarship process (Scholarship Reference Group, 2005). These were the Scholarship Processes Advisory Group (SPAG), and the Scholarship Technical Advisory Group (STAG). The latter group essentially comprised three leading academics: Professors Terry Crooks and John Hattie provided psychometric and assessment expertise, and Professor Gary Hawke acted as chair for both groups.

The STAG group designed a new examination process, which was then debated and approved by the SPAG. This process was first implemented in the 2005 examination round. It was a hybrid of standards-based and normative assessment, although of a different kind than the PEPs described in the previous chapter. Each Scholarship examination now comprised between two and six questions. Each question was marked on a scale of 0–8. Scores of 5 and 6 designated performance at the Scholarship level, and those of 7 and 8, performance at the Outstanding Scholarship level. The scores for the individual questions were aggregated to arrive at an overall distribution of total scores for each subject. With the guidance of STAG two cut-points were then drawn on this distribution, designating the minimum total scores for Scholarship and Outstanding Scholarship awards in each subject.

This system has standards-based elements. The questions and the criteria for achieving minimum marks for Scholarship (5) and Outstanding Scholarship (7) are based on documented standards. Furthermore any candidate awarded Scholarship or Outstanding Scholarship must have achieved at least one score of 5 (for Scholarship), or at least one score of 7 (for Outstanding Scholarship). This means that the cut points for the awards cannot be set below the point on the overall distribution at which those to be awarded satisfy these criteria.

The system designed by the STAG also has a normative component. As close as possible to 3 percent of the Level 3 cohort in each subject (defined as those students entering for at least 14 credits in achievement standards) are to receive Scholarship awards, and as close as possible to 0.3 percent of the Level 3 cohort, an Outstanding Scholarship award.

The standards-based and normative elements of the system can conflict. On occasion, the cut-point that would yield the desired percentage of the Level 3 cohort attaining an award would also result in some candidates receiving the award despite not having an individual question score at 5 or 7, as outlined above. However when this occurs, the standards-based criterion takes precedence. Thus, an award is never given to a candidate who has not demonstrated performance at the specified level.

Sometimes more than the desired proportion of the cohort might eligible to receive the award once the cut points are set. This conflict can arise, for example, if a subject cohort is very small but also academically talented. In such cases the normative element is relaxed. More often the proportion of candidates receiving an award is somewhat smaller than the proportion which has, on the basis of average performance in the assessment, met the standard. In other words, a greater proportion of candidates fairly often meet a standard than the 3 percent who are allowed, under the normative prescription of 3 percent of the Level 3 cohort, to gain a successful result. When this happens, the norm takes precedence and some students whose performance in the examination was technically at or above the standard nonetheless do not receive an award.

The new Scholarship system has been highly successful both from assessment and from political points of view. The psychometric data arising from the examinations show that, by-and-large, the system comprises assessments of very high quality, and it is widely acknowledged that this is so. Furthermore, the system distinguishes a hierarchy of scholars, from those who perform in the top few percent of students in individual subjects, to those who receive highly prestigious aggregate awards for high performance in multiple subjects. Scholarship is unashamedly a ranking exercise and, equally unashamedly, about defining an elite.

A quick comparison of Scholarship and NCEA processes

The measurement aspect of the Scholarship crisis, and its resolution, are similar to the corresponding crisis in respect of variability in the externally assessed achievement standards, although there are important differences in the detail.

For the NCEA standards, the normative element comes from the PEPs. When applied as intended, these work in concert with the standards-based underpinning of the assessment process. The overall process helps to ensure that any substantial change in distributions of grades in successive years is attributable to a change in the performance of candidates, rather than to a de facto change in the standard caused by (inevitable) variations in the difficulty of examinations.

In Scholarship, the normative element is more explicit; there are targets for the percentages of the Level 3 cohort attaining Scholarship and Outstanding Scholarship results in each subject. While there is some flexibility in the application of these norms, especially in small subjects, the norm usually takes precedence, with the exception that candidates never receive awards unless there is evidence of their having met the standard.

Pragmatism or essential elements of an assessment system

The early part of this chapter noted that the introduction of Scholarship examinations was, at least in part, an attempt to make the NCEA system more palatable to high-decile schools. High-decile boys' schools, in particular, had historically done well in competitive examination systems. Indeed they continue to do well in Scholarship. It was clear to some who were closely involved—for example Jim Strachan—that the leaders of high-decile boys' schools were fighting to maintain time-limited examinations as the predominant method of formal assessment. Furthermore these leaders constituted a powerful element within the Principals' Lead Group set up to discuss NCEA. With this context in mind, the pragmatism of introducing a competitive examination system to determine the prestigious Scholarship awards is difficult to deny. But this pragmatism is strongly at odds with the pure doctrine of the architects of standards-based assessment in New Zealand. Since the 2005 reforms Scholarship has been entirely externally assessed. It explicitly ranks students, and its norm-referenced element is weighted at least as strongly as its standards-based element when the two come into conflict.

Perhaps predictably, the introduction of Scholarship to appease NCEA's detractors amongst the principals of high-decile schools was only partially successful. Some of these detractors defected to alternative assessment systems anyway,[1] although most still encourage students at their schools to participate in Scholarship examinations. Nonetheless, there are erstwhile critics of NCEA who were won over to the entire system when Scholarship was seen to be functioning well in 2005 and beyond.[2]

Roger Moses: Champion of the classical liberal-arts education

Roger Moses is the principal of Wellington College, a high-decile boys' school. He stands as a salutary example of a critic who changed his view when Scholarship was reformed. Prior to this, he was a vocal public critic of NCEA. However, following the crisis in 2005, he became a member of SPAG, choosing to assist in reforming the system rather than continuing in his role as a public critic. When he was satisfied the Scholarship was operating well, he became a supporter of the entire NCEA system, albeit with some lingering reservations. His school has not adopted any alternative system, despite some pressure from his parent community to do so at the beginning of the NCEA system.

---

1 None of the principals who responded in 2012 NZCER National Survey of Secondary Schools said they used the International Baccalaureate qualification in their school. Nine percent said they used Cambridge examinations and a further 3 percent were considering doing so (Hipkins, 2013).

2 The National Survey has consistently showed very high levels of support for NCEA among secondary principals: 87% in 2003, 89% in 2006, 95% in 2009, 94% in 2012, 95% in 2015 (Wylie & Bonne, 2016).

For Moses, the Scholarship reforms saved NCEA. In his opinion, within 12 months of the crisis, enormous progress had been made in delivering a credible Scholarship system. This gave NZQA a breathing space within which further changes could be made. He does, however, note the irony that a norm-referenced examination can be credited with saving the standards-based approach.

Roger Moses' concerns with NCEA boiled down to two essential disagreements with the implementers of the new system. The first was epistemological in nature. An anecdote that he related when we spoke with him captures this in a passionate defence of liberal-arts educational values:

> We can underestimate the ability of students to grapple with difficult material. So we get rid of it and give them material that is more 'meaningful'. [But] that which initially appears remote might in the longer run be of great value. Under the current model we're subject to the *tyranny of the myth of relevance*. [However], an important part of secondary school should be the training of the mind—the liquidation of ignorance. At Waihi College, an old friend, Bill Snelling had come back into teaching in his sixties. He used to produce the most extraordinary Shakespeare plays [involving students]. The universality of Shakespeare is borne out by the fact that 400 years later, 12,000 miles away, in a little mining town, kids can still love his work.

What comes across here is anything but an elitist principal trying to shore up his students' privilege. Rather, Moses strongly believes that material often seen as being only for the elite, is actually important for all, because it serves the "liquidation of ignorance".

His other concern, one that he feels has been largely dealt with through the Scholarship reforms and endorsement initiatives, was the lack of a mechanism for able students to distinguish themselves. Again however, for him, such a mechanism isn't simply to allow students to engage in banal one-upmanship; rather, he believes that the possibility of being recognised as an outstanding scholar serves as a motivation for students to give of their best.

Is the salvation of NCEA through the reintroduction of normative elements really an "irony", as Roger Moses put it? Is Scholarship simply an example of the way in which radical reform can be made acceptable by reintroducing aspects of the familiar? Or are there sound arguments that such a competitive element is an important component of a comprehensive, modern, assessment system, not simply a pragmatic compromise with reactionary forces seeking to entrench existing privilege?

The impact on *student motivation* is one argument made for the competitive Scholarship system, or one like it. According to this argument, the most able students need to pit themselves competitively against their peers if they are to stretch themselves to their full ability. Like the many other issues discussed in this book, motivation constitutes a complex set of challenges.

Even so, might the competitive Scholarship system have been introduced on the basis of an assessment system that did not involve an external assessment or an explicit norm? Certainly it is conceivable that Scholarship could be based on a wider range of evidence than a time-limited examination and, in some subjects it already is. The visual arts subjects, graphics and technology are all based on portfolios of work, and the performing arts, including music, drama and dance, all have elements of performance contributing to the assessment. There is no reason in principle that project-based elements could not be incorporated in to the assessment process for other subjects. The main barrier to a widening of the assessment format for Scholarship is likely to be one of expense. It would cost a great deal to maintain the reliability required in an explicitly competitive assessment such as Scholarship on the basis of internally assessed portfolios of work across a wide range of subjects. It is much less expensive to mark an examination script than it is to mark a portfolio of work.

Explicit norms could also be dispensed with in theory, but only if a comprehensive moderation process was in place. Again, a strong moderation system is expensive to run. We discuss this challenge in Chapter 10. Even with such a system in place, if any substantial gaps appeared between subjects or years, the political consequences would be just as they were in 2005. And as we have already made clear, the ensuing criticism would be justified to some extent. Trying to justify comparisons of the relative difficulty of subjects quickly leads to epistemologically and statistically fraught arguments. Recall the political tensions, too, in the debate about te reo Māori vs traditional science subjects. The only way to prevent disputes about the fairness of outcomes is to maintain consistency in the success rate between subjects. Unless there is a substantial change in the characteristics of a cohort, results distributions under a standards-based system should not change much over time. A competitive system such as Scholarship, even if standards-based in conception, requires at least a tacit norm to prevent unacceptable variability, either over time or between subjects.

Another aspect of the previous assessment system that many early proponents of NCEA had hoped to see the end of—namely, ranking— fairly obviously cannot be dispensed with in an assessment that is designed to award money and prestige. As unpalatable as this might be to those arguing that social justice demands parity of esteem for all students' achievement, this viewpoint is difficult to reconcile with a positioning of the system as being for all New Zealanders, including those who do not believe that all learning is equally deserving of esteem, or who believe that "competition" is not a dirty word.

NCEA was designed by progressive educational policy makers who were rightly concerned at the proportions of young people leaving school without qualifications, particularly those whose families lack economic and intellectual capital. These policy makers also tended to hold highly egalitarian views about knowledge itself, according to which no learning ought to be valued more highly than any other learning. The concern about social equity is one with which just about any educator, whether progressive or conservative, would concur. The second, epistemological point however—the doctrine of parity-of-esteem—is far more contentious. Nonetheless, the implementation process for NCEA not only sidelined technical experts as we have discussed earlier in this chapter, but also more conservative educators. There was a tendency to disparage conservative critics as reactionaries seeking to entrench privilege, who had to be dragged kicking and screaming into the 21st century.

In some cases the disparagement might have been warranted; there may be some principals of high-decile schools who resented the way in which NCEA threatened to erode the qualifications advantage afforded to their students under the previous, norm-referenced, external examination-based system. Others—and we certainly count Roger

Moses among them—simply disagree that all learning has equal power to make a difference in the lives of young people, and believe that a competitive element brings out the best in many students. Whether or not these views are ultimately correct, they are views held by many experienced and thoughtful educators. In a democratic society, a balance between competing (informed) viewpoints must be struck. NCEA initially failed to do this, but the reform of Scholarship in 2005 marked the beginning of a move towards a greater balance of progressive and conservative values.

Chapter 9 A culture of continuous improvement

Many rolling adjustments to NCEA's processes have been introduced. For example, the process of using profiles of expected performance (PEPs) to manage year-on-year variability was explained in Chapter 7. In this chapter we discuss several more changes that have been made as NCEA's pressure points have been debated and clarified. The title of the chapter presumes that these changes have been for the better. In our view that is certainly the case with the first two changes that we introduce: the endorsement of certificates when Excellence or Merit grades have been achieved; and the process of grade score marking. Both have proactively and successfully addressed challenges that arose in the first decade of implementation. It is more debatable whether the revised process of awarding UE, introduced in 2015, really constitutes an improvement. One potential concern is that the UE requirement for 42 credits to be gained in approved subjects might act as a disincentive to using the flexibility of NCEA to design innovative courses of study. We will come back to this challenge in Part 3 of the book.

A key player recalls

Bali Haque joined NZQA early in 2006 as the senior manager with responsibility for school qualifications, as well as tertiary qualifications and qualifications recognition services (the appraisal of qualifications gained overseas). He moved to NZQA from a successful career as a secondary school principal and teacher. On arrival he found himself confronting the aftermath of the crisis that erupted when the 2005 Scholarship results were released (discussed above in Chapter 8).

In an earlier role as head of the commerce department in a large secondary school, Bali had been part of the trials of achievement-based assessment (ABA). From this experience he had developed an understanding of, and support for, the concept of standards-based assessment. Later, as a proactive secondary school leader, Bali was an advocate for NCEA in the face of opposition from many of his peers. He took the NZQA role following a major restructuring of the organisation. It was Bali's task to lead the development of detailed policy to enact reform and then to oversee its implementation. Karen Sewell, the acting chief executive who oversaw the restructuring, estimated that this would entail 4 to 5 years' work, an estimate that proved accurate.

The reform agenda included: introducing mechanisms to manage variability in results; providing endorsements for courses and certificates; changing moderation procedures; eliminating unit standards that duplicated the content of achievement standards; aligning achievement standards with *NZC*; and introducing the reporting of Not Achieved results for internally assessed standards.

Bali understood that a very different approach to that previously taken by NZQA would be required if standards-based assessment was to make sense to teachers and the wider public. This was not just a technical shift in practice: very important elements of his approach were consultation and communication. He understood that a great deal of the public criticism of NCEA came from people who had felt sidelined by NZQA during the development and implementation process. His much-more inclusive approach made many of those people feel as if they had been taken seriously at last, and he believes this was crucial to winning their support.

On the technical side, Bali looked for changes that would address some of the more strident criticisms of NCEA, while retaining the essence of its reforming intentions. He realised that these changes would be anathema to members of his team who were fully invested in a pure standards-based shift, but he was a pragmatist, and he pushed ahead in the face of sometimes very challenging internal opposition.

Bali credits the appointment of full-time moderators to improve the national consistency of teachers' judgements as being a critical factor in shoring up confidence in the internally assessed aspect of NCEA. While there had been some internal assessment as part of School Certificate and Bursary this was still unfamiliar territory for many New Zealand teachers and parents when NCEA was first implemented. One of the early mistakes had been to pay insufficient attention to public confidence in the reliability of teachers' judgements. The provision for endorsement of courses and qualifications was also a very important move: Bali commented that a fixation on percentage marks, inherited from English assessment systems, had led to widespread complaints that NCEA provided insufficient discrimination of students' performance. The endorsements went a considerable distance towards addressing these concerns, as well as those who argued that grade differentiation is necessary to motivate able students.

Certificate and course endorsements

As noted in Chapter 8, one of the criticisms of the early NCEA was that it did not provide sufficient incentive for students to distinguish themselves with high achievement. In fact, an early manifestation of this criticism was the development of the achievement standards before the implementation of NCEA; the original conception of the qualification was entirely unit-standards based, with just one passing grade available for each standard. Jim Strachan notes that, as early as 1996 it was clear that schools would not accept this model, and achievement standards, with three passing grades (Achieved, Merit, and Excellence) were developed. Nonetheless, at the aggregate level, there was no differentiation in reporting of the quality of results that had contributed to a certificate—one acquired with credits all at Achieved was reported in just the same way as one acquired with credits all at Excellence—and there was no aggregate reporting at the level of a course or subject at all.

The endorsements changed this. Certificate endorsements were introduced first in 2007, with NCEA qualifications endorsed with Merit if at least 50 contributing credits had been achieved with Merit or Excellence, and with Excellence if at least 50 contributing credits had been achieved with Excellence. Course endorsements were more difficult to design and faced greater political resistance. As a result their introduction was delayed until 2011.[1] They recognise high performance in specific courses of study, with 14 credits from the assessment programme required at Merit or Excellence for an endorsement with Merit, and 14 with Excellence, for endorsement with Excellence. There is an additional stipulation that at least three credits at the requisite level must be gained from internally assessed standards, and at least three credits must be gained from externally assessed standards—that is, a course cannot be totally internally or externally assessed.

There were three broad responses to the intention to introduce endorsements. The first is the supportive view, expressed by Roger Moses, that the endorsements were a necessary development to ensure that students of high ability were motivated to deploy that ability, and to recognise their achievement. The second, as expressed by Gregor Fountain, was pragmatic: while endorsements were contrary to a pure conception of standards-based assessment, they were nonetheless necessary to shore up support for the qualification. The third was outright opposition, as expressed by the PPTA executive (PPTA, 2007).

Opposition to certificate endorsement was based mainly on the argument that endorsements would reinforce a disparity of esteem for unit and achievement standards. Unit standards did not afford grades of Merit or Excellence, and would therefore not contribute to endorsements, exacerbating their already poor status in relation to achievement standards. The PPTA argued, probably correctly, that this would provide a further disincentive for the inclusion of unit standards in assessment programmes.

Course endorsements presented an especially difficult challenge, and encountered particularly stiff resistance from the PPTA. Originally, as noted above, the initiative was to be called subject endorsement and it would recognise high achievement in sets of achievement standards associated with a circumscribed number of school subjects. The PPTA argued, quite validly, that this model

---

1 A timeline of all major changes and improvements to NCEA can be found at: http://www.nzqa.govt.nz/qualifications-standards/qualifications/ncea/understanding-ncea/history-of-ncea/

would stifle the development of courses that drew upon standards from different subjects. After much internal debate involving rigorous discussions of the technical feasibility of various options, the present course endorsement option was developed. Under this model, each school declares to NZQA which standards are to be associated with which courses for the purposes of endorsement, and endorsements are awarded to students on the basis of achieving the requisite number of credits with Merit or Excellence from those declared sets of standards. This model was accepted, although not precisely embraced, by the PPTA.

Both the argument regarding the disparity of esteem for unit and achievement standards, and the argument regarding the reification of the subject canon, illustrate the way in which the NCEA system changed as it developed away from a model under which there would be just one type of standard with a single passing grade (the unit standard), with no subjects officially recognised at all. The NCEA model moved towards a tacit hierarchy of standards, and a de facto canon of subjects that, with some additions, looks much like the School Certificate/Bursary canon.

It should be noted that there is no inherent conflict between standards-based assessment per se, and either a hierarchy of grades or a canon of subjects. A hierarchy of grades can be accommodated by criteria of increasing sophistication (as is the case for the achievement standards), and criterion-referencing can be implemented on assessments for entire courses as well as fine-grained standards such as those used for NCEA. The perceived conflict was actually with the particular conception of standards-based assessment held by those who were involved in its early development in New Zealand.

One aspect of the idea of endorsements that sat uncomfortably with the proponents of the early conception of standards-based assessment was an ongoing attachment to the unit-standard model. The single passing grade afforded by unit standards had appeal to the social-justice agenda of the architects of the system, because it made it essentially impossible to rank or compare students. Their original vision was to apply the unit-standard model to all educational assessment in New Zealand, including assessment at degree level. In this regard, the adoption of the achievement standard model to contribute to NCEA was seen by many as a retrograde step, because it would provide a new mechanism for comparison and ranking. Endorsements, to this way of thinking, were another step in this direction.

While the capacity of an assessment system to support ranking of students (and by extension their schools) results in some undesirable consequences—most notably the corrosive effects of league tables in the press—the desire of those pursuing a radical social-justice agenda to eradicate any possibility of rankings was politically and epistemologically naïve.

On the political side, the endorsements did much to shore up the qualification. They were a factor in winning the support of moderate critics such as Roger Moses, and they actually did little, if any, damage to the social-justice agenda. In fact since the endorsements were introduced the disparity in the rate of qualifications achievement across the school-decile range has diminished (NZQA, 2014). While this correlation certainly does not imply a causal relationship between the two phenomena, it is possible that an improvement in students' motivation as a result of the endorsements is nonetheless a factor. In any event, while the availability of Merit and Excellence grades for achievement standards, for courses and for certificates certainly makes ranking possible, a critical difference with the School Certificate/Bursary system is that ranking is not used to manage pass rates, especially not at the level of courses or certificates.

The epistemological argument in favour of endorsements for courses and certificates based on achievement standards is similar to the argument for Merit and Excellence grades in the achievement standards themselves. Clearly the unit-standard design is suitable for certifying discrete skills. But in a discipline with epistemological depth a quite defensible argument can be made, from a standards-based point of view, to recognise qualitative differences in the sophistication of students' achievement with a hierarchy of grades. The extent to which every school subject is actually based in a discipline of any great epistemological depth might be debateable. However the point is that a crude obsession with ranking, or the pragmatic motive of motivating students, are not the only reasons to argue for a hierarchy of grades; there is a sound epistemological reason as well, and one that is no way contrary to broad principles of standards-based assessment.

Grade-score marking

A change to the marking system for externally assessed achievement standards was one of the less widely publicised changes to NCEA. The revised system uses an approach now known as *grade-score marking*. This approach was progressively implemented at the same time as the revised, curriculum-aligned standards: Level 1 in 2011; Level 2 in 2012; and Level 3 in 2013. The change was precipitated by a need to improve the reliability of external assessments. It was modelled to some extent on the process for Scholarship examinations, first implemented in 2005, but there are some important differences. Before we discuss what has changed, a description of the previous system for marking external NCEA assessments is in order.

The previous marking system for NCEA was known as *sufficiency marking*. Under sufficiency marking each examination question was marked as reflecting one of four levels of performance: not achieved (N); achieved (A); merit (M); or excellence (E). Some questions were written in such a way that they could attract only N or A grades, and others, only N, A, or M. Most examinations included multiple questions, so the individual N/A/M/E grades had to be aggregated into an overall grade. The aggregation process used in sufficiency marking was not as fair to students as it could have been, especially when only some of the questions allowed them the opportunity to perform at all these grade levels.

The examination schedules specified the numbers of questions that had to be answered at each grade level to attract each overall grade. This was known as *sufficiency* for each final grade. For example, in an examination comprising ten questions, sufficiency for each overall grade might have been as follows:

- **Achieved**: At least four questions with A or better.
- **Merit**: At least five questions with A or better and at least two questions with M or better
- **Excellence**: At least six questions with A or better, at least two questions with M or better and at least one question with E

There were four substantial problems with sufficiency marking. First, the method of aggregating the information across the paper entailed a count of categories (e.g., the number of questions with A). Statistically, this approach is expected to result in greater error of measurement in the final grade than the more traditional approach of summing scores (i.e., adding up individual question scores to produce a total). To understand why this is so, consider that all measurements in educational assessment entail a degree of error. That is, each response to an examination question is likely to over- or under-estimate the candidate's true level of achievement. When the scores associated with each question are summed, the positive and negative errors associated with the individual items tend to cancel out. However this cancellation does not occur to the same extent under the sufficiency approach of counting categories.

Secondly, because there were often a very small number of items that afforded an opportunity to demonstrate Excellence, or even Merit, the error of measurement associated with these grades was often particularly high.

Thirdly, the sufficiency marking process did not include a post-marking check to judge the extent to which students attaining each grade had actually met the criteria for that grade on a holistic reading of their work. To understand this point, it is necessary to appreciate that an external examination for NCEA is an *interpretation* of a standard, not the standard itself. Meeting the sufficiency criteria for a given grade is therefore a *proxy* for meeting the standard for that grade. However there was no check that the sufficiency criteria accurately reflected the standard on the basis of the quality of the work that students actually did in the examination. In other words, there was no way to ensure that the minimum performance for, say, Merit, under the sufficiency criteria was actually commensurate with the knowledge, skills, and abilities that the standard required for a Merit grade.

Finally, sufficiency-based marking was cumbersome to use in conjunction with profiles of expected performance (PEPs). If the marking process needed to be altered to bring a distribution of results in line with a PEP there were two available mechanisms; a change to the marking schedule for individual items, or a change to overall sufficiency requirements. The former was time-consuming for markers, because it would entail revisiting all previously marked work with a revised schedule. The latter was a blunt instrument. Very often a change of one item in the sufficiency criteria (e.g., requiring five rather than four questions at

A for an overall grade of *achieved*) would result in a large shift in the distribution, sometimes overshooting the PEP band in the other direction, or causing a problem at a different grade level.

Grade-score marking addressed each of these problems. Under this approach, all items must afford scope for achievement at all levels. Each item is marked and assigned a score from 0 to 8. A score of 0 means that there has been no substantial attempt at aanswering a question at all. Scores of 1 and 2 reflect performance at the Not Achieved level; scores of 3 and 4, performance at the Achieved level; scores of 5 and 6 reflect Merit-level performance; and scores of 7 and 8 reflect Excellence. When the scores have been assigned to the individual questions, a total score is calculated for a student by summing all of their individual question scores. This overcomes the problem that the category-counting method used in sufficiency marking unnecessarily exacerbates error of measurement.

Ensuring that each question can be answered at Achieved, Merit, or Excellence levels has resulted in a general reduction of the number of items in each examination. With sufficiency marking it was not unusual to have large numbers of items, some of which required no more than simple recall, and many of which required relatively insubstantial short-answer responses. Under grade score marking, there are typically fewer items, but they provide scope for more in-depth responses by students.

Cut scores

Late in the marking process there is a meeting of senior members of the marking panel to decide on *cut scores* for each final grade. Cut scores are used to differentiate between N, A, M, and E. The decision of where to position the cut between grades is made by selecting a sample of papers for each total score and reading them holistically (i.e., without consideration of the requirements of individual questions) to determine, using the professional judgement of these highly experienced markers, which pairs of scores should separate each final grade. For example, the meeting might decide that, whereas the majority of students with total scores of 13 are at the Achieved level according to the criteria of the standard, the majority of those with scores of 14 are at Merit level. They would therefore set 14 as the lowest score for a final grade of Merit.

This is a particularly valuable aspect of grade-score marking because it ensures that there is a final check of the grade distribution against the requirements of the standard itself, rather than relying solely on the examination, which, as noted above, is an interpretation of the standard, and an interpretation that inevitably changes from year to year.

It is possible for there to be a disagreement between the cut-score judged to best reflect a standard and a cut-score that yields an acceptable fit to a PEP. On the few occasions when results fall unacceptably outside a PEP range, the scale created by the score totals provides a relatively fine-grained mechanism to make small adjustments. However, disagreements of this kind are uncommon because grade-score marking affords high reliability. Large shifts in results distributions—the kind that result in unacceptable transgressions of PEP bands—are rare. Indeed, the statistical logic that underpins this system predicts that unacceptable levels of variation will be rare. But if they do happen it is necessary to balance the educational and political requirements of a national assessment system. This might sometimes result in a compromise between ensuring that results fall within the PEP bands and honouring the judgement of the cut-score meeting.

As a final note it is interesting that the aspect of grade-score marking that was initially most confronting for stakeholders was that grade-score marking involves numerical scores. There was a widespread fear that this would result in a return to the reporting of percentages, and the explicit ranking of students. This fear has proven to be unfounded, but it demonstrates the powerful mythologies that grow up around long-standing practices such as those that underpinned the School Certificate and Bursary systems. In fact, grade-score marking has only the most superficial resemblance to the scaling procedures used for School Certificate. The placement of grade boundaries under this system is done to align students' work with a standard, whereas the scaling system for School Certificate was done to ensure that norms (i.e., set proportions of students attaining each grade) were met. As is the case with a number of the post-2007 reforms to NCEA, what initially appeared to be a return to the past actually comprises a strengthening of standards-based assessment.

Determining who will be eligible for university study

The requirement to use school-qualifications results to determine who is eligible for university study is contested. In the middle decades of the 20th century UE was determined by a school-based accreditation process that took place in Year 12. The expectation that some unlucky students from each school—those who had just missed out on accreditation—would pass a set of UE examinations served as a check on each school's decision-making. Towards the end of the 20th century the determination of UE shifted to Year 13 and was based on results from the Bursary examination. A new method of determining UE was needed when NCEA was implemented. Bursary examinations were only offered in academic subjects, but NCEA credits could be gained across a very wide spectrum of learning experiences. For this reason, an NCEA Level 3 award could not necessarily be assumed to indicate that a student was ready for university study. A group representing the vice chancellors of New Zealand's universities worked with the Ministry of Education to design a means of differentiating UE from Level 3 NCEA.

The sorting mechanism this group devised harked back to the familiar distinction between academic and other subjects. The basic idea was that the source of the credits that made up the award could be used to determine its rigour, and hence suitability, as a basis for tertiary study. To this end an approved-subjects list was drawn up and published. Students aspiring to go to university needed to gain at least 14 credits from each of two Level 3 subjects on this list. They also needed to gain at least 14 further credits in another Level 3 subject, which could be on the list but did not have to be. Students also needed to provide evidence that they had achieved basic levels of literacy and numeracy, as indicated by credits gained in maths and English at Levels 1 and 2.

The composition of the approved subjects list was controversial. Initially, only traditional academic subjects were included—those that had previously been examined for UE, and then for Bursary. Teachers of subjects that missed out protested. In effect, any student who aspired to go to university would be discouraged from choosing to study their subject. A process was devised for updating and adding subjects to the list, but submission took some time and initially created anomalies. For example health, home economics and PE all have achievement standards written to the same achievement objectives in *NZC*. PE was on the list from the start because it had been an established Bursary subject. Health was added after strong submissions were made to the awarding panel, but it was to be some time before home economics was also added. This anomaly has now been addressed at the systems level. Following revisions to UE regulations made in 2010, any subject with its own suite of achievement standards at Level 3 was deemed to be approved. This does not mean however, that subjects with new suites of achievement standards arising from future senior secondary curriculum initiatives will be automatically added to the approved list.

The initial design for UE was debated and revised in 2010. A new set of regulations was published in 2011. These are shown in Figure 9.1. Notice that the importance of choosing approved subjects has tightened for students who aspire to be university-bound. Previously there was some wiggle room for course innovation because only two subjects needed to be on the approved subjects list. Now all three subjects need to be approved for the credits they carry to count for UE.

Figure 9.1. Current requirements for UE

University Entrance (UE) is the minimum requirement to go to a New Zealand university. To qualify you will need:
- NCEA Level 3
- Three subjects—at **Level 3**, made up of 14 credits each, in three approved subjects
- Literacy—10 credits at Level 2 or above, made up of 5 credits in reading; 5 credits in writing
- Numeracy—10 credits at Level 1 or above, made up of achievement standards—specified achievement standards available through a range of subjects, or unit standards—package of three numeracy unit standards (26623, 26626, 26627— **all** three required).

Source: http://www.nzqa.govt.nz/qualifications-standards/awards/university-entrance/

The classification into traditional subjects appears to assume that these traditional structures are necessary to demonstrate rigour. This assumption is problematic in several ways. First it assumes that all the achievement standards that make up a subject-based suite will furnish evidence of readiness for university, whereas we perceive considerable variation in their rigor and intellectual demand. Secondly, the stipulation discourages teachers from designing new cross-disciplinary subjects (two potential examples are English and media studies, or historical geography). It also discourages the design of courses designed to integrate elements from different subject suites to meet a specific curriculum purpose (examples are given in Chapter 12, where this issue is more fully elaborated).

Determining literacy and numeracy

The way in which students meet basic literacy and numeracy requirements was also updated when the UE regulations changed in 2011. There were two main reasons for making improvements in this aspect of UE regulations and associated practices.

One of the founding intentions of NCEA was that students could gain credits for naturally occurring evidence of learning. However, the principle of using classroom work as evidence for achievement never really took hold in many subjects. When the UE regulations changed, this principle was put to work on a more structured basis. Students taking traditional academic subjects should be able to demonstrate their literacy levels as they read and write during the learning and assessment work they already do. If they achieve credits in standards that require basic levels of literacy, these should be sufficient evidence that they are literate. That's the argument in principle. You can see it reflected in the current UE regulations in Figure 9.1 above. A list of suitable standards was drawn up to meet the needs of this regulation. Whereas previously literacy was determined by evidence generated only in the subject of English, now such evidence can come from right across the curriculum.

Numeracy for UE can be determined via naturally occurring evidence using the process we have just outlined for literacy. The catch is that fewer achievement standards require students to demonstrate aspects of numeracy.[2] The alternative is to use evidence from a small suite of unit standards that were specifically designed to assess aspects

---

2 Many teachers would say that even those on the list might not require a sufficient demonstration of the named skill set. Using a graph in an examination, for example, does not necessarily provide sufficient evidence of ability to "interpret statistical information for a purpose" (which is the title of the unit standard alternative).

of basic numeracy. There is a corresponding suite of unit standards for literacy. Both suites are set at NCEA Level 1 and were designed to be used to award basic literacy and numeracy as part of a Level 2 NCEA for students whose assessment has mainly been via unit standards.

Concluding comment

Certificate and course endorsement have been widely recognised as making a positive difference to motivation for many students. Grade-score marking was designed to improve the reliability of external assessment and provide a mechanism to check each distribution of results against its associated standard. It has not received similar acclaim to certificate and course endorsement, but it is less widely known and understood. Teachers and others directly involved in external assessment know and use the process, but do not necessarily interpret this within the wider assessment-principles framing employed by its designers. For others, the way in which grade-score marking works may only be familiar through hearsay. We had two aims in adding a detailed account of the process here. One was to ensure more people are aware of how grade-score marking works. The second—important to the overall agenda of our book—was to demonstrate how grade-score marking actually constitutes a strengthening of standards-based assessment processes rather than a return to practices of the past.

The fine-tuning of UE regulations is the third set of revisions we have discussed. These changes are more equivocal in terms of overall benefits. On the one hand there is now an alternative pathway to accommodate literacy and numeracy assessment for students who do not aspire to go to university. Another potential benefit is that a wider range of subjects can receive recognition for UE. On the other hand, the dual pathways have the potential to further consolidate and confirm deeply entrenched differentiation between "academic" and "vocational" students rather than lifting expectations for the latter group. And specification of credits is further confined within traditional subject groupings, which potentially discourages creative, but robust, curriculum innovation. We will return to these complex issues in Part 3.

Chapter 10 Moderation and teachers' professional learning

Moderation is a term that has a number of different meanings in educational assessment. One commonality is that moderation involves supporting the consistency (reliability) of assessment judgements. Beyond that high-level intention, the processes and philosophies of moderation are so varied that some moderation systems are almost incomparable with others. To illustrate the point, we begin this chapter by contrasting two very different approaches. One is the approach taken by the Ministry of Education to moderation for the National Standards in primary school reading, writing, and mathematics. The other is the NZQA process for the moderation of internally assessed achievement standards for NCEA in the senior secondary school. The contrast raises an important question, which we then go on to discuss in more detail: can a national moderation process undertaken to ensure reliable judgements also serve a valuable role in supporting teachers' professional learning?

As we recall

Some moderation processes offer important opportunities for professional learning, while others can only feasibly be used for accountability purposes.

Rose recalls a process that clearly led to an improvement in participants' understanding of how conflicting assessment evidence can be validly synthesised to arrive at a balanced judgement. Michael's account illustrates the way in which a statistical moderation process primarily designed to serve an accountability function was (wilfully) misunderstood by a journalist who used the information to unfairly damage the reputation of a school. Taken together, these accounts illustrate some of the tensions that arise when a moderation system is used to serve both professional learning and accountability purposes.

Michael: Internal assessment in the gutter press

When I was working at NZQA one of the most difficult conversations I had was with the principal of a high-decile girls' school. This school had been publically and unfairly accused in the press of poor internal assessment practice. The principal was understandably very upset, and there was nothing I could do to repair the situation. The accusations came on the back of the results of data analysis that I had undertaken, and which NZQA had been required to provide to a journalist under the Official Information Act. The analysis involved finding schools with internal assessment results that were outliers in comparison with their external assessment results. This analysis, described in more detail in this chapter, was not intended to become public, and certainly it did not provide hard evidence of poor practice. There are many perfectly valid reasons that a school might be an outlier in such an analysis, and it was intended to comprise just one source of information that NZQA could use to monitor the reliability of internal assessment for NCEA. The school in question had done nothing wrong; it simply had very able students who tended to excel in internal assessment. The incident highlights the difficulty of the job that NZQA faces in running the internal assessment system in the face of a media that is not only profoundly statistically ignorant, but which seeks to sensationalise minor—and in this case non-existent—incidents to generate headlines.

Rose: An encounter with a rich moderation conversation in English

Several years ago I was invited to present a keynote talk at a conference of English teachers. My talk was scheduled for after morning tea. I'd arrived the night before so I took the opportunity to sit in on a moderation workshop in the first slot of the day. The workshop was led by a highly experienced English teacher who had been appointed to the role of chief subject moderator. She showed several video clips of students making speeches in English. Together the 20 or so teachers present discussed the judgements they would make, based on the achievement standard criteria. One speech stands out in my memory. The student was confident and engaging—you could hear that her classmates were highly entertained (much laughter etc.). On reflection, however, she really said nothing of any substance about her topic. This presented some of the teachers with a dilemma because the criteria said that the speech had to be well presented and "convincing". Some teachers initially overlooked the lack of content. Seduced perhaps by the dramatic delivery, they leaned towards Achieved with Excellence (as the student's own teacher had done). Others wanted to dismiss the whole speech as not convincing and award a Not Achieved. The moderator skilfully led the discussion towards the making of a more holistic judgement. What sticks in my memory is the realisation of just how powerful such a conversation could be for teacher professional learning (see Hipkins, 2010b). Sadly, by this time moderation was already being discussed in the media as a process for checking-up on teachers.

Three different ways of carrying out moderation

> Moderation [for the National Standards] is the process of teachers sharing their expectations and understanding of standards with each other in order to improve the consistency of their decisions about student learning. (Ministry of Education, n.d.-a)

The process described in this Ministry of Education definition is sometimes called *social moderation*. Notice how it emphasises professional dialogue between assessors (in this case teachers), supported by exemplars and illustrations of the standards. This approach is designed to help teachers learn both about the process of assessment and the curriculum material being assessed. Rose's story is an example of a social-moderation activity. Typically, social moderation between groups of teachers does not involve an external moderator, or central authority, who makes decisions about whether or not teachers' assessment judgements are correct. (Rose's story is a bit unusual in this respect. In the context of a conference workshop teachers were working with a chief moderator who was an external authority.) While social moderation can promote consistency within moderation groups, if there is no external expert to review judgements, it cannot address consistency between moderation groups. This means that it is not really suitable for promoting consistency on a national basis.

NZQA carries out external school check moderation of internally assessed standards in secondary schools to ensure that:

- assessment judgements (marking of students' work) are at the national standard
- the assessment materials used (tasks, activities or tests) are at the national standard. (NZQA, 2015a)

The *check moderation* described in this NZQA definition involves the checking of a sample of teachers' assessment judgements by national moderators. They either endorse the grade allocated to each work item or judge that a different grade was appropriate. Schools are required to provide to NZQA a random sample of the work students have submitted for assessment against internally assessed achievement standards. Along with the work samples they must submit the assessment task which they used, and the grade allocated by teachers to each item of work. NZQA national moderators then check-moderate these samples and provide summary reports back to schools.

Check moderation is similar to check marking, which is a feature of almost all formal examination systems, including external assessment for NCEA. Check marking involves a senior marker checking a sample of marked work from each of the other markers to ensure that their marking is valid, and that it is not unduly harsh or generous. An obvious difference between check moderation and check marking is that the latter involves only the relatively small groups of teachers who are involved in marking external assessment. Thus the scope it affords for professional learning is considerably narrower than that of check moderation. Since check moderation applies to judgements made by a sample of teachers across the whole system it could also provide valuable professional learning. However, while moderators might indeed give helpful feedback about any discrepancies between a teacher's judgement and their own judgement of the same work, the main emphasis, at least in the NCEA system, is on accountability rather than professional learning. All check-moderation data are collated annually to provide a national agreement rate between moderators and teachers. This provides a check on the reliability of internal assessment at the systems level.

Statistical moderation is a different process to either social or check moderation. This involves moderating small-scale assessments against the results of a larger-scale assessment undertaken by all the students in the cohort to be moderated (typically a test or formal examination). The logic of this approach is that, if the reference assessment is a reliable predictor of performance in the smaller-scale assessments (i.e., if there is a strong enough correlation between the two assessments), it can be used to identify assessors whose judgements are out of step with the reference assessment. They might be harsher, or more lenient, or just less well correlated with the reference assessment. Like social moderation there is no person in an overall moderator role when statistical moderation is carried out. However the role of moderator is essentially fulfilled by the reference assessment.

NCEA moderation for internal assessment

In the remainder of this chapter, we explore the moderation processes for internal assessment in the NCEA system. Of all processes associated with NCEA, moderation of internal assessment provides the richest opportunity for teachers' professional learning, and that is our central concern in this chapter. It is worth noting however that moderation is not exclusive to internal assessment; profiles of expected performance (PEPs) (see Chapter 7) and check-marking are used to moderate external assessments, but these are largely invisible to most teachers, and are not further discussed in this chapter.

Moderation of internally assessed achievement standards for NCEA comprises several elements. The most expensive and visible element is check moderation, but this is supported by social moderation activities as well as (soft) statistical moderation.

Check moderation is the central and dominant element of the national moderation system for internally assessed achievement standards. NZQA employs assessment and subject experts as national moderators who check-moderate the grades allocated to between five and ten thousand items of work annually. They also check the validity of the tasks used to collect evidence of students' achievement (NZQA, 2015a) and provide reports to schools that show levels of agreement between teacher judgements and moderator judgements. NZQA's directives about how the process should be conducted and what should be done with their feedback make it clear that check moderation is done predominantly for accountability purposes:

> Schools are required to ensure that teachers have no opportunity to re-mark the sample of student work after it has been selected [for moderation].
>
> Schools must address issues that are identified in the external moderation process, including the use of invalid tasks and lack of agreement by the moderator with assessor judgements. (NZQA, 2015b)

Clearly the emphasis here is at the systems level. Moderation is conducted by specialist moderators under the auspices of a centralised authority (NZQA) to check on the consistency of teachers' decision-making. The system invests enormous power in moderators, and the quality of the accountability process is heavily dependent on their expertise, as are any professional learning opportunities afforded by moderation. A disagreement with a teacher's judgement with scant justification expressed is of very limited value from a professional learning point of view. Feedback from teachers suggests that some moderators are better than others at giving clear feedback about reasons for any disagreement with their judgements. National moderators also conduct best-practice workshops (see below). Thus their expertise in their respective subjects and disciplines, their knowledge of valid assessment processes, and their ability to work collaboratively with teachers all contribute to determining the quality of the professional learning opportunities.

There is little in the check moderation process that guarantees any professional learning. Reporting to schools is generally aggregated, and focuses on the rate of agreement between moderators and teachers. There are some missed opportunities here.

- Moderators investigate the process of assessment to check the validity of assessment tasks, but not the process used by the teacher to synthesise assessment evidence to make an overall judgement.
- Moderators focus on the grade awarded as the outcome of the assessment process, but not on ways in which assessment evidence might be used to enhance teachers' practice and students' learning.

Compared with the social moderation approach used for National Standards in primary schools, the NZQA approach might appear to be heavy-handed. However there is evidence that it has been successful in improving reliability of teachers' assessment decision-making. According to NZQA (2015c), moderators agreed with teachers' assessment judgements in 75.8 percent of cases in 2009. By 2014 the agreement rate was up to 82.8 percent. No parallel statistics are available to monitor the success or otherwise of social moderation for National Standards, but research from the National Standards School Sample Monitoring and Evaluation Project (Ward & Thomas, 2015) suggests that a lack of reliability is a persistent problem for that system.

There could well be hidden costs in the way that the reliability of internal assessment for NCEA is currently addressed. School senior leaders often place emphasis on a high agreement rate with moderators, which can make teachers risk averse and put them off attempting innovative approaches to internal assessment. On the other hand, the risk that students will not be assessed fairly—to say nothing of the political risk to the internal assessment system itself of not emphasising reliability—militates in favour of the approach taken by NZQA. Balancing innovation and reliability is a difficult political tightrope.

Other moderation activities in and for secondary schools

Every 4 years NZQA conducts managing-national-assessment (MNA) visits to every secondary school in New Zealand (or more often if NZQA deems it necessary). The focus of MNA visits is to discuss and assure the quality of school-wide internal assessment processes. While it would be a long bow to call the MNA programme a moderation process in itself, it is designed to ensure that each school conducts its internal assessment rigorously. This includes making sure that processes are in place for peer moderation of teachers' own judgements. Internal moderation varies in nature from school to school, but mostly relies heavily on social moderation activities. If strong assessment expertise is available within the school, if collaborative decision-making processes are in place, and if the opportunities for professional learning are perceived and valued by everyone involved, then genuine professional learning opportunities may be part of the overall moderation experience for teachers. These are three big ifs; a lack of any one of them could cause an opportunity for professional learning to go unrealised and moderation to be experienced as yet another imposed administrative pressure.

NZQA moderators run periodic best-practice workshops to assist teachers to improve their assessment judgements. Attendance at these workshops is optional for teachers, but they nonetheless constitute another social moderation activity associated with internal assessment for NCEA. Clearly the workshops are focused directly on professional learning, and national survey data indicate that they are very well received by teachers (Hipkins, 2013). In addition, NZQA publishes exemplar materials and clarification statements that make a contribution to moderation processes by conveying concrete examples of expectations in relation to standards-based criteria.

An annual analysis conducted by NZQA is the only element of statistical moderation used for internal assessment judgements. This analysis uses a statistical model to estimate, for each school, the average performance expected in internal assessments on the basis of its external assessment results. The analyses are run separately for each subject area and each New Zealand Qualifications Framework level. If a school varies from the statistically expected level of performance in internal assessment to a greater degree than 95 percent of other schools it is called an outlier. Schools identified as statistical outliers in this analysis are often contacted to seek further information, especially if moderators have also shown a relatively low level of agreement with teachers' grade decisions. This is a soft statistical moderation process in the sense that it never leads to internal assessment grades being changed. Neither is it assumed that there is anything wrong with the internal assessment practice of outlier schools. Given the definition of an outlier, 5 percent of schools will be so identified in every such analysis, even if no schools are engaged in faulty practice. Like other statistical moderation, this process offers no professional learning opportunities.

The shifting emphasis of NCEA moderation

The various aspects of moderation outlined above have developed over time. A strict social-moderation approach has never been used for moderating internal-assessment judgements. However, the general trajectory has moved from a system that embodied a commitment to professional learning and provided detailed feedback to teachers, to a system that emphasises accountability. The high-stakes nature of NCEA probably made this trajectory inevitable, but opportunities for professional learning have been lost along the way.

In the early years of NCEA, moderation was directly focused on improving assessment practice and specifically, the processes by which teachers made assessment decisions. The moderation system was much smaller in scale than is the case at present. There were no full-time moderators and no public reporting of agreement levels between teachers and moderators, as outlined above. Teachers were encouraged to submit the assessment judgements that they were least confident about, on the grounds that these judgements were likely to provide the richest opportunities for feedback from moderators.

The Scholarship crisis (see Chapter 8) led, among other things, to the preparation of a report by the State Services Commission (Martin, 2005) that focused on the delivery of secondary school qualifications. The following comments from this report illustrate the tension that the review team perceived between using moderation to improve practice and to improve reliability:

> Schools [could] choose which results to submit [for moderation, but] NZQA [continued] to persuade schools and teachers that borderline decisions submitted for moderation produce the most satisfactory professional outcomes. (p. 53)

> …schools select the examples of student work (but not the other material), raising concerns that only 'safe' marking decisions are put forward, a perception that has been reinforced by the unfortunate practice of some school principals who have used moderation outcomes as a measure of teacher competence. (p. 54)

> The Review Team accepts that in an optimal system teachers are best positioned to identify borderline cases for scrutiny, and positive, professional moderation invites the discussion that ensues… ….[but] it is a simple reality that new systems are viewed with suspicion and because unpredictable effects frequently occur, it is sensible to have safety nets that maximise stability. (p. 54)

If the system is primarily designed to enhance teachers' assessment practice, then difficult or borderline assessment cases are most desirable because they are likely to provide the richest information. From an accountability perspective, however, an emphasis on difficult assessment cases is undesirable because, by definition, these are the cases on which moderators are least likely to agree with teachers' judgements. However if the system is primarily designed to assure national reliability, a random-sampling approach would be preferable because it allows valid inferences to be made at the national level. Choosing borderline cases would result in a biased (unrepresentative) sample. The State Services Commission report inclined to the accountability purpose when it recommended revisiting a 2001 recommendation by government statistician David Rhoades (cited in Martin, 2005, p. 54) that random sampling be used to improve the validity of moderation.

Validity is always relative to purpose. If the purpose of moderation is to serve school accountability or to support public reporting of the reliability of internal assessment, then a random sample would indeed improve validity. But if, as seemed to be the case in the early NCEA years, the primary purpose is to serve teachers' professional learning, then focusing on borderline judgements—those with which teachers struggled the most—would constitute the most valid approach.

The pressure from schools and academic commentators to construe moderation purely in accountability terms was evident in the State Services Commission report (Martin, 2005):

> Some schools worried about the consistency of judgement between schools for internal assessment (p. 52)

> [Some schools have proposed] that the external examination [sic] be used to moderate school based assessments. (p. 51)

> [Some schools have proposed that] the average and range of ... internally assessed grades [should be] strictly controlled and limited (p. 51).

Had the latter proposal for heavy statistical moderation been adopted, it would certainly have eroded many of the gains that had been made in the early years of NCEA. Students in demographic groups who have not historically fared well in formal examinations would almost certainly have lost opportunities to have their achievements acknowledged. Furthermore, this type of moderation would have made nonsense of the notion that NCEA, or at least its internally assessed component, is standards-based.

Following the State Services Commission report (Martin, 2005) NZQA appointed full-time moderators to oversee a revised moderation process, but did not adopt full-scale statistical moderation as recommended. Initially, under this revised approach, 10 percent of all internal assessments conducted in schools, including both achievement standards and unit standards, were to be moderated. This marked a shift from an emphasis on professional learning to one on accountability. As we've already noted this shift was probably inevitable. While NZQA is to be commended on its previous commitment to using moderation for professional learning, it was probably unrealistic to think that this would, on its own, be publicly acceptable. However from a statistical point of view, the requirement to moderate 10 percent of all internally assessed work was a massive and expensive over-reaction. Schools found the new requirements onerous, and moderators found that all of their time was spent check marking; the entire process became focused on crisis management rather than professional learning or even on a rational approach to accountability. Fortunately, as time has passed and the political pressure has abated, NZQA has been able to adopt a much smaller—but nonetheless representative—random sample, sufficient to provide a very reliable estimate of the moderator–teacher agreement rate.

The scaling back of the size of the random moderation sample has left the moderators more time to engage in activities such as the Best Practice workshops. The moderation sample itself has been divided into two sets. One set constitutes an approximately random sample, and is used to support a national reliability check. The other is a sample of standards deliberately selected by NZQA's school relationship managers. This second sample allows NZQA to target standards and schools where teachers appear to require more feedback about the judgements they are making, and to ensure that all schools and standards undergo regular moderation. This targeted focus would not be possible with a pure random sampling approach. Aside from the optional workshops however, there is little in the NCEA moderation system as it stands that focuses specifically on professional learning.

Internal assessment was, and remains, controversial (see Chapter 4). We think that many of the reasons for this are unjustified. When properly designed and used, internal assessment affords opportunities to provide evidence of learning to students who do not thrive in time-limited examinations. Furthermore, internal assessment, because of its timing and potential scope, is much better placed to support teaching and learning than summative examinations. Nonetheless, by its nature, strong reliability is difficult to achieve and demonstrate for internal assessment. To achieve public acceptance of the NCEA system, a moderation system that, at the outset, entailed a balance of accountability and professional learning would have been wise. Ironically, the early focus on the latter, to the exclusion of the former, has resulted in a system that, today, focuses on the former at the expense of the latter.

Chapter 11 Assessment in context

During the 1980s and 1990s many educators around the world became actively interested in the role that contexts—that is, presenting abstract ideas and concepts in concrete situations—might play in supporting learning. This was a logical offshoot of the increasing prominence being given to constructivism as a theory of learning, with associated implications for pedagogy. Constructivism emphasises learning as a process of active sense-making by each individual. By implication, what students already know and believe, and the experiences they can already draw on, affect what they can learn next. Using familiar contexts was seen as one practical way to help students make active sense of their new learning (Hipkins & Arcus, 1997).[1]

A logical extension of this line of argument was that assessments should also be set in contexts that would provide opportunities for as many students as possible to demonstrate both what they know and what they can do. This chapter discusses the challenges that have arisen when this idea has been put into practice, in examination-type contexts, and in other assessment contexts (e.g., when achievement is

---

1 In New Zealand one prominent indicator of this interest was the inclusion of lists of "suggested contexts" in each section of the first outcomes-based curriculum developed for the science learning area (Ministry of Education, 1993).

internally assessed). We then look ahead to ask if NCEA provides fresh opportunities to achieve the type of engaged and active sense-making that allows students to demonstrate achievement to their full potential.

As we recall

Rose: The mysterious case of the coconut milk

When unit standards were being developed I attended a short series of workshops intended to introduce local biology teachers to the principles of standards-based assessment. We were shown how to use rubrics designed for achievement-based assessment (ABA) (see Chapter 5). As one learning task we were asked to design a simple investigation and then assess our own efforts using the five-level ABA rubric provided. I was flummoxed by this task. Titled "Coconut Milk" we were asked to design a means for testing whether storage conditions impacted on the amount of milk that could be retrieved from fresh coconuts. Coconuts were an exotic fruit in the small town where I grew up and I don't like them. I had no idea how to get the milk out, never having done it or seen it done. I didn't know where to start with the task. I couldn't believe how simple the expected answer was (drill a hole and pour the milk into a measuring device). I was anticipating something much more elaborate, though I wasn't sure what. This all seems a bit stupid to me looking back, but I haven't forgotten how the task made me feel. It was obviously a real enough dilemma at the time. The problem would have been quickly resolved if we had done an actual investigation instead of just planning one on paper. But assessment on paper often stands as a proxy for actually doing what is described. The problem I've sketched here is partly about the nature of the task itself, compounded by the use of an unfamiliar context.

Challenges for use of contexts in learning and assessment

Learning might be set in context for different reasons. The intent might be to motivate students—the context is of interest to them. A familiar context might be used to demonstrate the salience and usefulness of the intended learning as it applies to students' lives beyond school—the content is relevant to them. Some people argue that difficult concepts are more easily understood if the context in which they are introduced is familiar. (We think this is debatable, for reasons we discuss shortly.) Assessment might be also set in context for any of these reasons, or to test whether learning can be appropriately applied to new or unfamiliar contexts. Conceptual knowledge and skills are demonstrably more robust when they can be transferred in this manner (Hipkins, 1997).

However, as the coconut milk episode demonstrates, the manner in which contexts are actually used is critical. This recounted vignette is a classic example of what we think of as "candy wrapping". A bright shiny context is wrapped around a demonstration of learning that doesn't actually require it. For example, knowledge of simple experimental design would look much the same if a different context, or even no context at all, was used. In the coconut milk vignette the intended assessment target was of the ability to hold several variables constant while systematically changing another variable, then collecting data about the impact of making that change. This control of variables or fair testing strategy can be demonstrated in endless contexts, but in the school science laboratory settings familiar to students it is typically relatively context-free.

Contextual candy-wrapping can be confusing when students are not sure what they are supposed to be learning about—the context or the concepts. It can also add layers of conceptual complexity. Unanticipated challenges can arise because concepts seldom translate cleanly into different contexts when designing either learning or assessment tasks. The combination of the two can quickly surface questions that are not easily answered. It helps if a teacher has a deep practical knowledge of the context being used, but even then some questions could take the learning into deeper conceptual waters than the teacher intended. The validity of an assessment can be compromised if a student knows more than required and, as a result, picks up on a really tricky nuance to the question when something much more straightforward was anticipated. Hipkins (1997) discusses several examples of this in mid-1990s School Certificate science examinations.

Problems that arise when using contexts can impact variably on different groups of students. For example, there was some discussion in the 1990s of the possible gender impacts of contextualising science examination questions. One research team found that male students were more likely to attempt physics questions in context by selecting an algorithm to apply, even if they were not confident they had chosen the right one. Female students were more likely to be put off even attempting answer if they could not understand the relationship between the concept and the context (Rennie & Parker, 1996). Rose's vignette above exemplifies exactly such a response.

The challenge is applicable internationally

The use of contexts in international assessments is similarly controversial, with the added challenge that national contexts and the experiences of individuals within them are so diverse. The example that follows illustrates this challenge.

In 2010 an anthropologist was invited to accompany an international testing team employed by UNESCO to administer an adult literacy assessment to various nomadic herders living in the Gobi Desert (Maddox, 2014). One of the items in the assessment required participants to read about the Mongolian camel and to answer questions based on the text. Although this item was included to engage and interest Mongolian participants in the overall survey, it proved to be a case of too much context. Some of the herders knew far more about the camels than the text explained. But if they gave detailed answers that went beyond the text, these were marked incorrect. Expertise about camels increased enjoyment and participation for some of the herders, but test-taking conventions required them to privilege other people's knowledge, as set out in the text, while relegating their own knowledge to a place of secondary importance. To anyone unfamiliar with "playing the assessment game" this must seem like strange behaviour indeed.

Another item in the same test asked participants to complete an application form for a job in a fast-food restaurant. Maddox noted that inability to complete such forms is often cited as an indicator that adult literacy is lacking. However, as he also wryly observed, such restaurants are not a feature of life in the Gobi Desert. Herders taking the test were perplexed about how to respond. Should they pretend they wanted a job like that? Why would they do that? This highlights the opposite dilemma to that outlined in the previous paragraph. The assessment context is realistic (in the eyes of the assessment designers) but definitely not real for the intended assessment candidates.

Use of contexts in externally assessed NCEA standards

One problem with the use of contexts in tests and examinations is that difficulties that students might have in interpreting questions can't necessarily be predicted in advance. As the above examples illustrate, good intentions can go awry when people being assessed interact with the material presented in ways that were neither intended nor anticipated. Contexts afford additional scope for differences, unrelated to the knowledge that a question is designed to assess, to arise in the way that different groups of students understand and respond to an item.[2] In the case of high-stakes examinations for school qualifications, unexpected shifts in the spread and composition of assessment results can occur from year to year because more than just knowledge of the intended content is being assessed. Both validity and reliability are compromised when the use of contexts contributes to this type of response effect.

Potential advantages of contexts in external assessments

Terry Burrell, head of science at Onslow College in Wellington, was named New Zealand's science teacher of the year` in 2014. Rose met with her to explore the use of contexts in some recent NCEA examination papers. She said that "every year when I open the paper I'm either thrilled about the context(s) or I think 'how boring'".

Terry is an advocate for the use of interesting contexts in biology examinations. She noted that questions that don't have a context are often quite lexically dense. They can be hard to read and unpack if students don't immediately recognise what is required. A context can provide a way to engage the students' learning if they have been taught strategies to unpack unfamiliar contexts. These strategies help them work out how the context relates to the concept being tested. Terry noted that, compared to questions that just ask for a "brain dump", there is much scope in a question with an interesting context for well-prepared students to display deep understanding of the phenomena being examined. They will have more opportunities to provide

---

2 Psychometric analyses of large data sets can show up this effect. The technical term used is *differential item functioning* (DIF).

evidence that they have met the criteria for Merit or Excellence, which is of particular importance with grade-score marking (see Chapter 9).

Table 11.1 summarises selected questions from the papers Terry brought along to our meeting. It was indeed clear that able students would have more opportunities to demonstrate excellence in the questions with richer contexts.

Table 11.1. How contexts open up opportunities to display deeper learning

Examination year and AS number	Nature of context and question(s)	Task demands
Level 2 Biology 2010 AS 90461	No context—candidates discuss primary and secondary succession and explain why secondary succession often happens more quickly	Recall relevant concepts and shape explanation
Level 2 Biology 2014 AS 91156	Minimal context—a table that shows numbers of mitochondria in four different types of body cells. Candidates draw a mitochondrion then explain differences in numbers shown in the table.	Recall structure and use appropriate conventions to draw a biological diagram. Link knowledge of function of mitochondria to knowledge of likely functions of different cell types. Use links to explain differences in table.
Level 2 Biology 2012 AS 91157	Photos and information about three variants of a gene that impacts the appearance of Mallard ducks. Candidates are told there are six possible genotypes (pair-wise gene combinations) and three phenotypes (what they look like—each photo shows one of these).	Read and unpack the contextual information. Work out the six possible genotypes. Use genetic reasoning to complete the Punnett Square provided. Justify the solution with reference to the relevant gene expression concepts.

It could be argued that the potential advantage of challenging contexts for able students actually creates a disadvantage for those who have weaker academic skills if it is not clear to them which knowledge they should bring to bear. One rejoinder might be that lexically dense, more abstract questions are hard for such students to access too. A more positive response is that, with support, all students can access such questions, at least at the Achieved level, and they are more likely to be interested in answering them if the context is interesting to them. Terry stressed that she teaches students how to unpack an unfamiliar context so that they can accurately target the concept(s) being assessed. This essential part of their examination preparation ensures that they can engage with contextual questions and show what they know.

The promise and pitfalls of contexts in internal assessment

Internal assessment can open up interesting new opportunities to use contexts in more meaningful ways than is typically possible in examination settings. Problems arising from the use of contexts can be more easily managed by teachers who know their students than by an examiner who is writing an examination for thousands of diverse students. Teachers who are attuned to their students' lives can design learning and assessment tasks that engage and interest them. However, gender-based or cultural differences affecting the accessibility of contexts can still create inequities in the opportunities students have to show what they know and what they can do when everyone has to respond to the same task with the same context. Ideally, assessment design should be sufficiently open that students can choose their own contexts within the bounds of a common focus or framework. This is more feasible for some types of assessment tasks than for others, and critically, it requires teachers to hold deep subject expertise so that they can make sound judgements across a range of contexts and student responses. The following vignette illustrates just one of the challenges that might arise.

It can be challenging for teachers to make consistent judgements about the standard of students' work when some choose demanding topics and contexts for their work while others play it safe. One of us (Mark) documented this dilemma during a research project that focused on internally assessed achievement standards in history (Sheehan, 2013). The most recent versions of these standards require students to demonstrate aspects of historical thinking such as the ability to select and interpret diverse evidence sources. In one class some students chose the Springbok tour of New Zealand as a context. This was a controversial, protracted series of events, and it is not hard to find many different media sources that report or discuss what happened. In contrast one student in this class studied the rise of feminism in the 1980s, as reflected by writings in *Broadsheet*. This was a much more ambitious topic and the teacher noted that it would have been very difficult to judge it in comparison to the "safer" projects if he had not had a robust understanding of historical thinking. He noted that teachers who lacked deep disciplinary expertise tended to take a paint-by-numbers approach to judgements, relying on the semantics of the wording of the standards themselves (e.g., "x" number of sources used) instead of making more holistic judgements based on the quality of the disciplinary thinking displayed (Sheehan, 2014).

Contexts that pack an emotional punch

So far the implicit focus of this chapter has been on *cognitive* arguments for setting assessment in context. Now we turn to the potential for well-chosen contexts to *emotionally* engage students, helping them to lift their level of performance and to persevere with demanding tasks that require—and make space for—convincing demonstrations of achievement. The two stories that follow are different in their contextual specifics, but the dynamic at work is similar.

Case 1: Caring about safe driving

Digital technologies teacher Gerard MacManus is a member of the education reference group for the New Zealand Transport Agency (NZTA). Between them this group of teachers have expertise right across the learning areas of the curriculum. They have created a range of resources designed to increase students' awareness of various road and rail safety issues as a context for achieving other traditional learning goals (NZTA, n.d.).

In 2011 Gerard asked NZTA if he could access information in their crash database. He had in mind a specific learning and assessment task that required students to convert digital data to another programme that would then allow it to be displayed for a specific purpose. An NCEA Level 3 achievement standard in digital technologies assesses this ability (AS 91633: Implement complex procedures to develop a relational database embedded in a specified digital outcome). Gerard had been exploring various open data options. He was worried that databases used for assessment purposes were mostly too small and contained to give students a real sense-making challenge.

With access granted by NZTA, a small group of Gerard's Year 13 students began to explore the database and ask questions that could help them to identify rich "user stories" for the displays they were to build. The students already had experience of using Excel and MySQL open-source software but had never used CartoDB, the geographic-information system that would allow them to create interactive maps of New Zealand to display the data patterns for the specific story they chose to tell. Once the draft themes for their user stories had been identified, Gerard's students began to dig into the details behind the data, to find out what had been going on when each crash occurred. He noted that this was the point at which the "why" questions began to flow and the students (all boys) became emotionally engaged. He said they now "dropped their Year 13 bravado" and became deeply engaged with the task and the associated digital learning challenges. They were "hungry to develop a good visualisation" and all of them did so.

In Gerard's experience rich contexts are "enablers" of Merit- and Excellence-level achievement. They allow students to make the task their own and this helps them lift their perseverance and performance. Some students did initially ask about the number of credits the task could yield (see Chapter 14). However, Gerard said that students no longer ask about credits once they get deeply immersed in a rich context such as this. The learning had the desired ongoing impact on students' road safety awareness. For example, every second year, students at the school took part in the Canteen organisation's Run for Life fundraising event. After doing the digital learning exercise, the Year 13 students were much more aware of the dangers of running on the road verge. They took a leadership role in developing safer practices for all students who took part in the run.

Case 2: Caring about young children's physical development
Physical education teacher Helen Lowther teaches interpersonal and coaching skills to Year 11 PE students at Queens High School in Dunedin. The students use their growing skills to plan and provide coaching in PE programmes at a local primary school, which generates evidence towards gaining a Level 1 achievement standard (AS 90966: Demonstrate interpersonal skills in a group and explain how these skills impact on others). In an interesting departure from this usual scenario, Helen varied the context in one instance. She was working with a small group of students who had been identified as being at risk of disengaging and not achieving the NCEA credits they needed. In contrast to the usual practice of having her students work in primary schools to demonstrate achievement for this standard, Helen arranged

for this group to work with 3 and 4 year olds from a daycare facility on the school grounds. They were challenged to research and plan fundamental movement activities suitable for these children and then to coach the children to carry out the activities appropriately.

Helen had initially made the contextual change from working with primary school children to working with preschoolers for pragmatic reasons—the children were on site, making access easier to manage at a busy late-year stage of the school calendar. What she had not anticipated was the *emotional* impact of this change, which she quickly observed. In contrast to their earlier work at the primary schools, the students interacted much more readily with the younger children. They chose innovative activities and used more varied equipment. Their coaching was more hands-on. They got down at the children's level, joining in the activities and communicating readily with them. They weren't afraid to sing or dance or model actions. They also involved the children in the decision-making process, asking them what activities they would like to do. Small children are typically open and honest so the students got immediate feedback on their planning and coaching. They needed to use their initiative and problem-solve on the spot.

Improved NCEA results were one consequence of this positive emotional engagement with young children's developmental needs. All students gained the achievement standard, and half gained it with Excellence. Helen was intrigued by the difference that the early childhood context appeared to make. In her view, working with the preschool children provided a context where students who were not always engaged in other settings could see themselves as positive role models and hence demonstrate strong achievement gains. She intended to use this type of context again.

The potential to integrate assessments in rich contexts

Richly contextualised learning experiences will often cross multiple areas of the traditional curriculum. When this happens it is possible, at least in theory, to draw out the different aspects within different subjects and then use multiple achievement standards to assess different aspects of a common rich task. A statistical inquiry might be part of an investigation of a social issue, for example, or a specific aspect of English (report writing, making a speech, developing a static image) might be combined with a research project in a different curriculum area.

The potential to develop integrated assessment tasks has been present since the inception of NCEA. It could help address the fragmentation of the curriculum that arises when NCEA (assessment) standards are treated as (curriculum) topics. Integrated assessment tasks also have the potential to alleviate problematic student workloads (see Chapter 14). However, this type of innovation seems to have been largely overlooked in the first decade of NCEA. No doubt there are good reasons for this. Curriculum integration requires a degree of collaborative planning that can be hard to achieve in a busy working day. Interestingly, we have noticed a shift in practice during 2014–2015. NZQA has begun to publish approved examples of integrated tasks such as this one:

> This activity requires students to critically examine the significance of skateboarding, for self, others and society in developing a justified conceptual design for a skateboard park, that has the potential to be fit for purpose. (Ministry of Education, n.d.-b)

While skateboarding is the suggested context, this type of task could work equally well in many different contexts where young people are physically active or engaged in rich leisure pursuits. The specific standards brought together— AS 91331: Examine the significance for self, others and society of a sporting event, a physical activity, or a festival; and AS 91356: Develop a conceptual design for an outcome —are from different learning areas of the curriculum. The first of these assesses an aspect of the PE curriculum area and the second, an aspect of the technology curriculum. This example was generated when teachers from different subject areas worked together during the Sport in Education initiative (Sport New Zealand, 2014). This project had an overarching aim of using sports-related contexts to lift engagement and achievement for students at risk of low or under-achievement. The project afforded time for participating teachers to plan together, and in some cases to co-teach a class. Creative ideas for integrated assessment were an interesting output from the project in its second and third years of implementation (Boyd & Hipkins, 2015).

Concluding discussion

In principle, the design of NCEA lends itself to ongoing developments in the appropriate contextualisation of assessment tasks. There are certainly pitfalls to be avoided, as we outlined in the earlier parts of the chapter. But there are also real potential benefits and gains.

Task designers need to be very clear about *why* they are using a context. Often a context will be integral to what is being assessed; without a context of some sort the assessment would be conceptually meaningless. This is true of all the vignettes above. For example, any demonstration of statistical inquiry or reasoning must be set in a context: the data being explored must be *about* something concrete and measurable (see for example Neill, 2012). The internally assessed component of NCEA is an important enabler here because teachers have the freedom to select contexts that engage their students and allow them to demonstrate their learning achievements.

In the next chapter we turn our attention to the senior secondary curriculum, beginning with a short discussion of important recent shifts to a 21st century framework as the overarching guidance for all subjects. Traditionally, learning has mostly focused on cognitive issues and challenges, with the tacit assumption that such knowledge will be a sufficient preparation for life beyond school. Now there is a focus on how students use their growing knowledge and skill base to demonstrate more complex competencies in actual or virtual contextual settings. Competencies add dispositional components to the learning and assessment mix (Hipkins, 2008). For example, if we want to educate good citizens we need them to *care* about their learning, to see ways they can be proactive in contributing to a better society, and to then use their knowledge and skills to act appropriately in actual contexts.

PART 3. THE CURRICULUM AS A CONTEXT FOR NCEA

In Part 3 we turn our attention to the senior secondary curriculum as a context for NCEA. Now that the assessment dilemmas have been outlined it is time to turn back to some of the curriculum challenges we briefly outlined in Part 1, to see how they have played out as NCEA has bedded in. Recall that the senior secondary curriculum was in a somewhat parlous state in the pre-NCEA years, and that NCEA was designed and developed several years before *NZC*—the current national curriculum framework. Given this mismatched timing (among other reasons) the achievement standards have continued to stand as a proxy for curriculum content in many subjects.

This might not be such an issue if *NZC* had continued the content-focused curriculum traditions of the past. But as we outlined in Part 1 it is a document of two halves, and the front half has a transformative intent. *NZC* declares an intention to prepare students for the 21st century, not the one that has passed. The signals are clear that learning should prepare students in multiple ways for life beyond school. NZC also clearly signals that teachers should design varied programmes of learning that will challenge and extend all the school's own students. The latter intent stands in stark contrast to the one-size-fits-all examination prescriptions of the past. To meet this change agenda, teachers to think more broadly yet also more explicitly about the purposes for which they teach specific content. Arguably, there needs to be a streamlining and reduction of selected content, so that the topics which remain can be more deeply explored, and stronger interconnections can be built between different parts of an overall learning programme. In the chapters to come we'll see some examples of what such a programme might include.

Letting go of some traditional content is not easy for teachers, given the long history of thinking about a curriculum as a list of topics to be covered and then assessed. But the burgeoning knowledge that confronts us in today's world cannot possibly be covered in any curriculum, not even in the most sketchy of details. Coverage is not even an option any more. So how do we choose from the plethora of material that could be taught—and is seen to be important—in any specific subject area? It is important that selections are made in a principled way because there can be no one right way to do this. Here is where we come back to the idea of "lifeworthy" learning, which we briefly introduced in Chapter 3.

David Perkins' agenda in *Future Wise* (2014) was to offer a set of broad principles and processes for choosing what to keep and what to discard from an over-full curriculum. Recall his argument that lifeworthy learning should centre around big understandings that: generate insights into how the world works; empower the taking of action in appropriate ways; support the development of ethical and more humane mindsets; and be likely to come up in a range of circumstances. This seems to us to be a simple but powerful manifesto for selecting, from an overfull curriculum, content that really matters. The front half of *NZC* conveys the same intent, but as we have already noted, its two-halves structure can act as a barrier to seeing the innovative potential of our national curriculum.

Once lifeworthy content has been identified, students need to learn in ways that allow the intended knowledge to become what Perkins calls "life-ready". To render learning life-ready Perkins suggests that big understandings should be developed in ways that allow students to think with them, not just think about them. Further, learners need to learn to notice when the understanding is relevant to a situation, and they need to care sufficiently to want to use this understanding as they respond. He differentiates between a bounded framing of learning (learning for now) and an expansive framing of learning (for now and the future). Only the latter is likely to support the development of life-ready understandings.

We see this as a useful manifesto for guiding decisions and actions related to NCEA. At the intersection of a visionary and flexible curriculum framework (i.e., *NZC*) and a modular NCEA system, it ought to be possible to design courses of learning that have powerful salience (lifeworthy and life-ready) for each and every senior secondary student. Furthermore, it ought to be possible to design (internal) assessment tasks that reflect and enhance this salience. Readers familiar with what actually happens in our secondary schools may raise an eyebrow at this point, or smile gently at what seems like hopeless optimism. However, we are realists, not naïve optimists. We know there are many potential barriers in the way of achieving the ideal of powerful learning for every student. This section is the place where we tackle issues related to the way in which NCEA is understood and enacted in our schools. In every chapter we include examples where innovative school leaders and teachers are showing new ways forward.

Chapter 12 Aligning curriculum and assessment

NCEA was implemented from 2002 to 2004, and its general structures and processes were worked out across several years prior to that. The national curriculum (*NZC*) was not released in its final form until 2007, although work on it had begun earlier in the decade. Thus, by the time *NZC* came into teachers' sights NCEA was well embedded. Teachers' curriculum thinking and planning now tended to centre around the assessment requirements specified in the achievement standards and unit standards. The purposes envisaged for learning were all too often articulated in terms of credits to be gained. The assessment cart was already well and truly in front of the curriculum horse, as is so often the case in environments of high-stakes assessment

The Ministry of Education and NZQA belatedly addressed this challenge by carrying out a systematic alignment exercise several years after *NZC* was released. Teams of teachers, advisors, and teacher educators worked to re-examine the suites of achievement standards in every subject in the light of *NZC*. The mix of expertise in each team varied, and some teams seemed better placed than others to understand the implications of *NZC* for their subject. The mix of standards at each of Levels 1 to 3 in each subject was also open to scrutiny and change.

A consultation exercise was carried out so that other teachers would be aware of the proposed changes. As a result of all this activity some achievement standards were tweaked and some were more extensively redeveloped.

A short time after this exercise had been completed, 16 percent of teachers who responded to NZCER's National Survey of Secondary Schools disagreed with the statement that "the realigned standards successfully capture the intent of the New Zealand Curriculum". Science and mathematics teachers were overrepresented among those who disagreed with this statement. A further 30 percent of the teachers were unsure whether the alignment exercise had achieved its stated purpose. Agreement that the alignment had achieved its purpose came from just over half of the respondents (Hipkins, 2013, pp. 28–29).

While survey data cannot tell us why teachers responded as they did, we suspect that at least some of the uncertainty resides in the complexities of working with a curriculum that provides a framework for school-based curriculum design rather than a more detailed prescription of what should be learned. In Chapter 3 we explained that *NZC* is a document of two halves. The visionary front half was widely endorsed and supported across the whole education sector.[1] However, as implementation of *NZC* proceeded it became increasingly evident that planning a responsive curriculum, based on a framework that permits multiple possible combinations of the various curriculum elements, is a highly complex design task. To take one core design dilemma, the structure does not (cannot) show how to integrate aspects such as key competencies with the more traditional curriculum content. Even researchers working actively on understanding the potential of key competencies and building resources to support new curriculum thinking have found this challenging (Hipkins & Boyd, 2011). How was it ever envisaged that schools and teachers could independently do this for themselves? With this challenge in mind, we now turn our attention to what is actually now being demanded of teachers as they work between *NZC* and NCEA in the context of senior secondary

---

[1] A team based at the University of Auckland carried out a systematic survey as part of the Monitoring and Evaluating Curriculum Implementation (MECI) project (Sinnema, 2011).

school years. Reconciling the demands of these two potential sources for informing curriculum thinking can be easier said than done.

Bringing NZC and NCEA together

NCEA was intended to allow flexibility in the design of programmes of learning or courses. The range of available standards was intended to ensure that schools could provide and assess meaningful learning for every student in the senior secondary years, and that when the intended learning had been successfully demonstrated, they would have a fair opportunity to gain a qualification. For most students this was expected to be an NCEA qualification, but the seamless National Qualifications Framework also allowed some students to aim for industry-owned qualifications such as the National Certificate in Employment Skills. *NZC* was also designed as a flexible, minimal framework—in effect a conceptual backbone on which a more detailed local curriculum could be built by each school. Again, the intention was to encourage schools to build varied learning programmes to meet the specific needs of all their students.

There were costs and drawbacks to this flexibility. A modular assessment system, in combination with a flexible minimal curriculum framework, can result in a highly fragmented approach to course design. Teachers could and often did create courses that were simply loose aggregations of standards approached as separate curriculum topics.

One way to counter this tendency is to support teachers to design courses with a clear rationale that they can explain. But doing this requires an expansive sense of *purposes for learning*—something more than simply building credits towards qualifications (see Chapter 14). Ideally the standards themselves would encompass something of the aspirational purposes for learning to be found in a more holistic reading of *NZC*. But many of the standards do not do this, at least in part because of poorly aligned timing that resulted in the deployment of NCEA before *NZC*. Bad timing is not solely to blame however. The potential opportunity to really challenge and change traditional curriculum thinking during the alignment project was unevenly taken up across the learning areas. Teams with bolder leadership did make progress, as we'll see in the next chapter. Others simply made small improvements to the status quo, leaving traditional thinking about purposes for learning in the senior secondary school largely unchallenged.

Designing coherent courses

NZC was designed to provide a framework on which teachers could build their own local curricula. NCEA was designed as a modular-assessment system, in which different assessment standards can be mixed and matched to design assessment programmes for courses that meet the learning needs of specific groups of students. Why, then, have we seen so little creative curriculum thinking that brings these two flexible elements of the system together? In most schools, traditional subject courses continue to predominate and alternatives to those tend to be seen as suitable for less-academic students. Meanwhile, in the 21st-century world, epistemological processes of actual knowledge-building continue to evolve apace, often in hybrid spaces between the more traditional subjects. Such hybrids include biophysics, place-based history, and "big data" mining at the intersection of statistics and any other content area. Some disciplines that have been neglected in the traditional school curriculum could make a useful contribution to life-worthy learning, given the opportunity. For example, Perkins identifies behavioural economics, which he describes as "a marriage of psychology and economics" (Perkins, 2014, p. 178) as a hybrid discipline that is rich in insight, action, ethics, and opportunity. It offers a counter-account to a key idea underpinning classical economics—namely that we make rational choices and mostly exercise sound judgement when self-interest is implicated. Of course, to work in the intersections between established disciplines, at least a working knowledge of the epistemological structure of the separate disciplines is required. All too often this basic knowledge is lacking, even in the treatment of powerful disciplines as separate school subjects.

Could it be that long-established but tacitly held assumptions about the nature of subject coherence are also acting as a barrier to change? When people talk about the importance of traditional curriculum knowledge, they often have in mind the sort of content knowledge that they themselves learned at school. There seems to be an assumption that a curriculum built of pieces of the same traditional subject area will be coherent, while other courses will not. We think this assumption is worth holding up to critical scrutiny and we now do this via three case studies. The first explores the potential for coherence in traditional and newer science subjects and their translation into NCEA achievement standards. The second and third cases then unsettle the problematic assumption that a collection of content to be assessed (whether it is expressed as an examination prescription or as a set of achievement standards) can realistically be expected to ensure coherence in course design or in a student's learning experience. These cases will bring us back to the critical importance of teachers' thinking about purposes for learning.

Case 1: Coherence within science subjects?

In the early 1990s, when outcome-based curricula were introduced for the first time, *Science in the New Zealand Curriculum* added a fourth subject strand called Making Sense of Planet Earth and Beyond.[2] This strand was made up of an interesting amalgam of topics that science educators and leading teachers believed to be important, but that were not easily accommodated under the umbrella of the three heritage subjects, biology, chemistry, or physics. Topics addressed included: aspects of geological history (acknowledging for example, young children's fascination with fossils and dinosaurs); active geological processes (especially earthquakes and volcanic activity, but also erosion, flooding and so forth); weather patterns and dynamics; and basic astronomy and the night sky. By the time *NZC* was developed a decade after this ground-breaking work, science teachers who had relished the challenge of working with this new strand were ready to address the criticism that it lacked coherence and was simply a grab-bag of topics. Over the decade they had come to recognise the potential for refocusing the strand to emphasise learning about the complex systems that sustain life on earth:

> The **Planet Earth and Beyond** strand is about the interconnecting systems and processes of the earth, the other parts of the solar system, and the universe beyond. Students learn that Earth's subsystems of geosphere (land), hydrosphere (water), atmosphere (air), and biosphere

---

2 All the subject strands began with the phrase "Making sense of…" This was one way in which the importance of students' active sense-making was highlighted for teacher attention. This focus controversially reflected the predominance of ideas underpinned by constructivist theories of learning in science education research at the time.

(life), are interdependent and that all are important. They come to appreciate that humans can affect this interdependence in both positive and negative ways. (Ministry of Education, 2007, p. 28)

The signal that learning should cohere around the idea of interconnecting systems is strong and unequivocal. It's interesting to contrast this with the equivalent statement for physics, one of the heritage subjects in the science curriculum:

> The **Physical World** strand provides explanations for a wide range of physical phenomena, including light, sound, heat, electricity, magnetism, waves, forces and motion, united by the concept of energy, which is transformed from one form to another without loss. By studying physics, student gain an understanding of interactions between parts of the physical world and of the ways they can be presented. Knowing about physics enables people to understand a wide range of contemporary issues and challenges and potential technological solutions. (Ministry of Education, 2007, pp. 28–29)

There are also several signals about coherence here—if teachers are attuned to them. This, however, is quite a big if. We are told that diverse physics topics are "united by the concept of energy". However this potential for coherence is neither further explained nor developed, and could be easy to miss, coming as it does at the end of a long string of topic names. The phrase "interactions between parts of the physical world" suggests one avenue for creating links between topics. The phrase "ways they can be represented" draws attention to a potentially unifying set of communication and meaning-making capabilities subsumed under the key competency titled *using language, symbols and texts*.

Default course design—based on assessment rather than curriculum thinking—would simply aggregate topics based on individual standards from either of these science subjects. Coherence in such a course is possible, but would require considerable thought on the part of a teacher, precisely because the standards titles mostly continue to reflect a traditional topic-based division of content. It could be that conceptual coherence is signalled at the more detailed level of criteria for Achieved, Merit, and Excellence within each standard. Standards that specify more than one concept area provide a good test of this. For example, one physics standard at Level 2 has the title Electricity and electromagnetism. If coherence really is valued, we should see criteria that specify connections between these two conceptual areas. Interestingly, the criterion for excellence in this standard specifies a demonstration of *comprehensive* understanding. And comprehensiveness is defined in the explanatory notes to the standard as "writing statements that demonstrate understanding of connections between concepts". In other words, awareness of conceptual coherence is reserved as a hallmark of excellence—it is not for the average student.

Thinking differently about course coherence

The science example above suggests that collections of standards themselves, or for that matter, collections of topics, do not automatically invest courses with coherence. Any coherence has to come from skilful course design, followed up with teaching and learning experiences appropriate to the stated aims of the course. The next two case studies provide examples of carefully designed courses, with explicitly articulated immediate and longer-term outcomes that each teacher would like students to take away from their learning.

Case 2: Coherence via an intention to build capabilities for the future

The overarching reason for including science in *NZC* is stated as follows:

> In science, students explore how both the natural physical world and science itself work so that they can participate as critical, informed, and responsible citizens in a society in which science plays a significant role. (p.17)

What might this fine-sounding aspiration mean in practice? To address this question, even briefly, we need to introduce another element of the science learning area into the discussion. As well as the four strands that specify learning from biology, chemistry, physics and earth sciences, there is an overarching Nature of Science (NOS) strand that is supposed to be woven through these other four strands as teachers create courses of learning. This asks a great deal of teachers. The science education literature has thoroughly documented how hard it is for teachers to do this weaving in ways that achieve the intended aim of developing insights into science as a knowledge system (i.e., a discipline) (Lederman & Lederman, 2014). How best to do this when beginning with NOS ideas is still an area of active debate among science education researchers (see for example Duschl & Grandy, 2013). Yet doing so is arguably necessary if students are going to become the "critical informed and responsible citizens" that *NZC* demands (Hipkins & Bull, 2015).

If teachers do understand this dilemma, and have the necessary intellectual insights to plan courses that address the citizenship challenge, a type of coherence can be forged that looks quite different from the coherence assumed to reside in a collection of topics from the same discipline area. The example in Figure 12.1 illustrates this point. It shows the bare bones of a Level 2, Year 12 course designed by biology teacher Kirsty Farrant, from Newlands College in Wellington. Kirsty has been working on refining this course for 4 years now and this is version three, to be implemented in 2016.

Figure 12.1. An example of innovative course design in science

Assessment	Unit title and focus of learning	Credits
Ag/Hort 2.10 (AS 91298) I Report on the environmental impact of the production of a locally produced primary product.	**Wasted Waterways** A look at how farming impacts on the waterways of the area.	4
Biology 2.2 (AS 91154) I Analyse the biological validity of information presented to the public	**Paradise in Peril** New Zealand is a user of the chemical 1080 to try and control introduced pests. How is information conveyed to the public, on both sides of the argument?	3
ESS 2.4 (AS 91190) I Investigate how organisms survive in an extreme environment	**Life on Mars** When Earth becomes too small to sustain human's population growth, is Mars a viable option?	4
ESS 2.5 (AS 91191) E Demonstrate understanding of the causes of extreme Earth events in New Zealand	**Shake, Rattle and Roll** NZ is affected by a number of types of extreme Earth events—earthquakes, volcanos and tsunamis. Here we will learn what causes all of these events.	4
ESS 2.7 (AS 91193) E Demonstrate understanding of physical principles related to the Earth System	**Climate Crisis** The climate is changing, and this is creating some significant issues. Here we will explore the principles of heat and the impact on Earth.	4
OR ESS 2.2 (AS 91188) I Examine an Earth and Space Science issue and the validity of the information communicated to the public	**Context undecided at the time of writing**	4

At a superficial level, it is not obvious that there is coherence here. The achievement standards Kirsty has selected come from three different suites which are more typically grouped in separate courses: biology; earth and space science (ESS); and agriculture/horticulture. The original course also included one achievement standard from the Education for Sustainability suite but Kirsty removed this from version 3 because students found it too hard to sustain their learning momentum over the extended period required. There is a one-to-one mapping between course topics and achievement standards, with no explicit connections between them. But coherence in this course is conferred via Kirsty's stated overarching aim of supporting students to become better decision-makers, able to use their growing awareness of how science works in the world, and to take these new capabilities into their years beyond school. The purpose for which each area is introduced and the pedagogy used to develop that purpose become twin vehicles for coherence.

Version 1 of this course had included only one externally assessed achievement standard. Because course endorsement requires at least one contributing standard to be externally assessed, if students did not achieve at least Merit in this assessment they could not gain a Merit or Excellence endorsement for the course, no matter how well they might have done in the internally assessed standards. Version 2 added a second externally assessed standard, but Kirsty was aware that achieving it could be challenging for some of the lower-ability students, who tend to choose this course if they want to keep one science subject in their course mix. To address this dilemma, she added an option of completing an additional internally assessed standard instead. Like the biology standard, the newly added Earth and space science standard assesses students' ability to analyse the validity of information. Kirsty reasoned that giving her lower ability students two attempts at doing so—in very different contexts—would help them to build valuable capabilities for life beyond school at the same time as experiencing success in gaining credits. Meanwhile, more academic students who chose the course as an interesting adjunct to their traditional science studies could also experience a mix of learning and assessment options that challenged and extended their citizenship capabilities.

The detail of this example illustrates the sort of curriculum thinking that *NZC*'s framework structure encourages. Doing this sort of course planning requires a deep intellectual engagement with the subject, the overall curriculum, and the needs of the learners in the class. Furthermore, there are likely to be NCEA-related obstacles to be overcome, in this case not least that the Nature of Science strand receives only a very token treatment, if any, in the various achievement standards. Kirsty designed this course for students who might be discouraged from taking a traditional single-subject science course, yet she was also aware that she needed to meet the needs of more academic students. There is a double-dipping regulation which precludes an individual student from gaining credits for the same standard twice. This meant in practice that Kirsty had to negotiate which achievement standards she could use—in effect those that were not wanted by other teachers for the traditional science subject courses.

Case 3. Contextual *and* conceptual integration within a course

Shelley Gilman, from St Matthews Collegiate in Masterton, chose "sugar" as the overarching context for her 2015 Year 13 Home Economics course. This proved to be prescient. Throughout 2015 the excessive amount of sugar in our diets and the potential consequences for our health were often in the news. Shelley wanted her students to leave school with a more nuanced and critical understanding of food systems—how they work and where leverage points for change might reside. This intent reflects a strong grasp of the sociocritical approach used to conceptualise the Health and Physical Education learning area, which subsumes the subject of home economics.

Careful thought went into Shelley's choice and sequencing of the year's work and the achievement standards that would be used to assess the student's learning. Shelley chose three internally assessed standards. Figure 12.2 summarises the course and the standards used to assess the intended learning.

Figure 12.2 An example of innovative course design in home economics

Assessment	Unit title and focus of learning	Credits
AS 91469: Investigate the influence of multinational food corporations on eating patterns in New Zealand Written report and practical task	**Cereal Killers:** Building on knowledge of nutrition and data associated with nutrition related disease in NZ students examine the evidence and make links to demonstrate how cereal companies encourage consumption of breakfast cereals, why they use these methods of promotion/marketing and the impact on the wellbeing of New Zealand society.	5
AS 91619: Demonstrate understanding of the application of a technical area to a specific field Individual research project	**Fiddling with food:** Each student researched a specific Functional Food, its purpose, challenges and opportunities. They investigated legislation around functional foods and how manufacturers can make the claims they do. This aspect of the study made strong links to one of the externally assessed standards.	4
AS 91468: Analyse a food related ethical dilemma for New Zealand society Written report and practical task	**Sugar tax:** This unit examined how both ethical principles and health promotion methods might apply to the idea of a sugar tax. Students encountered the idea that altering food environments can help people to make good decisions and take personal responsibility in a supported way. Examining a range of perspectives and the reasons for people/groups having different positions was essential to be successful in this unit.	5
AS 91470: Evaluate conflicting nutritional information relevant to well-being in New Zealand society Examination	**How true?** Students learned to unpack research findings/messages/information and misinformation. Skills overlapped with those for the advertising paper. Students developed a check list as a group on help spot a believable research report.	4
AS 91471: Analyse the influences of food advertising on well-being Examination	**Advertising: Lies, lies and more lies:** Students learned to unpack and analyse food-related advertisements to develop and practise a set of skills applicable to any advertising.	4

Note that two of the internally assessed achievement standards are from the home economics suite but the third one is from a suite of generic technology standards where food is one potential context for learning. Shelley challenged her students to investigate a *functional food* of their own choice (i.e., one that purports to have enhanced nutritional value added during the manufacturing process). Such foods are often high in sugar and Shelley anticipated that this standard would serve to weave together and consolidate learning from the other two. In addition, all three internally assessed standards introduced aspects that would come into the foreground later in the year as students began to prepare for the external assessment in two more home economics standards.

There is an evident conceptual coherence in this collection. Furthermore, the choice of one overarching highly topical context serves to weave the collection of standards into a tight multifaceted whole. The envisaged learning should have real salience for students' lives now and in the future. It should also be evident from the brief descriptions in Figure 12.2 that supporting students to build strong critical thinking and systems-thinking skills were unifying aims across the whole course. Shelley noted that students particularly enjoyed the critical-thinking challenges presented by the advertising unit. They came to realise the power of visual cues. Feedback from students who had left school suggested they continued to use these skills often.

Having designed the course in-principle, Shelley said she would be able to readily change the context in 2016, so that her next group of students experienced learning that was conceptually similar but different in its specifics. This would keep the course fresh and intellectually stimulating for her and while also addressing the challenge of ensuring authenticity because students could not borrow work from those in the previous year. When we were completing the writing of the book her preliminary thinking was that the marketing of food to children, juxtaposed with the challenging issue of some children going hungry in New Zealand, would make a rich course context for her 2016 class.

Concluding comment

In this chapter we set out to provide some insights into the complex nature of the challenges entailed in designing a course of learning based on *NZC*, which is subsequently assessed using NCEA achievement standards. Not least of these challenges is that this complexity can be invisible once a coherent and elegant course design has been achieved.

Not surprisingly, many teachers still default to traditional experience, seeing curriculum as a specification of topics to be covered, as prescribed by examination requirements. This observation should not be read as a criticism of individual teachers. For a number of reasons they have not been well served with targeted support to develop their curriculum thinking. The lack of alignment in the development of NCEA and *NZC* has been one problem. As we've outlined, a belated attempt was made to align these two vital policies but the manner in which this was done did not necessarily work well to align curriculum and assessment thinking. A lack of secondary resources to illustrate how *NZC* might be expected to play out in the senior secondary school has been another problem. Such resources were promised to support the initial implementation of *NZC* but in the event did not begin to appear for some years. In this vacuum NCEA materials (model assessments, examiners' comments etc.) served as curriculum support materials to which all teachers could gain ready access. This small set of materials has too often become the national point of reference, constraining the development of the local curriculum design in the process.

Another big challenge can be traced back to teacher's learning as they gained their subject-based qualifications. The second and third case studies above give some indications of the intellectual sophistication needed to design the sorts of courses described here. An education that provides a strong focus on how knowledge is built within a discipline is a necessary foundation for this sort of curriculum thinking. Finally, as we have already noted, these highly innovative courses were infused with a clear sense of purposes that aspire to help students build lifeworthy knowledge and skills. We elaborate on the challenges inherent in this aspect of teachers' curriculum thinking in the next two chapters.

Chapter 13 The washback from NCEA to teaching and learning

High-stakes assessments have always conveyed strong messages to teachers, students, and families about what is important. Whether intended or not, these messages can then "wash back" into the learning experiences that teachers plan and orchestrate. Our aim in this chapter is to develop a more nuanced conversation about the washback dynamic than we typically see in commentary about NCEA. As we have said a number of times, there was no golden age in which curriculum led the way and examinations simply followed along. Indeed, as Chapter 3 outlined, in the pre-NCEA years the senior secondary curriculum was in a somewhat parlous state. Given the messy and uneven curriculum context in the senior secondary school, it is hardly surprising that teachers continued to look to NCEA for curriculum guidance, as they had looked to external examinations in the pre-NCEA years.

In NZCER's past national surveys a clear majority of secondary teachers have agreed that NCEA drives the curriculum: 80 percent agreement in 2006, 75 percent in 2009, 76 percent in 2012 (Hipkins, 2013). In the face of this pervasive belief we begin this chapter with an argument that such washback need not be a negative influence. How NCEA influences the curriculum depends at least in part on how achievement is framed by the achievement standards in each subject. There are instances where the focus of the achievement standards has been a positive force for change. We illustrate this dynamic in the Learning Languages *NZC* learning area, drawing on the work of Martin East and Adele Scott, who are prominent in the learning languages research community in New Zealand.

Subject-specific matters are not the only influences on the classroom curriculum. This chapter also takes account of a small selection of NCEA regulations that have the potential to influence teaching, learning, and assessment decisions in every subject. Regulations can be changed of course and we've already seen in Chapter 9 that NCEA has been modified over the years in a culture of continuous improvement. In this spirit, we have pinpointed regulations that would benefit from further modification or substantive rethinking.

Achievement standards as a positive change influence

Many teachers feel frustrated that the achievement standards for their subjects do not reflect the scope and promise indicated in *NZC*. As we've already noted, an *NZC*–NCEA alignment exercise was carried out in the 3 years immediately preceding the 2012 NZCER National Survey of Secondary Schools. Yet only half the teachers who responded to the survey in 2012 agreed that the realigned standards had captured the intent of *NZC* (see previous chapter). If the view of these respondents is accurate, there seems to have been a missed opportunity here for powerful across-the-board change. However our interest lies with a counter-instance. What might we learn from a whole learning area where NCEA and *NZC* do seem to be better aligned?

Traditional examination prescriptions for languages in addition to the student's mother tongue typically emphasise such matters as knowledge of grammar and ability to translate text from English to the chosen language and vice versa. Researchers describe this rather formal set of experiences as a "grammar-translation" approach to teaching and learning additional languages. A more contemporary view is that the teaching of languages should emphasise communication—i.e., using languages for authentic contextualised purposes. This is called a "communicative" approach to teaching and learning.

Across the languages that can be assessed in the NCEA system, the achievement standards are now shaped to reflect achievements in various aspects of communication. Table 13.1 illustrates this emphasis by showing the full suite of achievement standards for the subject of French. Researchers of languages learning argue that there have been positive washback effects as a consequence of the communicative focus of achievement standards in this curriculum area. They say that this emphasis has prompted changes in pedagogy as teachers prepare students to use their growing mastery of the target language, demonstrating their communication skills in a range of engaging tasks (East & Scott, 2011).

Table 13.1. The matrix of achievement standards for French

	Level 1	Level 2	Level 3
Listen and Respond	AS 90878 (1.1) Demonstrate understanding of a variety of spoken French texts on areas of most immediate relevance.	AS 91118 (2.1) Demonstrate understanding of a variety of spoken French texts on familiar matters.	AS 91543 (3.1) Demonstrate understanding of a variety of extended spoken French texts.
Speak, Present	AS 90879 (1.2) Give a spoken presentation in French that communicates a personal response.	AS 91120 (2.2) Give a spoken presentation in French that communicates information, ideas and opinions.	AS 91544 (3.2) Give a clear spoken presentation in French that communicates a critical response to stimulus material.
Interact	AS 90880 (1.3) Interact using spoken French to communicate personal information, ideas and opinions in different situations. *Internal*	AS 91119 (2.3) Interact using spoken French to share information and justify ideas and opinions in different situations.	AS 91545 (3.3) Interact clearly using spoken French to explore and justify varied ideas and perspectives in different situations.
View and Respond	AS 90881 (1.4) Demonstrate understanding of a variety of French texts on areas of most immediate relevance.	AS 91121 (2.4) Demonstrate understanding of a variety of written and/or visual French text(s) on familiar matters. *External*	AS 91546 (3.4) Demonstrate understanding of a variety of extended written and/or visual French texts. *External*
Write	AS 90882 (1.5) Write a variety of text types in French on areas of most immediate relevance.	AS 91122 (2.5) Write a variety of text types in French to convey information, ideas, and opinions in genuine contexts.	AS 91547 (3.5) Write a variety of text types in clear French to explore and justify varied ideas and perspectives.

This appears to be a case of evolution rather than revolution, with some serendipity in the timing. The decade between the introduction of the 1993 curriculum framework and the implementation of Learning Languages as the eighth learning area in the *NZC* has been described as a time of consolidation and growth for languages-learning approaches in New Zealand (Scott & East, 2009). The key shift to communicative approaches during this decade coincided with the development of the first sets of achievement standards and hence presented an opportunity to begin moving away from the grammar-translation approach that fitted comfortably with the traditional examinations of the past. However, the shift was not without controversy. Scott and East noted that resistance to change was expressed by principals and teachers who were concerned about the reliability of the new internal assessments and also about increased workload. But the door to change had been opened and the alignment exercise which took place between 2009 and 2012 pushed it further open still.

Importantly, the alignment exercise in Learning Languages was informed by a systematic review undertaken by the New Zealand Association of Languages Teachers. This project enabled the association members to have a voice in the changes subsequently proposed and to understand the thrust of these changes once they came. Hence the languages community was able to develop matrices of achievement standards with an emphasis on aspects of communication, such as that shown in Table 13.1 (East & Scott, 2011). The innovative matrix of Level 1 achievement standards initially developed for science makes an interesting contrast. The initial developers were a small group from the New Zealand Association for Science Education. Rose recalls that they produced a matrix that departed from the traditional subject-based structure but reflected the new emphasis in *NZC* on science for citizenship. This matrix was withdrawn after a strong backlash from many science teachers who were not ready for the shift. The traditional separate-subject, content-based structure was restored and an opportunity was lost to move the science curriculum forward.

The changes made by the languages teachers also placed a stronger emphasis on collection of evidence of learning over time. In 2014 Martin East surveyed languages teachers to find out how they felt about these changes (East, 2014). Around 150 teachers responded. They appeared to hold mixed views about the *interact* achievement standards (middle row of Table 13.1). They said that the main advantage of these standards was their authenticity—they require a meaningful interaction for a specific purpose. However their main disadvantage was seen to reside in impracticalities such as the technical challenges of recording interactions (which is required for moderation purposes). Whereas some teachers liked the fact that assessing interactions is less test-like, and therefore less stressful for students, others thought that the increased emphasis on internal assessments was more stressful for students. Interestingly, teachers who chose to use the *interact* standards were more likely to comment on their positive attributes than on their problems. This reminds us that the very same pressure for change might be perceived as positive by some teachers and negative by others, depending on their curriculum beliefs and values. It is also another example of the way in which NCEA's flexibility does allow teachers to design courses that emphasise, and are assessed by, aspects of learning that align most comfortably with their own curriculum thinking, as discussed in the previous chapter.

The impact of system-wide influences on NCEA

Some washback pressures relate to the manner in which NCEA is administered and NCEA results are used to make decisions that go beyond individual students' demonstrations of their achievement. Such purposes include making high-stakes sorting decisions such as who will be eligible to go to university (see also Chapter 9). However, before discussing these more visible perverse incentives, we begin with a regulation that might be less visible to those not working closely with NCEA.

Authenticity/conditions of assessment

Authenticity is the assurance that evidence of achievement produced by a learner is their own. There are three broad categories of authenticity challenges that need to be managed during the assessment process. Education organisations and assessors must be aware of the potential for learners to: copy from another person or source (plagiarism); have too much guidance from the teacher or assessor; get specific answers for the assessment activity because it is publicly available (such as Ministry of Education/Te Kete Ipurangi activities on the internet). Assessors must verify that the work submitted for assessment has been produced by the learner. Assessors must consider (and manage) the potential for work to have been copied, borrowed from another learner, photocopied from a book or downloaded from the internet. (NZQA, n.d.)

This quote has been taken from NZQA's website. Teachers are held accountable for ensuring that their students do not cheat in any of the three possible ways described. They are expected to manage assessment processes so that they can say hand-on-heart that the assessed work is the student's own. Teachers take this responsibility seriously. The simplest and time-honoured way to attest to the type of authenticity envisaged by NZQA is to sit students down under test conditions and make them write—in effect to make an assessment event into an examination. David Hood, who lead the early NCEA thinking in his role as the founding chief executive of NZQA, captures the potential absurdities of this in the following reflection, which we quote verbatim from his recent book.

Scientific method—NCEA style

Recently I was told of an "investigative" project all students had to do as part of NCEA Level 1 Science. The students were allowed only four hours in the classroom to do the project, I assume because the Achievement Standard has little credit value and there is much more "stuff" to cover during the year.

Students could spend as much "preparation" time at home as they wished, and use their computers to find and gather relevant research, data, diagrams etc. However the project had to be done in the classroom; during those four hours they could not use their computers, and the students had to start from scratch and write up their project on paper in long hand. If they wanted to use anything they had "discovered" as support material it had to be printed off beforehand.

The reason why? Because the work had to be seen as authentic—done by the student and no-one else. Hence the handwriting, non-use of computers, attaching evidence separately, all done in the classroom.

Equally alarming is that students were expected to do the learning in their own time at home, and the four hours in the classroom was in reality being used totally for assessment purposes.

Scientific method? Hardly. Authentic, valuable, purposeful in-depth learning or real-life way of working? I don't think so. Absurd? Most definitely. (Hood, 2015, p. 49)

Innovative teachers will, and do, design assessments that enable students to investigate in ways that are more authentically reflect the practices of scientists (i.e., messy, iterative, collaborative, multi-method, cross-disciplinary, digitally supported and documented, to name a few potential characteristics).[1] However, the method of ensuring the type of "authenticity" prescribed by NZQA, and justifiably ridiculed by David Hood, is all too common. Arguably, this view of authenticity rests on an outdated view of learning as something that happens only in the brains of individuals and content acquisition as the end goal of all learning that matters. Both of these assumptions are overly simple. For example, contemporary learning theory draws attention to the *distributed* nature of thinking. Indeed, the visionary front-half of *NZC* describes learning and capability-building as being enabled by interactions between "people, places, ideas and things" (Ministry of Education, 2007, p. 12).

While employers look for people who can work collaboratively, building new ideas between them, many teachers feel they cannot assess group work for NCEA because they cannot separate out individual contributions. There are some exceptions. For example, drama and music have achievement standards that allow the work of a group to be assessed in a way that also allows for individual contributions to be judged. So it is technically possible to create group-assessment standards and processes and it should be possible to transfer this knowledge to other learning areas.

Information technologies add several layers to the authenticity challenge. The ease with which students can find and plagiarise the work of others is an obvious negative example. As we have just seen, NZQA

---

[1] The nature of "science practices" is the subject of lively debate in the international science education community, prompted by the recent shift from a focus on "science inquiry" to a focus on "science practices" in the Common Core Standards for school assessment in the United States (see for example Osborne, 2014).

warns teachers about this. We think that this challenge can be solved more creatively than making students work under examination conditions. Assessment tasks can be (we would say should be) designed in ways that require students to draw disparate threads of their learning together, such that "copy and paste" is simply not an option. However, creating such tasks requires teachers to envisage purposes for learning (and assessment) that go well beyond the correct recall and understanding of a body of content.

The widespread use of IT for collaborative purposes brings a new and interesting challenge to light. At the cutting edge of assessment design, experts are working on ways to assess online collaboration as one critical aspect of an individual's IT capabilities. What's more these assessments will be *stealth assessments*, that is, students won't need to do anything in addition to their everyday coursework for the purpose of being assessed. As they work together on some meaningful online task (either in the same physical space or virtually), metrics gathered behind the scenes will judge the nature of their contributions to the group. These developments are in their infancy, but they are coming. They will change the face of the authenticity debate in ways we are only just beginning to comprehend (see for example Shute & Ventura, 2013).

The washback effect of approved subjects for UE

The manner in which UE is determined was outlined in Chapter 9. Whether or not a subject is on the approved list for UE can have a washback effect into school planning and student choices. Subjects not on the list are seen to be of lower status and hence risky choices for students who aspire to tertiary study. To make school timetables work these alternative subjects are often paired with subjects seen as central to academic courses (such as maths, English, sciences, history). This effectively rules out alternatives to traditional academic subjects as choices for students who need to keep open pathways into high-status courses such as engineering, medicine, or veterinary studies (Hipkins, Vaughan, Beals, & Ferral, 2004).

The potential for NCEA to contribute to curriculum innovation can also be negatively impacted by the manner in which credits must be distributed across three traditional subjects from the approved subjects list. Chapter 12 introduced two examples of innovative courses, each with a clearly articulated sense of purpose. These courses were devised *in spite of* these UE regulations. For example, the addition of a food technology standard to a home economics suite would be seen by many teachers as a risky move because any credits gained from that achievement standard cannot count towards UE, even though they can count for Level 3 NCEA. Yet as we outlined in Chapter 12 this course had a tight contextual and conceptual coherence that arguably made it more intellectually rigorous than, say, a loose aggregation of topics within one subject. The problematic assumption here is that academic rigour inherently resides in traditional subject arrangements.

The Year 12 socioscientific course described in Chapter 12 is also vulnerable to UE pressures, even though students who take it usually have one more year at school if they are university-bound. In the interests of continuity for students, most Year 12 courses are expected to lead into similar Year 13 courses. But credits gained from a follow-on Year 13 course compiled along the lines of the Year 12 socioscientific course would not count towards UE. The credits would be too widely distributed across traditional subjects. The teacher who designed the Year 12 course explained that she included two standards from the ESS (earth and space science) suite so that students could have the option of transitioning to a Year 13 course in this subject if they needed UE and did not have a second science course in their Year 12 subject mix.

Around a third of Year 13 students actually transition into university studies. Yet the structure of most courses in Year 13 curriculum has been designed to meet the need of this group to gain UE, regardless of the impact on choices available for other students. In effect, the Year 13 curriculum is held hostage by the UE regulations unless teachers are brave enough, or creative enough, to design innovative alternatives despite UE. It can be done, but we don't often see the sort of creative thinking with which we ended Chapter 12.

All said, the negative washback of UE requirements on curriculum need not be especially serious. UE requires only 42 credits to come from approved subjects, whereas at least 60 Level 3 credits are required for NCEA Level 3, and a typical student undertakes about 100 credits during Year 13. Furthermore, only 14 credits must be gained in each of three approved subjects, and a typical course is assessed with about 18–22 credits, leaving at least some room to use credits from different subject areas in a course. Certainly, with careful course planning and more innovative timetabling, it ought to be possible for a student to undertake at least some courses with cross-disciplinary assessment programmes, without seriously compromising their UE prospects.

The washback effect of literacy and numeracy requirements

Some tertiary teachers have found a mismatch when students have gained a UE award but score at low levels on an independent measure such as the TEC (Tertiary Education Commission) online tool for assessing basic adult literacy. This impression was confirmed by a recent statistical study funded by TEC. This study found that around half the students in the study were below the level of literacy or numeracy that might be expected given their NCEA Level 1 or 2 awards when they were subsequently assessed using the TEC tool (Thomas, Johnston & Ward, 2015). Needless to say, this is a threat to the credibility of NCEA, even though the dynamic in play is rather complex. We suspect that this situation reflects a tricky set of perverse incentives related to the recent move to use naturally occurring evidence of literacy and numeracy (as outlined in Chapter 9).

When teachers are under great pressure to help students achieve a certain number of credits from externally assessed standards they may resort to coaching them in formulaic response patterns. Students simply apply the relevant pattern to the question as presented on the day. In this way they give a semblance of literacy, regardless of their actual ability to write fluently. There is no way of knowing how widespread this practice of coaching to a formula actually is, but many teachers will grumpily own up to it. In our experience they don't like doing this sort of cynical coaching but feel they have no option given the pressure they are under to increase their students' achievement successes (about which we will say more very shortly). Coaching in examination-answering techniques is not new of course. It was a routine part of examination preparation in pre-NCEA times. What is different in the case of NCEA is that, across a wide range of standards, formulaic responses patterns are taken as a proxy for literacy, not just as evidence that the student knows the content being examined.

One casualty of this washback effect could be the opportunity for students to build stronger literacy skills. A related effect is the lost opportunity to develop critical-thinking skills in areas such as argumentation. Teachers need the courage and persistence to get past the hand-holding instincts that come with the territory of supporting young people to succeed in NCEA. It is not easy to push back when students expect and demand short-term success. But the case study with which we end this chapter shows it can be done.

Those students who do not aspire to gain UE must still achieve certain levels of literacy and numeracy to gain their NCEA award (see Chapter 9). Purpose-designed literacy or numeracy unit standards can be used when a student is unlikely to gain success via an achievement-standard pathway. However, unit standards are always internally assessed so the judgement of sufficiency of the evidence is made at the teacher/school level. Given that such evidence should be naturally occurring (i.e., could come from any part of the student's learning) the judgement could well be made by a teacher who does not have specific literacy or numeracy expertise. When mixed with pressures to get students over the Level 2 hurdle (see below), inappropriate judgements can and do get made. Again NCEA's reputation is at stake when students cannot demonstrate the levels of skill their certificate says they should have.

To balance the negatives, we also need to note one positive type of washback opportunity. The nature of the literacy demands inherent in many academic achievement standards has been investigated by one team from the University of Auckland. They have used their research findings to work with teachers in low-decile schools. The aim is to raise teachers' awareness of the literacy demands of their subjects, helping them to more constructively support students to build new levels of literacy to meet these demands (Wilson & McNaughton, 2014). With a similar aim, some schools have devised strong processes to support teachers who are not literacy or numeracy experts as they select sufficiently robust evidence from students' work (Hipkins, 2012). These processes combine an element of professional learning with NCEA decision-making, in the best tradition of moderation that supports teacher learning (see Chapter 10).

Specifying targets for NCEA success

In 2012 the National government set a target for at least 85 percent of 18 year olds to achieve NCEA Level 2, or an equivalent qualification, in

2017 and thereafter. This target constituted one part of a policy package outlined in a short document titled *Delivering Better Public Services: Boosting Skills and Employment by Increasing Educational Achievement for Young People* (New Zealand Government, 2012). This title speaks for the positive intention, grounded in the argument that gaining a Level 2 qualification is the minimum required to keep a range of ongoing learning options open. Evidence from the longitudinal Competent Learners study supports this assumption:

> Leaving school with NCEA Level 2 or Level 3 was worthwhile, and was more likely to support a more satisfying pathway into early adulthood. Leaving school without a qualification was not only associated with greater likelihood of unemployment in the post-school years, but also with more major regrets, less happiness and optimism and more experience of depression and mental ill health. Post-school study did not improve the opportunities for these young people: instead, they had higher rates of not completing courses they undertook, indicating their need for support with learning, and building habits of learning that they had not built in school. Simply changing the environment of learning without addressing these needs would not suffice. (Wylie & Hodgen, 2011, p. xvi)

An important additional insight from the Competent Learners research was that gaining NCEA Level 2 is at least as important for the *attitudes* to learning needed for success as it is for the actual subject-related achievements. This is an important consideration in the light of the potential for washback effects when schools are under pressure to lift achievement overall rates, exacerbated by league-table reporting of their actual results.

An additional source of pressure comes from a subsequent Ministry of Education initiative with the acronym ART (Achievement, Retention, Transition). Ministry of Education officials target schools seen to be in need of help to lift overall achievement levels. They work with these schools to devise strategies to help borderline students get over the Level 2 bar. The secondary teachers' union (PPTA) has expressed concerns that ART is damaging to the credibility of NCEA.[2]

---

2 See for example http://www.ppta.org.nz/resources pptanews/
2868-pptanews-dubious-focus-2013

Some school leaders who responded to NZCER's 2012 National Survey of Secondary Schools believed this scale of change cannot be achieved without recourse to undesirable practices (Hipkins, 2013). However, 3 years on just 10 percent of principals responding to the 2015 National Survey of Secondary Schools agreed that the ART initiative compromises the credibility of NCEA. Note, however, that 33 percent held a neutral view and a further 10 percent either did not answer or were unsure. Interestingly, when the same issue was framed in terms of student success rather than credibility, 60 percent of the principals agreed that ART was a positive way to support students to achieve a Level 2 NCEA (Wylie & Bonne, 2016).

NCEA's flexibility becomes a two-edged sword when intense pressure is applied to schools. For example, they could resort to directing borderline students into courses with a lower academic demand in order to ensure their success. A related strategy might be to cherry-pick standards perceived to be easy and then encourage borderline students to add these to their credit totals. However both of these types of response could result in students gaining a Level 2 NCEA award with little or no coherence or relevance to their future learning needs and plans. This flies in the face of the intent of the policy to keep learning pathways open, and is unlikely to foster the dispositions for learning highlighted in the Competent Learners research.

Many teachers are now telling us that their own school sets them targets to lift overall NCEA achievement rates year-on-year. When such targets become part of their performance review teachers may work to achieve them in any way they can. This is one source of the pressure for the teaching of formulaic writing frames, for example. The Competent Learner findings, as well as common sense, seriously question the wisdom of putting teachers and students in this difficult position. Recall that this research team said one of NCEA's most important attributes was that it provided an indication of strong learning *habits and attitudes*. Any sort of shortcut to unwarranted success will actively undermine the development of strong learning capabilities. The challenges of shifting the assessment emphasis from sorting students by relative achievement successes, to seeking evidence of the learning gains that all students have genuinely made, should not be underestimated.

One important counter-argument is that teachers will not necessarily resort to expediency. Those who are supported to take students' learning challenges seriously can help them to make genuine achievement gains. They could for example support students to improve their literacy levels before they undertake examinations for standards with high literacy demands (see Wilson & McNaughton, 2014). In any case, setting high expectations for *all* students is one of the eight foundational principles of *NZC*. As we saw in Chapter 12, teachers who are skilful curriculum thinkers can design coherent, intellectually demanding courses while meeting a range of learning needs. The case study that concludes the chapter illustrates the way in which powerful changes in practice can be prompted when carefully targeted support from outside the school supports willing teachers to rethink their typical pedagogical responses to common NCEA pressures. The caution here—as in the case of the languages teachers above—is that teachers need to be convinced rather than coerced if the changes they make really do support achievement gains that have power and meaning for students' lives. Such changes have the potential to be lifeworthy, rather than simply focused on getting students over the line.

Case study: A growing appreciation for NCEA's flexibility

Massey University's Professor Lisa Emerson's first experiences of NCEA were shaped through the eyes of a parent. With a daughter in the very first NCEA cohort, she formed the distinct impression that teachers could not explain the new system. How NCEA worked remained a mystery to her and other parents.

Over the next few years Lisa and her colleagues noticed a change in the readiness of transitioning students to make the step up from secondary to tertiary study. They were inclined to lay three specific issues at the door of NCEA: a lack of understanding of the implications of failing an assignment; an expectation of individual attention; and continual requests for exemplars that students could follow in shaping their own work. The first of these they attributed to the allowance of resubmission for internally assessed work in senior secondary. They attributed the second issue to too much "hand-holding" in secondary classrooms, and the third to the NCEA exemplar tasks in common use in those classrooms. Lisa and her colleagues were aware that differences in the cohort coming into the university might account for some of these effects, but in general NCEA was seen as the "baddie" that left students poorly prepared for tertiary study.

Lisa's view changed when she began to research more effective ways to support the transition of students from secondary school to university (Emerson, Kilpin, & Feekery, 2014, 2015). With space to step back to review the big picture, she saw that the demands of first-year university study had increased considerably and that this change was directly related to an "explosion in the amount of information available". Students were not expected to work with primary sources a decade ago, nor did they undertake independent library-based research using a range of databases until at least their second or third year of university study. However, in response to the escalation of published information across the last decade or so, a critical engagement with source texts is now a routine expectation of first-year students (at least in arts-based courses).

These differences in expectations of first-year university students shift the way the transition issue is framed. Lisa's team now recognised that lack of readiness of students is not about NCEA per se. Rather, from their perspective secondary teaching and expectations have not changed fast enough to keep pace with changes in tertiary teaching and expectations. While there is some emphasis placed on information literacy, critical thinking, and so on, in senior secondary classrooms, these positive shifts have not gone far enough, or fast enough, to keep up with the demands of rapidly evolving university study.

Lisa and her team began to work with secondary teachers to do something about closing this gap in expectations. They then began to see at first hand the "extraordinary pressure" that secondary teachers are under to ensure their students gain the NCEA credits they need. More importantly, Lisa also began to see how the perverse effects of this pressure had masked her view of the remarkable flexibility inherent in the NCEA system as a whole. She could see that teachers are free—at least in theory—to design programmes that meet any combination of learning needs, and they have the skills and knowledge to do so. It isn't that teachers can't foster greater independence, critical thinking, and information literacy. However, the need to *ensure* student success acts to discourage secondary teachers from taking what they see as a risk—fostering greater student independence in learning.

A similar dynamic appeared to be limiting students' opportunities to practice extended writing tasks. Secondary teachers tend to work around a common reluctance of students to engage with such tasks. They find ways to scaffold writing that allow students to show what they know, which is a legitimate assessment goal. But the perverse consequence is that students intending to transition to university may not develop the strong independent writing skills they will need. NCEA's flexibility contributes to this dilemma, while the pressure on teachers to sustain achievement rates can work against addressing it proactively.

Fortuitously, Lisa's team did find a way to persuade teachers taking part in their research to boost the time students spent practising extended academic writing. During orientation sessions at the university, they showed the final-year school students what they could expect to be doing in their first year of tertiary study. Students went back to school asking for chances to build their independent writing skills. They didn't necessarily enjoy academic writing any more than they had before, but the goal was clear. With the students now asking for more challenging writing opportunities, NCEA's flexibility allowed teachers to respond proactively and offer students the types of extended assignments and associated writing tasks both groups (students and teachers) could see they needed to undertake.

Concluding comment

In this chapter we have endeavoured to strike a balance between clearly presenting the potential for perverse effects from aspects of the way NCEA is put into operation, and showing that these effects are not an *inevitable* consequence of NCEA. In every case we have been able to include examples of teachers who resist the pressures as presented, making principled teaching decisions with their students' learning needs in mind.

The curriculum and assessment development in the Learning Languages learning area of *NZC* and the secondary to tertiary transition study conducted by Lisa Emerson's team both involved partnerships between tertiary-based subject specialists and classroom teachers. The tertiary researchers/advisers are able to hold up a critical mirror in which teachers can see their practice as reflected through others' eyes and a wider framing. They are supported to think differently about the teaching and learning that happens in their classrooms, to push back when ideas are a step too far or not practical, and to push forward when there is resistance from curriculum traditionalists. The point we are making here is that teachers should not be left to figure out these sorts of changes without careful and purposeful support, and that support has not been widely forthcoming, either when NCEA was implemented or when *NZC* followed.

Chapter 14 The learning experience for students

This chapter foregrounds the experiences of students and, in particular, two commonly heard complaints about NCEA, both of which have the potential to impact negatively on adolescent learners. The first complaint is that the steady diet of internal assessment in every subject, across all 3 years of senior secondary schooling, places students (and teachers) under relentless pressure and eats up time that could otherwise be devoted to teaching and learning. The second complaint is that the flexibility of NCEA requires students to make quite complex decisions about matters such as productive learning pathways and whether to submit work for specific assessments. The concern here is that making these kinds of choices places too much responsibility in the hands of young people who lack the life experience to understand the far-reaching consequences of their decisions. These two challenges interact with each other. Students who are under pressure from too many internal assessments, or who simply consider that they have enough to meet the requirements for a certificate, are likely to make spontaneous decisions to skip one or more assessments, often to the distress of their teachers and parents, and sometimes to the cost of their own learning progress. This remains a serious issue for NCEA internal assessment.

With this conundrum in mind, we consider NCEA from the perspective of students' learning opportunities, decisions, and actions. We place concerns about these matters in a wider contextual frame that asks critical questions about how NCEA has been represented to students and their families, and how it has been managed in schools. In particular, we question the seemingly common assumption that the main value in learning is to gain qualifications. Where are the visionary purposes for learning that matters, as clearly signalled in *NZC*? In this chapter we make the case that the only viable solution to the twin dilemmas sketched above is to run courses that engage students through their content, rather than relying on credit accumulation as a motivating force.

Another assumption—that *NZC* does not apply to the senior secondary years and that its place is taken by achievement standards—also seems quite pervasive. When this sort of thinking prevails, assessment considerations tend to replace other curriculum signals in teachers' thinking and planning. However *NZC* clearly signals that the curriculum framework sets directions for learning which will be put into effect in the senior secondary school and not just during the years leading up to this time. There is also a very explicit expectation that schools should be leveraging the potential for flexibility that exists at the intersection of curriculum and assessment, so that meaningful and valuable learning experiences are provided for all students in the senior secondary school:

> The *New Zealand Curriculum*, together with the Qualifications Framework, gives schools the flexibility to design and deliver programmes that will engage all students and offer them appropriate learning pathways. The flexibility of the qualifications system also allows schools to keep assessment to levels that are manageable and reasonable for both students and teachers. Not all aspects of the curriculum need to be formally assessed, and excessive high-stakes assessment in years 11–13 is to be avoided. (Ministry of Education, 2007, p. 41)

Unfortunately, the pressures on students that we discuss next suggest this advice about avoiding excessive assessment has often gone unheeded. Many people seem to hold NCEA directly to blame for this unfortunate state of affairs, but we think there is a need to ask more critical questions about the curriculum, assessment, and learning dynamics in play. By keeping the question of the purposes envisaged for learning in our sights, we aim to present a more nuanced account of what really constitutes over-assessment.

Gaining qualifications as the primary purpose for learning

In the pre-NCEA years the use of examination prescriptions as the de facto curriculum reinforced the commonly held assumption that students stayed on into senior secondary school primarily to gain the qualifications required to move on to tertiary study. As we outlined in Part 1 this sorting purpose was already under pressure by the mid-20th century because more students, with a greater range of learning abilities and needs, were staying longer at school. NCEA partially addressed this challenge by allowing for achievement to be acknowledged in much more varied types of learning experiences. However, underlying assumptions about purposes for learning were not explicitly addressed as the assessment system began to evolve, and problems soon arose.

Chapter 6 explained that the original suites of achievement standards were predominantly designed by a process of chunking previous examination prescriptions. The teams who developed these first suites of standards were reassured that only the method of assessment would change and that teaching and learning itself could go on fairly much as it had in the past.[1] The learning areas developed towards the end of the 1990s were arguably better served in the NCEA development process because their more recent curriculum debates influenced the focus of the standards being developed, at least to some extent. The discussion in Chapter 13 about the achievement standards developed for Learning Languages illustrates this point. However in curriculum subjects for which initial outcomes-based curriculum documents had been

---

1 Interestingly this situation quickly changed once implementation was actually underway. The Ministry of Education soon commissioned consecutive rounds of research that investigated the impact of NCEA on the pedagogy of innovative teachers in science and mathematics (first round) and geography and home economics (second round) (Hipkins, Conner, & Neill, 2006; Hipkins & Neill, 2006).

developed in the early 1990s, the long-held but mostly tacit assumption that gaining qualifications was the primary purpose of senior secondary learning continued much as before.

As soon as NCEA was introduced many teachers began to modify the motivational "carrot" they offered in conversations with their students. In the lead-up to the formal examinations under the previous examination-based system, it would be common to hear phrases such as "you'll need to know this, it could be in the exam". Once NCEA was in place, greater student effort began to be encouraged via the incentive of more immediate rewards in the form of a small bundle of credits for each internally assessed standard achieved. Furthermore, all students could be offered this type of reward, regardless of their academic abilities. NCEA was designed to encourage all students to see themselves as successful learners. We do not see this inclusive intent as the problem that has led to complaints about over-assessment. The issue is that value of the intended learning quickly came to be framed almost exclusively in terms of credits to be gained. This is clearly an impoverished view of what makes learning worthwhile. It almost certainly results in teachers approaching assessment standards as if they were designed to be curriculum topics, and then to assess them with generic tasks. When this happens—and it is the norm rather than the exception at present—the belief that students have to be motivated by the promise of credit accumulation leads directly to curriculum fragmentation and assessment-driven courses. As we saw in Chapter 12 the development of NCEA before *NZC* did not help matters, but neither did the quick uptake of credits as the predominant motivational frame for learning.

A bumper credit harvest

One of the most obvious issues with offering credits as the reward for learning is that teachers' motivational talk very quickly became self-fulfilling. The belief that students were not prepared to make an effort in the classroom unless there were credits on offer quickly spread. Several research projects conducted in those first few years of NCEA documented the large numbers of credits that some students had begun to amass. The following comment from the age 16 phase of the Competent Learners study illustrates the point:

> We found little evidence that students were taking the easy route to NCEA by doing the minimum amount of work necessary. In fact, the more academically inclined students gained far more than the 80 credits they needed to achieve NCEA Level 1, with many gaining 138 credits or more. (Wylie, Hodgen, Hipkins, & Vaughan, 2008, p. 21)

In the third year of the Learning Curves project[2] the researchers spoke to 54 different focus groups of students in the six schools. The nine groups of students interviewed in each school were carefully selected to represent the different sorts of learning experiences that more and less academic students might encounter. As part of the wider discussion, every group was asked to respond to the following prompt: "Some people say students don't want to learn anything unless they can get credits. Do you think that's true?" From every group, the immediate response was almost inevitably "yes". However, when pushed to consider what they had just said: "really, you don't want to learn anything unless you can get credits?" students would open up and begin to talk about the sorts of learning experiences they enjoyed (Hipkins et al. 2005). The researchers were quite easily able to push past the knee-jerk response. But this is not necessarily as easy to do in the classroom, when students might need to apply considerable effort to learn things whose benefit to them does not become clear until later on.

Both the Learning Curves project and the age 16 phase of Competent Learners were conducted before certificate and course endorsements were introduced (see Chapter 9). In this context, both research projects reported that more able students saw high credit totals as a way of differentiating themselves from other learners.

The credits-for-learning equation was also reinforced by the need for teachers to attract sufficient numbers of students to courses they designed. It was common for faculty heads to tell the Learning Curves researchers that they would like to offer fewer credits in their courses (and hence expend less time and effort on assessment) but they were worried that students would preferentially choose courses that continued to yield a higher credit harvest (Hipkins et al., 2004). This is

---

2 The second Learning Curves report discusses the issue of excessive credit totals in some detail: http://www.nzcer.org.nz/research/publications/learning-curves-meeting-student-learning-needs-evolving-qualifications-regime-

another self-fulfilling argument. It is a brave teacher who stands against the flow of such a commonly held view. Reducing the numbers of credits assessed in courses needs a strong collegial culture in which everyone agrees to lower totals in order to enhance students' learning experience. Furthermore, a lower number of credits cannot be an end in itself undertaken simply to alleviate over-assessment or teachers' workloads. The credits that *are* available need to be generated from tasks that are integrated into a motivating course that conveys powerful knowledge. If this does not happen the only difference from the *status quo* will be that students will have the opportunity to undertake fewer credits, and the credit-accumulation mentality will persist. The case study at the end of this chapter shows what can be achieved when curriculum design in the senior secondary school becomes a collective endeavour rather than a competition amongst the staff of a school.

It is also important to acknowledge the dilemma teachers face when a coverage imperative dominates their curriculum thinking. The assumption that students won't learn unless they can gain credits aligns closely with the assumption that anything worth learning should be assessed. Teachers can be reluctant to omit achievement standards from their course design if this leads them to believe that students will then miss out on something they see as an important aspect of their subject. However, as we noted in the introduction to Part 3, the burgeoning of new knowledge in every discipline makes in-principle coverage of everything important impossible. Teachers need access to curriculum-thinking tools, such as the "lifeworthy" principles, which help them make carefully reasoned reductions in content. In Chapter 12 we introduced the idea that there can be valid alternatives to coverage when assembling a collection of disciplinary content to create a coherent course. Carefully reasoned alternative course designs can provide a more critical frame for exploring and enabling course coherence. Nevertheless, it is important to acknowledge that subject coverage can be a genuine concern. It is hard for teachers to see their way to reduce credit totals, even if they see a need to do so, when they hold a default coverage view of the purposes for learning their subject. Again, in this regard, careful course design is the key. Ultimately, the course should define which standards ought to be assessed; assessment reduction is not an end in itself.

When it appears that any credits will do

The challenge we now address follows logically from the credit-harvesting issue. If the real value in learning lies in the credits gained and the qualification awarded, it is not such a big step for some people to begin to think that any credits will do—i.e., that it doesn't matter how the various standards are combined to build the overall qualification, or how much effort is put into attaining them. We could argue that this view was a not-quite-explicit founding assumption of NCEA. It should come as no surprise that we want to hold this perception up to critical scrutiny as we develop a more nuanced account of the dynamics in play.

In the early years of NCEA some researchers believed that many students would do the bare minimum necessary to gain their NCEA credits, and hence the quality of their learning would suffer (see for example Meyer, McClure, Walkey, McKenzie, & Weir, 2006). The short excerpt from the Competent Learners project, cited above, begins by challenging this belief. Nevertheless, levels of concern about motivation were such that the issue provided an important impetus for course endorsement. Endorsement was undoubtedly successful in ameliorating concerns about the motivation of more academically inclined students.[3] However, by addressing only the obvious challenge to extrinsic motivation yet another opportunity was lost to broaden the debate both about reasons for valuing learning, and about when and why students might willingly expend learning efforts regardless of immediate rewards.

Some years after NCEA was introduced a new research project explored the forms that course innovation took in three quite different secondary school settings (Hipkins & Spiller, 2012). One of these case studies investigated an early version of the socioscientific issues course discussed in Chapter 12. The second case explored the impact on course design of new achievement standards in history. The third case looked at the remixing of traditional learning experiences and

---

3 The NZCER National Survey of Secondary Schools in 2009 reported widespread consensus that "endorsing NCEA certificates with excellence or merit was a worthwhile change to make" (96 percent of principals, 90 percent of board of trustee members, and 86 percent of teachers agreed with this statement. Note, however, that just 50 percent of parents agreed and 29 percent were unsure) (Hipkins, 2010a).

different pacing of learning. The focus was a one-off course designed to attract back into school students who had drifted away in the chaos that followed the Christchurch earthquakes. Looking across these three quite different case studies the researchers questioned the simply binary distinction between extrinsic and intrinsic motivation:

> The ways in which the teachers in this study sought to motivate students were nuanced and strategic. A simple differentiation between extrinsic and intrinsic motivation is not particularly helpful here. All the teachers saw early success as important: they worked hard to help their students gain credits from internally assessed standards early in each course. However, their reasons for doing so related more to changing learners' expectations of themselves than to simply gaining credits as the reward for learning effort. Students come to their NCEA years with "learning careers" and "assessment careers" already well established. For some students these cumulative "career" experiences point to confidence in their own ability and ongoing success, but others perceive disappointment, failure and low expectations in their personal track record over time. Early success—provided it is real success in the form of worthwhile learning seen to be of value to self and others—can be a circuit breaker here. (Hipkins & Spiller, 2012, p. 37)

The proviso in the last sentence of this quote is an important one. Students in the Learning Curves focus groups were very aware of the relative value of the credits they had gained. In those fledgling years of NCEA many students in alternative courses were not convinced that their NCEA award was worthwhile. The very structure of school kept them firmly in place on the bottom of the learning heap (as they saw it). The exception to this were students who had gained their credits from a strategic, carefully compiled mix of unit standards that moved them along a pathway they wanted to follow anyway, beyond school and into the world of work or vocational training. Their motivation came from a sense of purpose, and a strong fit between their learning and their goals, not just from the promise of rewards in the form of credits. Similarly, history students interviewed some years later during the innovations project spoke of their passion for their personal historical inquiries and the effort they were willing to put into their learning, regardless of any credit rewards.

Who actually chooses?

Now we turn to the question of how much choice students actually have when they choose specific actions that carry NCEA-related consequences. It is certainly the case that spontaneous decisions to skip assessments can be taken by students unilaterally, although, as we have already noted, some of the pressures that lead to skipping might be averted if the teachers planned together more carefully and avoided excessive assessment pressure points. Not so straightforward is the choice of subjects, and hence the type of pathway through NCEA that will be open to the student. Although students typically think that they have a free choice, behind the scenes school structures can act to open up or constrain options, and those structures embed assumptions about the capabilities of different learners. The actual choices available to a student might be more constrained than they and their parents are aware, and there could well be very real consequences for their achievement, and for how they perceive themselves as learners.

The Health and Physical Education learning area of *NZC* (HPE) provides the main context for the discussion that follows. This learning area surfaces interesting issues because the subjects it includes (health, PE, outdoor education, home economics) are typically seen as less academic, and therefore of lower value or status, than some other curriculum subjects. It follows from this assumption that these subjects might be seen as more suitable for students who could struggle to gain an NCEA with a mix of subjects such as languages, history, mathematics, and sciences. There are embedded assumptions here about the relative value of knowledge from different learning areas. These assumptions shine a critical light on the problematic notion of parity of esteem. All subjects can and should offer learning of real value that extends the students who take them. The *NZC* messages about worthwhile achievement, including the principle of *high expectations* for all students, demand no less.

In this part of the discussion we draw on recent research by a classroom teacher and a teacher educator who both raise critical questions about teachers' curriculum choices and their perceptions about the best options for supporting students to successfully gain NCEA.

Case 1: Choosing achievement standards for an HPE course

HPE teacher Sally Hart recently completed a postgraduate dissertation based on an investigation of teacher decision-making about which achievement standards to use to assess their students' work (Hart, 2014). She began with a quantitative analysis of NZQA data and found that, compared with numbers attempting more practically oriented achievement standards in PE, fewer candidates were attempting the sociocritical standards.[4] She then focused on four PE standards that do assess the sociocritical aspects of the learning area[5] so that she could learn more about teachers' reasons for choosing them or not. Sally undertook case studies in two schools, one that used the sociocritical standards to assess learning and one that did not. Teachers who avoided these standards tended to make a binary distinction between practical and academic learning. For them these standards were not practical and therefore not likely to readily yield learning success (at least in the form of NCEA credits). But the teachers who did use these standards enjoyed challenging their students to successfully step up to more-demanding learning.

Recall the home economics case study in Chapter 12 (pp. 160–162). This study presented a snapshot of a challenging course where learning was also assessed using sociocritical standards from the HPE learning area. Clearly some teachers can, but some cannot, envisage a successful pathway through such a course. In her thesis Sally suggested that teachers need access to "quality teaching and learning programmes, where curriculum, assessment and pedagogy are considered and aligned" (Hart, 2014, p. 91). We couldn't have put it better ourselves.

---

4 This comment should not be taken to mean that these standards only assess practical achievements. Most will also have theoretical components. It is the balance between theory and practice, and the focus of the more theoretical components that is at issue here.

5 Level 1–AS 90070: Explore how the body is portrayed in physical activity; Level 2–AS 90432: Examine the relationship between physical activity and health, and implications for self and society; Level 2–AS 90437: Investigate the sociological significance of a sporting event, physical activity or festival; Level 3–AS 90743: Examine a current physical activity event, trend or issue impacting on New Zealand society.

The languages researchers, whose work we considered in Chapter 13, came to similar conclusions, especially in relation to achievement standards that assess students' ability to interact in the language they are learning. In this type of activity practical communication skills and more theoretical aspects of language knowledge are inescapably intertwined. A binary distinction between theory and practice has little meaning in this context.

The point about interaction illustrates why it is important not to undervalue the practical components of lifeworthy learning. Both practical and theoretical components of learning are important *for all students*, but achieving a well-reasoned balance between them can be problematic. For "academic" students the balance tips in favour of theoretical learning. For "vocational" students it tips to the practical side. Furthermore, this type of labelling of students is a big problem in itself. It can narrow the scope of learning for students labelled as academic, and become self-fulfilling for students labelled as "alternative" or "vocational" or some similar label. The second case study illustrates this dynamic from another perspective.

Case 2: Motivating "sporty" kids

A recent study by health educator Katie Fitzpatrick discusses challenges and opportunities for underachieving Māori and Pasifika students who opt for a mix of HPE courses in their senior secondary years (Fitzpatrick, 2011). On the one hand NCEA records show that these students are experiencing success in gaining credits for HPE achievements, whereas in pre-NCEA years many of them would not have gained any qualifications before leaving school. This success is usually attributed to learning experiences that are seen to be meaningful for "sporty" kids. On the other hand, if teachers (and students) adhere to stereotypes that position Māori and Pasifika youth as successful because of their natural sporting abilities, there is a risk that the students will be "trapped in the physical" at the expense of engaging with the intellectual dimensions of the learning area. Katie concludes that HPE teachers need to engage more critically with the academic aspects of HPE subjects so that students are not disenfranchised by their NCEA "success" (i.e., it is a hollow success that actually takes them nowhere in terms of ongoing learning pathways). Given the systematic undervaluing of the learning area as a whole, she questions whether achievement in HPE really does challenge perceptions of underachievement of Māori and Pasifika students in New Zealand *or actually reinforces this*.

We've highlighted the last point to emphasise the potential for assumptions about "less academic" learners to become self-fulfilling. Nor is this effect limited to the HPE learning area. For example, the Learning Curves project discussed what some teachers saw as the "intellectualisation" of assessment of previously practical subjects subsumed into the technology learning area, at least when achievement standards were used to assess learning. Unit standards can be used instead and their focus is highly practical. But does this substitution leave practical technology students "trapped in the vocational" (to echo Katie's PE point above)? A related, and intriguing, question is whether students can become "trapped in the academic". When the term *academic* is a euphemism for a focus on traditional content-heavy subjects that have their basis in powerful epistemology hollowed out, it is tempting to conclude that they can.

One of the challenges of achievement standards such as the HPE sociocritical ones, or the more "intellectual" ones in technology, is that they demand sustained critical thought or higher order thinking. The reward for this intellectual hard work is that learning can be really illuminating about ways society is organised and the complexity of socially based issues. Such learning takes students beyond their own lives and experiences. David Perkins would say the learning is lifeworthy because it fosters *insight* and engages *ethical thinking*. Almost all students can access such thinking given the right types of support and sufficient motivation to want to try. For example, carefully designed research has shown that pedagogy with a strong metacognitive element supports lower achieving students to make much more rapid gains in higher order thinking than those already succeeding academically (Zohar & Ben David, 2008). These Israeli researchers emphasise that it is important that teachers do not write off these students as being academically too weak to cope with intellectually demanding learning with a strong metacognitive component. Expectations that students will not cope become self-fulfilling when they are not supported to try and develop their higher order thinking capabilities.

NCEA's modular assessment structure effectively renders schools' sorting assumptions invisible, even while consolidating them. The two HPE research projects we have outlined in this chapter illustrate why students may not even be aware of the ways their learning choices are being narrowed by decisions their teachers take when, with all good intentions, they smooth the path to credit acquisition by avoiding more intellectually demanding assessments. Challenging teachers' ability-based beliefs about the achievement limitations of weaker students has real potential to open up a wider range of lifeworthy learning.

Support for making better pathways choices

Students do make choices of course. Within the constraints of schools' timetable structures they are free to choose their subject combinations. Research conducted by the Starpath team at Auckland University investigated reasons that Māori and Pasifika students were more likely to fall by the wayside than other students, leaving school with no qualifications or none beyond Level 1 NCEA. They soon reported that these students more frequently opted for subject combinations that closed off rather than opened pathways to further learning (Madjar, McKinley, Jensen, & Van Der Merwe, 2009). For example, students who are encouraged to take an alternative version of science in Year 11 could well find that they are not eligible to enrol for any Year 12 specialist science subject because they have not gained the achievement standards specified as prerequisites for those courses (by the schools themselves—NZQA imposes no prerequisites).

This dilemma can be seen as yet another consequence of the labelling we have already discussed. But forewarned is forearmed, and it is important that students and their families are aware of what is at stake as they make their choices. The Starpath researchers were so concerned about what they found that they shaped a series of simple narratives to help make the common pitfalls in making NCEA-related choices easily understandable for students and families (Madjar & McKinley, 2011). Ensuring that all families with children in Years 11–13 have an adequate understanding of NCEA remains a work in progress.

As we have already noted, students can also unilaterally choose to skip assessments. If they do this too often, they risk arriving at the end of the year short of the credits they need for an NCEA award. The Starpath team found that some students seemed to be unaware of the consequences of these choices. As a proactive response, the research team designed processes for systematically tracking progress of all students in a school. The intention was that the tracking would be supported by processes for advising students and supporting them to keep their progress on track towards gaining the credit total needed for an NCEA award. Achievement rates for Māori and Pasifika students in the Starpath schools began to improve once such systems were in place (McKinley et al., 2009).

This success was soon noted and taken up by other schools, especially after the 85 percent NCEA Level 2 target was announced (Chapter 13). But a focus on credits can be a two-edged sword. On one hand vulnerable students can be better supported to make sound learning and assessment decisions. On the other, the tracking processes can act to keep the focus on gaining credits as the predominant purpose for learning. There is a tricky balance to be achieved between a focus on lifeworthy purposes for learning, credit accumulation, and keeping learning pathways open. To achieve a strategic balance between these purposes for learning, assumptions underpinning choices made by and on behalf of students need to be candidly aired and debated.

Case 3: Innovative school-wide NCEA design

We now draw together the various threads of this chapter, and indeed of the book as a whole, with a case study that illuminates possibilities for leveraging NCEA's flexibility to address the dilemmas outlined above. Hobsonville Point is a new secondary school established to serve a rapidly growing area of mid-density new housing in Auckland. In 2014 the school opened with a cohort of Year 9 students, and expanded to Years 9 and 10 in 2015. Along the way a small group of Year 11 students was also enrolled. (Their parents did not want them to miss out on the rich opportunities afforded by the school's innovative curriculum design.) By mid-2015 planning was well underway for the first full cohort of students, who entered Year 11 in 2016.

In most secondary schools Year 11 formally signals the beginning of 3 years of NCEA assessments.[6] Students following typical learning pathways work towards Level 1 NCEA in Year 11, Level 2 NCEA in Year 12, and then Level 3 NCEA in Year 13 (with or without also gaining UE). Hobsonville Point does not intend to follow these established traditions. The school community wants to keep its singular vision for the junior secondary curriculum alive into the senior secondary years. Thus to understand the school's NCEA thinking it is first necessary to understand something of their curriculum design.

A rich integrated curriculum has been brought to life as the school has evolved. Students mix and remix their learning groups across Years 9 and 10, choosing between richly contextualised modules of learning that combine at least two curriculum subjects and are co-taught by pairs of teachers with the necessary disciplinary expertise. A careful mapping has been undertaken to ensure that students will encounter what the teachers perceive to be the most important concepts of each learning area. This mapping ensures that the basics can be covered via different module combinations, thus catering for the different strengths and interests that students bring to their learning.

It is evident that careful guidance is needed to make a system like this work well for every student. Such guidance is built into the curriculum via several time slots allocated each week when students can work with their assigned learning coach to review their progress and choices, and to organise for additional learning support if needed. As their capabilities in self-regulation grow stronger, the intention is that students will experience greater autonomy in the learning decisions they make, so that they leave school well-equipped to become the lifelong and life-wide learners that the curriculum intends (Hipkins & Cowie, 2014).

This is a complex and ambitious curriculum design that appears to be serving the students well. The teachers say that most students are highly engaged with their learning, often producing work that exceeds their teachers' expectations (which are grounded in their experiences of

---

6 In fact, NCEA assessments often begin in Year 10. Teachers claim students need practice in the assessment methods and terminology they will encounter, and any credits gained can be "banked" for awarding in Year 11.

teaching junior secondary students in other schools). This success is one factor in the thinking that has encouraged the school leaders to extend their curriculum structure into Year 11, although perhaps with not as much cross-subject integration. Importantly, most Year 11 students will aim to achieve a total of just 20 credits in areas of their passions and strengths.[7] This is a long way short of the 80 credits required for a Level 1 qualification.[8] The intent is to give the Year 11 students a positive and manageable introduction to the qualifications framework. They will not need a Level 1 award for any credentialing purpose and the "carrot" of gaining NCEA credits is not needed when the learning on offer is rich and engaging for its own sake. Effectively NCEA will not noticeably intrude on the learning of most students at Hobsonville Point until Year 12.

As they solidified their NCEA implementation plan the senior leaders at Hobsonville Point were mindful of a challenge issued by the Education Review Office (ERO) in early 2015 (Education Review Office, 2015). ERO noted the impact of excessive NCEA assessment pressures on students' wellbeing. Indeed, some teachers had noted instances of students coming into Year 9 already stressed by the mere possibility that they might need to sit practice exams in that year. During an interview in mid-2015 the principal said that wellbeing was "at the centre" of the school's NCEA design planning.

The intention is that individual Year 12 courses will be assessed by a mix of achievement standards that can each yield 16–18 Level 2 NCEA credits at most. Opportunities to gain these credits will mostly come from internally assessed standards, with evidence gathered wherever possible from rich learning tasks. Students who aspire to gain Merit or Excellence endorsement for a course will need to have an opportunity to gain at least one externally assessed achievement standard (see Chapter 9). Other externally assessed material will still be taught if teachers deem it important. The motivational dividend of the school's curriculum approach should be such that students will recognise that

---

7 Individualised plans can allow for more Level 1 assessment when circumstances make this relevant and worthwhile.

8 The choice of total is strategic—a maximum of 20 Level 1 credits can count towards a Level 2 NCEA, if needed.

the learning is worthwhile in and of itself, and curriculum components addressed by externally assessed standards should be valued by students even though they will not receive credits for this learning.

In mid-2015, with an actual Year 13 cohort still several years in the future, the school was conceptualising this as a "launch-pad" year in which the potential for flexibly supporting individual programmes of learning afforded by NCEA could be fully realised. Students who aspire to enter competitive university courses (e.g., in engineering and medical schools) will follow a traditional learning/assessment plan, much as students in other schools might. However those on different learning/career/life pathways will also be able to negotiate programmes of learning and assessment that match their needs. Again, it is obvious that access to critical, engaged, and ongoing academic mentoring will be an essential cornerstone of this ambitious plan, along with a carefully constructed modular and flexible curriculum. The salient point here is that this is *possible now*, if a school is courageous enough to radically depart from tradition and habit.

As might be predicted this plan was initially a source of concern for some teachers, students, and parents. The principal identified the following as underlying beliefs that troubled people:

- Level 1 is necessary preparation for Levels 2 and 3. Students need to learn how to handle NCEA assessment procedures at this time.
- If we assume that learning won't happen unless it is assessed, then Level 1 can be seen as a necessary precursor to Level 2.
- The NCEA standards are the curriculum in the senior secondary school.

All three beliefs can be countered when people have the chance to surface and debate their assumptions and concerns. The senior leaders at Hobsonville Point have worked hard on these conversations. They designed a robust interactive workshop which they used first with their teachers, then with Year 11 parents (a small group), then with all parents, and then with students. In 2014 the principal estimated that he would have received "challenging emails" about this topic at least once a week. By mid-2015 the level of concern was much lower, although several families who wanted a more traditional experience for their children had removed them from the school at the end of Year 9.

Building a complex whole

It will be evident that a number of factors need to come together to enable the full potential for NCEA's flexibility to be realised in a school. In the first place, there is an actual *assessment plan*—it is not taken for granted that assessment is simply the logical follow-on from learning (or indeed the driver of learning). Logically, the school-wide assessment plan follows from and is embedded in, a strong coherent school-wide *curriculum plan*. There is a shared story to be told about the learning that matters, for whom, and why. In turn, this point highlights the presence of an overt conversation about the learning needs and potential achievement trajectories of different students. It is not taken for granted that whole cohorts will follow a lock-step curriculum into which they must fit (or not). Next, it logically follows that the potential for differentiation must be supported by access for every student to ongoing academic mentoring, so that they make good choices and have opportunities to develop their full learning potential. Finally, the wholeness of these intersecting pieces needs to be perceived and understood by all those with a direct stake in the success of the school and its students. Given this demanding manifesto, it is not surprising that Hobsonville Point stands out as an exceptional case study of what is already possible within the NCEA assessment system.

Concluding comment

NCEA was set up as a flexible, standards-based, high-stakes assessment model that was inclusive of all students, including those who had previously been excluded from gaining qualifications and for whom the schooling process was typically an alienating, negative experience. In this regard NCEA has been an undoubted success. Young people are motivated to stay at school longer than they ever have before (though high youth unemployment rates have also contributed to this trend). The number of them achieving qualifications is increasing. This increase includes students who would have been disadvantaged by the previous school system, and who typically left school without any qualifications. This is the good news about NCEA, but it is an equivocal story.

On closer inspection it is not altogether clear whether the increase in students gaining NCEA qualifications translates as an improvement in learning that matters—what we have called lifeworthy learning. For

David Perkins (2014) such learning introduces students to knowledge that is powerful because it is: rich in insight; prompts ethical thinking; links meaningfully to students' lives; and equips them with knowledge and skills for taking action. If students' senior school courses of study are made up of subjects that are not informed by a robust body of knowledge (which is typically, but not exclusively, informed by disciplinary knowledge) then they are unlikely to be equipped with the skills, dispositions, and knowledge that prepare them to think independently and participate constructively in 21st-century democratic society. These are qualities that lie at the heart of what it means to be educated and they are important for every student, not just the most able (Biesta, 2014).

In summary, our unfolding story is of a new qualification system that has been only partially successful in its attempt to address the challenges and practices of the past. Many positive gains have been made, especially in the evolving systems and processes that support the use of NCEA. But not everything is working as it should. Now we need to up the ante. It is time for new *curriculum* thinking to be brought to bear on NCEA's mix of achievement standards, and the processes for course construction that these standards support. It is time to think again about features that create perverse incentives and to look for ways to support teachers to surface tacit thinking about why they do what they do. We address these next challenges in the final section.

PART 4. (RE)IMAGINING NCEA AS A COMPLEX SYSTEM

In the introduction we described NCEA as being the most complicated school-exit qualification system we know of. In Part 2 we worked our way systematically through the complications of NCEA, documenting both the challenges and the opportunities they might confer. In Part 3 we lifted our gaze to discuss the potential of NCEA at its innovative best. It was important to us that we kept this conversation grounded in the context in which NCEA was introduced in the first place (i.e., the discussion in Part 1). If anything, the imperatives that led to its introduction have become even more acute in the intervening years. There can be no going backwards, but how best to continue forwards calls for a tricky balancing of critique and innovation.

Over the course of the 2 years that it took to shape this text we have been constantly surprised and stimulated by the insights that emerged in the spaces between our individual professional experiences and knowledge. Each of us brought something unique and something shared to the table. Writing this book was a genuine collaboration. We make this point to emphasise that the vision for NCEA and the recommendations we make in this final section have emerged from our work-in-progress conversations. They are not what we thought we knew at the start of our writing journey.

In the final chapter we use the lens of *complexity thinking* to look back over the NCEA journey we have recounted in this book. We think this comparatively recent field of theory can offer some useful pointers as we ask "where to next for NCEA?" For those unfamiliar with the main ideas, the following notes are a brief overview of features of complex systems. Possibly the best-known idea is that change in a complex system cannot be predicted by analysing the functioning of its individual parts. Rather, there is an emphasis on the dynamic interconnections and interactions between the various system components. Some complex systems evolve in response to changes to the conditions in which they are situated. In an evolving complex system, the greater the diversity of types of interactions that can occur between the different parts of the system, the more resilient it is likely to be in the face of new challenges and pressures.

Examples of complex systems in the natural world include ecosystems, climate, biological evolution, and the geological forces that govern tectonic movements. Many systems in the social world are also complex (as well as frequently also being complicated). Human social interactions act as feedback mechanisms on economic, political, and professional systems, to name but a few examples.

The various parts of a complex system can interact in a range of ways. A critical concept in understanding how complex systems work is that of *feedback*, meaning that information produced by the system re-enters the system and modifies its functioning. Sometimes feedback amplifies a system's processes, and sometimes it dampens them. Sometimes it can do either, depending on the system's current state. In any event, in complex systems that evolve, feedback mechanisms allow the system to keep adapting as conditions change. Some systems theorists call this the capacity of a system to *learn*. Such a system evolves dynamically over time, and the changes that come about are said to be *emergent*, which means that they are non-linear and are not brought about by properties of the system's individual components, but by interactions between them. Thus, small changes to the state of the system at a point in time can have dramatic effects at a later time, changes which might not have been anticipated or predicted. Sometimes change in a complex system occurs incrementally, although always unpredictably. In other situations a system can maintain a fairly steady state for a time, before abruptly and again, unpredictably, transiting to a radically different state. The state of a system as it makes such an abrupt change is sometimes referred to as a *tipping point*.

It is important to note that complex systems need not be complicated. They don't necessarily have a lot of components or processes. An example is the celebrated Mandelbrot set. This is generated by quite a simple mathematical algorithm and can, in turn, be used to generate endless different fractal patterns of great beauty and, literally, infinite detail. It is the presence of certain kinds of feedback mechanisms that give rise to complexity, not the number of parts. Some complex systems however, *are* complicated. We have said that NCEA is complicated; we also believe that some interesting insights into its past and future can be gained by considering it as complex. The final chapter does this.

Chapter 15 Reimagining NCEA

Our original aim for this book was to demonstrate the contextually complex nature of assessment challenges in any assessment system. As we have said a number of times, there was no golden age before NCEA. Every known system has its challenges. However, a number of structural and process decisions were taken when NCEA was first implemented. These decisions papered over some cracks that, with hindsight, would have been better opened up and proactively addressed. Even so, the rolling improvements made as these issues re-emerged have taken the NCEA system to a more sophisticated level of assessment thinking and practice, at least in terms of the official structures and processes. In the end, though, what really matters is how people talk about and use its flexibility, in the context of the national curriculum, to build meaningful programmes of learning for each and every student. This is arguably the most neglected aspect of NCEA debate and development to date. In this final chapter we position NCEA at the complex intersection of curriculum and assessment.

A complex intersection between curriculum and assessment

The leaders, trustees, and teachers in New Zealand's self-managing schools are charged with making decisions about the structure of the courses they offer, including those that will be assessed for qualifications. Given the flexibility of the NCEA model, teachers are effectively the curriculum builders. For internally assessed standards, teachers are also curriculum assessors of their students' work. As we've seen, using this freedom and flexibility to provide lifeworthy learning for each and every student is possible, but doing so requires nuanced and sophisticated thinking about what knowledge counts, and which purposes for learning are worthy of the intellectual and practical efforts they demand.

With some notable exceptions teachers have not been well supported to develop the level of next curriculum thinking that would allow them to do these things well. If we could wave a magic wand over the next decade of NCEA, we would wish for collective resourcing and intellectual effort to go into supporting robust professional knowledge development in the context of NCEA's various standards and practices.

We would like to leave our readers with an even more radical vision for NCEA than those that have already been realised by innovative curriculum thinkers whose work we have described in earlier chapters, although elements of their approaches will be evident in this vision. One of the intentions of this vision is for assessment to become so enmeshed in the everyday work of students that they would not even know that they were being assessed. Indeed, all of the work that they undertook during a course would potentially be evidence that could contribute to credits. Concepts such as fragmentation, over-assessment, credit-counting and selective disengagement from assessment would all evaporate because there would be no formal assessment events at all—with the singular exception of external assessments. Even the preparation for these, however, could be radically transformed if it was integrated deeply with the coursework. It goes without saying that this approach could only be taken by confident teachers, with the full support of their colleagues and school leaders, and a firm command of the discipline or disciplines informing the course content.

How might one design a course that was to be taught and assessed in such a way? It would surely have to start with the objective of conveying a deep understanding of a disciplinary epistemology, by engaging students directly in using that epistemology in ways that were relevant to them. This is the diametric opposite of starting with a set of standards to be taught and assessed. (This is not to say that the standards ought to be ignored in course design, just that they ought not to lead it.) Such a course would take into account the circumstances of the students for whom it is designed; that is, their cultural backgrounds, their interests, and their prior understandings. The sequence of teaching would be determined by a structure designed to serve pedagogical ends, rather than assessment ends.

Next, a series of tasks and activities, to be undertaken by the students in the course, would be designed to develop the envisaged learning. Like the course itself, these tasks would not be designed with assessment at the forefront, but would be created to serve as learning experiences in which students would have opportunities to put into practice the concepts of the course, and in so doing, to build their understanding of the discipline thinking underpinning it. These tasks would also serve a formative purpose, giving teachers and students a basis on which to discuss students' progress and to identify their challenges and difficulties. Finally, as if as an afterthought, standards would be selected as the formal assessment for the course, on the basis of the evidence of achievement that a teacher expects to be elicited by the tasks and activities.

It is unlikely under this scenario that there would usually be a one-to-one mapping between the tasks and the standards. Rather, the work undertaken by students to accomplish the tasks would collectively comprise a portfolio of evidence from which a teacher could make judgements about achievement against a set of standards.

A vision within our grasp: Reimagining NCEA through the lens of complexity thinking

We are well aware that the approach we have sketched would certainly have its challenges on pedagogical and political levels. It would not be possible for a single teacher, or probably even a single department, to undertake this approach alone; it would have to be adopted as a school-wide approach. There might well be resistance from students and parents because they are used to credits being awarded in a sequential manner, on the basis of discrete assessments, rather than on the basis of accumulated evidence. The national moderators might have difficulty in making their judgements, for similar reasons. Nonetheless, if the NCEA system is to work as it was intended to, if internal assessment is to be used to best effect, and if the fragmentation problem is to be solved without sacrificing the piecemeal nature of NCEA assessment along with the flexibility that it affords, then an approach like this is probably necessary.

The good news is that no formal change to the NCEA system would be required. This approach could be undertaken forthwith, within all of the existing rules and guidelines. We'll say it again to be really clear—we are not calling for big policy changes. Rather, our plea is to work smarter to consolidate on the remarkable achievements of our assessment system over the last decade, while not sweeping challenges under the carpet and hoping they will go away. With this aim in mind, we now identify promising areas where the system might be most effectively leveraged to kickstart a new round of evolution and adaptation for the ground-breaking NCEA. As a starting point we begin by thinking about similarities and differences between the previous assessment system and the NCEA system in terms of their complex system dynamics.

The School Certificate and Bursary assessment system was certainly impacted by social feedback in a wide range of areas. These included: changes in teacher demographics, education, and cultural backgrounds/beliefs; developments in curriculum; the political environment of the day; and the changing aspirations of students. However the system was held in a state of near-equilibrium for a number of decades. During this time changes in social feedback were insufficient to result in substantial change to policy or practice. As a consequence, feedback pressure built up over time. Eventually this pressure became strong enough to precipitate the comparatively sudden shift to the NCEA system. We could say, a tipping point was reached.

The comparative rigidity of the previous system helps explains its resistance to adaptive change. Under School Certificate and Bursary, there was almost no flexibility in the way in which students were assessed. There was a single assessment event—almost always a time-limited (externally assessed) examination at the end of the school year—for each subject in a defined curriculum canon. Interdisciplinary courses were practically impossible to run. The examination constituted a one-off, all-or-nothing, opportunity for students to be credentialed for what they had learned in each course of study.

In contrast, NCEA is much more susceptible to changes in policy and practice as a result of social-feedback mechanisms. This is partly because the system is still relatively new and has not yet reached a point of comparatively stable interactions between the parts.[1] In addition, the characteristics of the system itself, in particular its flexibility, its disaggregation, and the comparative autonomy it affords teachers in terms of developing programmes of study, are such that it is likely to remain more open to the influence of feedback.

NCEA as a diverse and resilient system

Diversity is an important feature of responsive, resilient, complex systems. In Part 2 of this book we discussed technical challenges associated with the smaller grain size of NCEA assessments, compared to the one-off examinations of the former assessment system. However, reframed in complexity terms, these multiple and diverse components confer very real advantages in rapidly changing times.

The multiple assessment events associated with each course of study make the overall programme highly flexible and responsive to feedback, both within the system and from outside it. Because more than half of the standards in almost every disciplinary area are internally assessed, students can engage in a great variety of tasks and activities to provide evidence for achievement, and different courses of study within a single discipline can employ a great many combinations of standards. Even within a single course, different students can undertake different standards. Courses themselves can therefore also be much more variable, both in terms of their content and of their epistemological underpinnings. Furthermore, standards can be drawn from more than one disciplinary area, so assessing interdisciplinary courses is much more feasible than it was previously.

Furthermore, assessment under NCEA no longer carries quite such high stakes as it did previously. Students can show their achievement in a piecemeal fashion, and they need not repeat an entire school year

---

1 Complexity theorists say that complex systems exist in states that are far from equilibrium. Apparent stability occurs when the dynamic interactions within the system are in relative balance, but it is always changing and adapting—never staying exactly the same.

if they do not achieve a certificate; rather, they can continue to build on whatever achievement they have attained, and potentially gain that certificate in a subsequent year.

All these features point to the potential for NCEA to remain resilient and responsive to the learning needs of students in the face of rapidly changing social conditions—a defining feature of life in the 21st century. However it is important to acknowledge the impact of this dynamism on teachers' working conditions. They have experienced a decade of imposed changes, often with minimal consultation. Those who feel overwhelmed and "done to" by the system are less likely to want to take up their potential agency to effect yet more change. There is a pressing need to ask whether and how the learning potential of the system as a whole might be more effectively leveraged to support all teachers, wherever they work, to make best use of NCEA's dynamic flexibility.

NCEA as a system that can learn

A defining characteristic of complex systems is unpredictability in the way they change—and potentially evolve—over time. One central idea of biological evolution is that a great many possibilities (for both parts and processes) might emerge, but many of them will be likely to fail, and only some will prove highly successful. This basic principle has been applied to management theory as the idea of "safe to fail" experiments (Garvey Berger & Johnston, 2015). In essence, many things get tried in response to a challenge, and those that don't work out are quickly abandoned before any real harm is done. The ones that do work can then be refined and applied more widely.

We don't for one moment think that the dynamic of safe-to-fail experiments was deliberately used to manage the rolling changes to NCEA that have taken place so far. But the events we have recounted in this book can be seen to serendipitously fit the idea. The important point is that the dynamic seems to have worked—things that didn't work out fell away, and useful changes stuck. Out of this seemingly tortuous journey, a more resilient high-stakes assessment system has emerged. Compared with the previous assessment system, the one we have now could yet be more responsive to the complex and unpredictable times ahead—times that will be our young people's futures.

Implications for ongoing policy work

As we've already noted, policy changes can be *expected* to have unanticipated and unpredictable effects on practice in a complex evolving system. Attempting to control the system using rigid rules and regulations is unlikely to yield the intended results. Instead, rigidity is likely to produce perverse incentives and outcomes, as we saw in Chapter 13.

All users of the system must be prepared to tolerate failure as an inevitable by-product of the evolution of successful practice. This isn't something that happens just because a policy hasn't been thought through carefully enough (although as we've seen there certainly have been instances of that along the way). Everyone with a role inside the system is an active agent and their activities will generate feedback that influences the system, sometimes in ways that simply couldn't be predicted. One important implication is that we all need to think differently about "mistakes" and "fix-ups". There have been plenty of both, and they have helped NCEA adapt and evolve.

These are very challenging ideas in the current political and bureaucratic environment within which the wider New Zealand education system is situated. Of course policy-makers know that policies can have unanticipated effects. However, the notion that a system is not particularly responsive to top-down control is likely to sit very uncomfortably with them. Politicians, the media and the public expect the Ministry of Education and NZQA to control educational practice and assessment for qualifications. Furthermore, the State Services Commission holds public agencies responsible for quite specific outcomes through mechanisms such as Better Public Service targets and key performance indicators. Such an accountability regime does not sit well with the notion that a system should be allowed to evolve in its own way or that failure ought to be tolerated and indeed expected. Mistakes are a complete anathema in a political environment in which politicians and the media are respectively driven by the avoidance and exposure of scandal. Thus, even if the principle of bottom-up evolution was to be accepted by the agencies responsible for NCEA, from a political perspective, they would put themselves at great risk by allowing more of it to occur.

One important caveat is that substantive concerns about natural justice arise when a system is prepared to tolerate some (minor) failure in the pursuit of success. Each time there is a "failure" of practice in high-stakes assessment, there is a risk that there will be detrimental consequences for the young people affected by that failure, at that moment in time. Indeed, the first round of Scholarship provided an example of this (Chapter 8). There are no easy answers to this dilemma. Probably the best and most pragmatic approach that can be taken by agencies in light of the complex and evolutionary nature of the NCEA system is first, to resist policy changes that restrict innovation, while carefully managing the political risk of this approach; second, to transmit the correct signals to the sector about what constitutes success, and to publicise successful practice wherever it can be identified; and, third, to maximise the conditions under which successful innovation is likely to take place.

Government agencies can potentially be highly effective in communicating ideas about successful practice within an adapting, evolving system. But as we've just noted the political environment does not necessarily make this easy. Furthermore, *success* can be defined in a number of ways. It might, for example, be defined in terms of proportions of students gaining qualifications. The present Better Public Service target for 85 percent of students to gain an NCEA Level 2 qualification by the age of 18 does this, and is thus the definition that the agencies are constrained to work with. However as we've seen the system has—quite predictably—evolved in ways that maximise the attainment of credits, without necessarily ensuring that their accumulation reflects lifeworthy learning. What might happen if we were to reset the definition of success?

Alternative goals could be to build strong vocational skills or robust epistemological understanding of at least two discipline areas. (Readers will no doubt be aware that the latter is a definition of success that we would favour.) Yet another possibility is to foreground the success of the system in terms of the extent to which qualifications are valued and trusted by employers and tertiary education institutions. This would tend to promote vocational skills and preparation for further study, but might or might not promote courses that build epistemological understanding. Epistemological insights and ongoing learning skills and dispositions could be co-developed, but only if critical thinking and mastery of knowledge-creation processes were explicitly valued by employers and tertiary institutions.

Unfortunately, the most facile of these success definitions—the counting of credits and qualifications—is also the easiest to measure, and hence to set targets for. The most sophisticated—the building of strong epistemological understanding—is the most difficult and the least well understood. Epistemological competence is unlikely to register across the policy agenda any time soon, even though it is implicit in many of the stated aims of curriculum subjects (e.g., to educate for informed citizenship). All is not lost however. Systems often evolve from the bottom up. We are aware of instances of epistemological shifts in senior secondary subjects that have been driven by informed subject association groups operating within the current curriculum structure. The shift to an emphasis on historical thinking is one such example, as discussed in earlier chapters. The shift to foreground the building of robust statistical reasoning, before introducing the more traditional statistical computation, is another example. The latter case is particularly instructive of what can be achieved when disciplinary experts from outside the school sector stand behind the education specialists to jointly lobby for change, guided by a clear sense of the intellectual contribution the specific subject area might make to most students' future lives (Hipkins, 2014).

Leadership at the policy–practice intersection

The challenges we've just outlined segue inevitably into a consideration of leadership. Even if the policy system itself was successful in resetting definitions of success, who should take the lead in communicating the implications of this shift, both within the education sector and to the wider public? A related question concerns how we might achieve stronger *curriculum* leadership in the NCEA space. At the moment the potential for curriculum leadership is widely distributed.

- The Ministry of Education owns the school curriculum and all the associated policy work.
- The New Zealand Qualifications Authority enacts all the processes that enable NCEA assessments to happen, and maintains the policies associated with assessment in action.
- Every school has autonomy to build a local curriculum, based on *NZC*, to meet the learning needs of all their students. The way

the school's senior leaders go about supporting this vital curriculum-building work is critical to its comparative success.

- The Education Review Office has responsibility for evaluating how well each school does build and deliver a local curriculum that meets the learning needs of all their students.
- Individual universities and professional learning consortia have autonomy over the teacher education programmes they offer.
- Some subject associations provide bold curriculum leadership to their members, but others are more invested in supporting the status quo.

We think that leadership which is presumed to be everywhere can too easily end up actually being nowhere. In our experience of NCEA to date, this division of responsibilities has impeded the more widespread development of the types of cutting edge practice that we sought out as illustrations of NCEA's potential (Part 3). What could, and should, we do about this? In complexity terms, we might say that local interactions between different parts of the system should be more deliberately supported and leveraged to ensure rapid-fire experimentation and spreading of successful innovation across the system as a whole. We wonder if the collaborative process we followed in writing this book could work for the ongoing evolution of NCEA. None of us held all the pieces needed to do this work. None of us could have written the book by ourselves. As we discussed issues and challenges over and over again, new ideas emerged in the spaces between our different areas of expertise/insight/practical experiences. Could a similar model of collaboration work for NCEA's next steps? What would it look like? Who would need to be involved? How would we ensure variety in the spaces between and that some voices did not dominate as has tended to happen in the past? As the curriculum policy-holder, the Ministry of Education is arguably the agency that should take a proactive leadership role in setting up these types of opportunities. Complex systems theory would also say that the more diverse these opportunities can be, the better the chances of fostering the emergence of real and sustainable change.

How could the various government agencies and representative leadership groups work together in ways that ensure matters of curriculum and knowledge leadership are taken as serious inquiry questions (i.e., not just technical matters)? To give one specific example, we wonder who might ensure that individual NCEA subject moderators, who are employed by NZQA, have regular opportunities to engage in deep curriculum conversation with a range of other leaders who have a holistic understanding of *NZC* and/or deep education expertise in their subject area (as in the case of the statistics educators or the history educators).

Might it be possible to provide more support for subject associations? Within the status quo, it seems to us that smaller groups, such as the languages teachers, are able to be more successful in supporting/brokering real change. For some of the larger subject associations, we wonder if additional support for the subject leaders (who are usually volunteers) could help them to work with factions within their membership who want to preserve the status quo. At the same time these volunteer leaders need to ensure that teachers feel they have a voice and are appreciated. Support as they walk this particular leadership tightrope could well make a difference.

How can policy and best-practice work led by the various agencies leverage the opportunity to make more effective use of challenging input from the visionary teachers and school leaders we know are out there? How might these innovators be better supported so that they don't, by default, carry the burden of leading the curriculum/assessment system into the future? Whoever takes up this challenge will need to have the mandate to proactively seek out, critique, and spread best-practice ideas. The place of critique is crucial here, and we don't just mean criticism—though criticism is certainly needed when the loudest voices are free to proclaim the virtues of their practice without the balance of strong counter-narratives being heard. Informed and robust critique is needed to pinpoint the critical aspects of innovation, and to lead carefully nuanced conversations about the practical realities of spreading good ideas into the diverse contexts of secondary schools embedded in very different communities.

To take just one example of a complex and nuanced challenge that is particularly tricky to address, we return briefly to the issue of parity of esteem for different types of learning. This design feature, which sits at the heart of NCEA, is integral to the ability of the system to be responsive to a wide range of learning needs. However it is also central to the misuse of NCEA's flexibility when credit accumulation is seen as the most important goal of learning and indication of success. It would be wrong to take away NCEA's flexibility to be responsive to the learning needs of the widest possible range of students, so the leadership challenge lies in showing how to use this flexibility wisely and well. For this to happen, it will be necessary to ensure that all teachers have the epistemic strengths in their own subject areas. In turn, this points to the final set of challenges we address—how to initiate and sustain effective teacher professional learning.

Implications for the teaching profession

Teacher expertise will be of paramount importance to maximising the probability that successful practice will evolve. Perhaps the most effective and the least politically risky approach to ongoing adaptation of the system is for the government agencies, and the Ministry of Education in particular, to press for a better trained and more knowledgeable teacher workforce. In practical terms this could involve resourcing the universities to design and implement courses that educate the best available candidates in ways that deepen their epistemological knowledge while building their confidence and abilities to innovate within a complex learning system such as NCEA. We think that recent initiatives to establish master's degrees in teaching are a step in the right direction. However, this is an opportunity now open only to comparatively few new teachers because these courses are highly selective in their intake. We must also consider ways in which the majority of new teachers who undertake more traditional training, as well as in-service teachers, can be encouraged and supported to improve their epistemological sophistication and to engage in innovative practice.

Again it will come as no surprise that we see the necessity to be more proactive in supporting all teachers to more flexibly and fluently join the dots between their curriculum and assessment understandings and practice. Currently, too much time and effort is vested in trying to pin down the sense of where a standard resides because there is insufficient trust in teacher judgements. As we saw in Part 2, recourse to more and more detailed semantics will almost certainly have the opposite effect to that intended—the more finely the standard is specified, the more it will slip away in the welter of words. Teachers who feel they must wrestle with semantics will try to second-guess examiners, or moderators, or both. And if these officials take their own interpretation as gospel, there will be high-stakes rewards for second-guessing correctly. In systems terms we could say that the feedback operating at multiple levels within the system is having an escalating negative impact that drives adaptive change in what we see as an undesirable direction. The compounding results will include: higher workloads; greater stress levels; and greater chances that unjust or unhelpful decisions will be made, which in turn will undermine public confidence in NCEA overall. Unjust decisions could include assessing student work on nit-picking detail rather than on its holistic strengths, while unwise decisions might include interpreting a standard in such a narrow frame that the actual intent of the relevant part of the curriculum disappears from the assessment focus altogether. Negative systems dynamics like these do no good for anyone—officials, teachers, learners, potential employers, and so on.

What is the alternative? This question takes us back to the vision we sketched at the start of this chapter. In short, any professional learning opportunities and resources should support teachers in ways that take full cognisance of their role as the curriculum builders for their students. NCEA's flexibility can't be used to its full potential unless and until every teacher of senior secondary students is a confident curriculum builder with a strong epistemological base on which to draw. This implies that every teacher needs to be, to echo *NZC*'s vision, a "confident, connected, actively involved, lifelong learner" themselves. The system as a whole needs to explore what it might take to make this happen. The more diverse the range of policy and practice responses, the more likely it will be that emergent change will occur at the nexus of *NZC* and NCEA. Such change is needed to ensure ongoing responsiveness in the system so that students' learning needs continue to be met appropriately in rapidly changing times. This is the great promise of both *NZC* and NCEA, and already some great things have been achieved. The massive shifts in policy over the last couple of decades, though, are just the beginning. The ongoing journey must now involve adaptive change to the knowledge and culture of educators.

References

Abbiss, J. (2011). Social sciences in the New Zealand curriculum: Mixed messages. *Curriculum Matters, 7*, 118–137.

Alison, J. (2005). *Teachers talk about NCEA: Research report on focus groups with secondary teachers.* Retrieved from http://www.ppta.org.nz/2013-12-03-23-14-37/publications/doc_view/32-teachers-talk-about-ncea-summary-version

Alison, J. (2007). *Mind the gap! Policy change in practice: School qualifications reform in New Zealand, 1980–2002.* Unpublished doctoral thesis, Massey University, Palmerston North.

Alison, J. (2008). The NCEA and how we got there: The role of PPTA in school qualifications reform 1980–2002. *New Zealand Journal of Teachers' Work, 5*(2), 119–138.

Apple, M. (1979). *Ideology and curriculum.* London, United Kingdom: Routledge. http://dx.doi.org/10.4324/9780203241219

Beare, H., & Slaughter, R. (1993). *Education for the twenty-first century.* London, United Kingdom: Routledge.

Biesta, G. (2014). Pragmatising the curriculum: Bringing knowledge back into the curriculum conversation, but via pragmatism. *The Curriculum Journal, 25*(1), 29–49. http://dx.doi.org/10.1080/09585176.2013.874954

Bolstad, R., & Gilbert, J. (2008). *Disciplining and drafting, or 21st century learning?: Rethinking the New Zealand senior secondary curriculum for the future.* Wellington: NZCER Press.

Boyd, S., & Hipkins, R. (2015). *Getting runs on the board: Stories of successful practice from two years of the Sport in Education initiative.* Retrieved from http://www.sportnz.org.nz/assets/Uploads/attachments/managing-sport/sport-in-education/SiE-Getting-Runs-on-the-Board.pdf

Coddington, D. (2005). Questions to ministers: National Certificate of Educational Achievement—results. *New Zealand Parliamentary Debates, 623*, 18,575.

Coddington, D. (2011, July). Blowing the whistle. *North & South, 304*, 50–56.

Duschl, R., & Grandy, R. (2013). Two views about explicitly teaching nature of science. *Science & Education, 22*, 2109–2139. http://dx.doi.org/10.1007/s11191-012-9539-4

East, M. (2014). Working for positive outcomes? The standards–curriculum alignment for learning languages, and its reception by teachers. *Assessment Matters, 6,* 65–85.

East, M., & Scott, A. (2011). Working for positive washback: The potential and challenge of the standards–curriculum alignment project for learning languages. *Assessment Matters, 3,* 93–115.

Editorial: Performance pay for teachers has caveats. (2012, 24 March). *NZ Listener.* Retrieved from http://www.listener.co.nz/commentary/features/editorial-performance-pay-for-teachers-has-caveats/#print

Education Review Office. (2015). *Wellbeing for young people's success at secondary school.* Wellington: Author. Retrieved from http://www.ero.govt.nz/National-Reports/Wellbeing-for-Young-People-s-Success-at-Secondary-School-February-2015

Elley, W., Hall, C., & Marsh, R. (2004). Rescuing NCEA: Some possible ways forward. *New Zealand Annual Review of Education, 14,* 5–25.

Emerson, L., Kilpin, K., & Feekery, A. (2014). Starting the conversation: Student transition from secondary to academic literacy. *Curriculum Matters, 10,* 94–114.

Emerson, L., Kilpin, K., & Feekery, A. (2015). Let's talk about literacy: Preparing students for the transition to tertiary learning. *set: Research Information for Teachers, 1,* 3–8. http://dx.doi.org/10.18296/set.0002

Fitzpatrick, K. (2011). Trapped in the physical: Maori and Pasifika achievement in HPE. *Asia-Pacific Journal of Health, Sport and Physical Education, 2*(3–4), 35–51. http://dx.doi.org/10.1080/18377122.2011.9730358

Fountain, G. (2012). *Caught in-between: The impact of different forms of mandated national assessment for qualifications on teacher decision-making in year 12 history in New Zealand, 1986–2005.* Unpublished master's thesis, Victoria University of Wellington.

Garvey Berger, J., & Johnston, K. (2015). *Simple habits for complex times: Powerful practices for leaders.* Redwood, CA: Stanford University Press.

Gilbert, J. (2005). *Catching the knowledge wave: The knowledge society and the future of education.* Wellington: NZCER Press.

Goodson, I. (1987). *School subjects and curriculum change: Studies in curriculum history.* London: Falmer Press.

Haque, B. (2015). *Changing our secondary schools.* Wellington: NZCER Press.

Hart, S. (2014). *Investigating socio-critical discourses in assessment of senior physical education in New Zealand.* Unpublished masters thesis, University of Waikato, Hamilton. Retrieved from http://researchcommons.waikato.ac.nz/handle/10289/8984

Hipkins, R. (1997). Should contexts be used in science examinations? A critical review of current practice. *New Zealand Science Teacher, 86,* 31–35.

Hipkins, R. (2008). The something more in key competencies. *set: Research Information for Teachers, 3,* 35–37.

Hipkins, R. (2010a). *The evolving NCEA.* Wellington: New Zealand Council for Educational Research. Retrieved from http://www.nzcer.org.nz/research/publications/evolving-ncea

Hipkins, R. (2010b). Learning through moderation: Minding our language. *set: Research Information for Teachers, 1,* 18–19.

Hipkins, R. (2012). Assessment of naturally occurring evidence of literacy. *Assessment Matters, 4,* 95–109.

Hipkins, R. (2013). *NCEA one decade on.* Wellington: New Zealand Council for Educational Research. Retrieved from http://www.nzcer.org.nz/research/publications/ncea-one-decade

Hipkins, R. (2014). *Doing research that matters: A success story from statistics education.* Wellington: Teaching and Learning Research Initiative. Retrieved from http://www.tlri.org.nz/tlri-research/research-completed/cross-sector/doing-research-matters-success-story-statistics

Hipkins, R., & Arcus, C. (1997). Teaching science in context: Challenges and choices. In B. Bell & R. Baker (Eds.), *Developing the science curriculum in Aotearoa New Zealand* (pp. 101–113). Auckland: Addison Wesley Longman.

Hipkins, R., & Boyd, S. (2011). The recursive elaboration of key competencies as agents of curriculum change. *Curriculum Matters, 7,* 70–86.

Hipkins, R., & Bull, A. (2015). Science capabilities for a functional understanding of the nature of science. *Curriculum Matters, 11,* 117–133. http://dx.doi.org/10.18296/cm.0007

Hipkins, R., Conner, L., & Neill, A. (2006). *Shifting balances 2: The impact of NCEA implementation on the teaching of geography and home economics.* Wellington: Ministry of Education. Retrieved from http://www.educationcounts.govt.nz/publications/schooling/5343

Hipkins, R., & Cowie, B. (2014). Learning to learn, lifewide and lifelong learning: Reflections on the New Zealand experience. In R. Deakin-Crick, C. Stringher & K. Ren (Eds.), *Learning to learn: Perspectives from theory and practice* (pp. 303–320). London, United Kingdom: Routledge.

Hipkins, R., & Neill, A. (2006). *Shifting balances: The impact of level 1 NCEA on the teaching of mathematics and science*. Wellington: New Zealand Council for Educational Research. Retrieved from http://www.educationcounts.govt.nz/publications/schooling/5339

Hipkins, R., & Spiller, L. (2012). *NCEA and curriculum innovation: Learning from change in three schools*. Wellington: New Zealand Council for Educational Research. Retrieved from http://www.nzcer.org.nz/system/files/NCEA%20and%20Curriculum%20Innovation%20final_1.pdf

Hipkins, R., Vaughan, K., Beals, F., & Ferral, H. (2004). *Learning curves: Meeting student learning needs in an evolving qualifications regime: Shared pathways and multiple tracks: A second report*. Wellington: New Zealand Council for Educational Research. Retrieved from http://www.nzcer.org.nz/research/publications/learning-curves-meeting-student-learning-needs-evolving-qualifications-regime-

Hipkins, R., Vaughan, K., Beals, F., Ferral, H., & Gardiner, B. (2005). *Shaping our futures: Meeting secondary students' learning needs in a time of evolving qualifications*. Wellington: New Zealand Council for Educational Research. Retrieved from http://www.nzcer.org.nz/research/publications/shaping-our-futures-meeting-secondary-students-learning-needs-time-evolving-qu

Hood, D. (2015). *The rhetoric and the reality: New Zealand schools and schooling in the 21st century*. Masterton: Fraser Books.

Hood, D. (1998). *Our secondary schools don't work anymore: Why and how New Zealand schools must change for the 21st century*. Auckland: Profile Books.

Keown, P., Parker, L., & Tiakiwai, S. (2005). *Values in the New Zealand curriculum: A literature review on values in the curriculum: Report for the Ministry of Education*. Hamilton: Wilf Malcolm Institute of Educational Research, The University of Waikato. Retrieved from http://nzcurriculum.tki.org.nz/Archives/Curriculum-project-archives/References#vision

Lederman, N., & Lederman, J. (2014). Research on teaching and learning of nature of science. In N. Lederman & S. Abell (Eds.), *Handbook of research on science education* (vol. 2) (pp. 600–620). New York & London: Routledge.

McKinley, E., Madjar, I., van der Merwe, A., Smith, S., Sutherland, S., & Yuan, J. (2009). *Targets and talk: Evaluation of an evidence-based academic counselling programme*. Auckland: Starpath Project, The University of Auckland. Retrieved from http://www.education.auckland.ac.nz/en/about/research/starpath-home/starpath-research/targets-and-talk.html

Maddox, B. (2014). Globalising assessment: An ethnography of literacy assessment, camels and fast food in the Mongolian Gobi. *Comparative Education, 50*(4), 474–489. http://dx.doi.org/10.1080/03050068.2013.871440

Madjar, I., & McKinley, E. (2011). *Understanding NCEA: A relatively short and very useful guide for secondary school students and their parents.* Wellington: NZCER Press.

Madjar, I., McKinley, E., Jensen, S., & Van Der Merwe, A. (2009). *Towards university: Navigating NCEA course choices in low-mid decile schools.* Auckland: University of Auckland, Starpath Project. Retrieved from https://cdn.auckland.ac.nz/assets/education/about/research/docs/starpath/Towards-university-Navigating-NCEA-course-choices-in-low-mid-decile-schools.pdf

Mallard, T. (2004, April). *Education for the changing world.* Address given to the PPTA Charting the Future Conference, Wellington. Retrieved from http://www.beehive.govt.nz/speech/education-changing-world

Martin, D. (2005). *Report on the performance of the New Zealand Qualifications Authority in the delivery of secondary school qualifications.* Wellington: State Services Commission. Retrieved from http://www.ssc.govt.nz/review-nzqa-part-two

Meyer, L., McClure, J., Walkey, F., McKenzie, L., & Weir, K. (2006). *The impact of NCEA on student motivation.* [Report to Ministry of Education]. Wellington: Victoria University of Wellington. Retrieved from https://www.educationcounts.govt.nz/publications/schooling/29252

Minister of Education. (2007, 6 November). *Letter accompanying release of New Zealand curriculum.* Wellington: Ministry of Education.

Ministry of Education. (n.d.-a). *What is moderation?* Retrieved from http://assessment.tki.org.nz/Moderation/Moderation-professional-learning-modules/What-is-moderation/Definition

Ministry of Education. (n.d.-b). *Level 2 physical education assessment resources.* Retrieved from http://ncea.tki.org.nz/Resources-for-Internally-Assessed-Achievement-Standards/Health-and-physical-education/Physical-education/Level-2-Physical-education

Ministry of Education. (1993a). *New Zealand curriculum framework.* Wellington: Learning Media.

Ministry of Education. (1993b). *Science in the New Zealand curriculum.* Wellington: Learning Media.

Ministry of Education. (1996). *Biology* in the *New Zealand curriculum*. Wellington: Learning Media.

Ministry of Education. (2007). *The New Zealand curriculum*. Wellington: Learning Media.

Morris, J. (2008). NCEA: An ill-planned recipe for academic anorexia. Retrieved from https://web.archive.org/web/20081014123308/http://ags.school.nz/content/about/headmasters_articles_speeches/ncea_an_ill_planned_recipe_for_academic_anorexia.html

Moses, R. (2005, 16 February). Silent shame is scholarship debacle. *The Dominion Post*.

Muller, J. (2012). *Every picture tells a story: Epistemological access and knowledge*. Paper presented at the Knowledge and Curriculum Symposium, University of Cape Town, South Africa.

Nash R. (2005). A change of direction for NCEA: On re-marking, scaling and norm-referencing. *New Zealand Journal of Teachers' Work*, 2(2), 100–106.

Neill, A. (2012). Developing statistical numeracy in primary schools. *set: Research Information for Teachers, 1*, 9–16.

New Zealand Government. (2012). *Delivering better public services: Boosting skills and employment by increasing educational achievement for young people*. Wellington: Author. Retrieved from http://www.education.govt.nz/assets/Documents/Ministry/BPS/BPSYoungPeopleWEB.pdf

New Zealand Qualifications Authority. (n.d.). *Authenticity*. Retrieved from http://www.nzqa.govt.nz/providers-partners/assessment-and-moderation/assessment-of-standards/generic-resources/authenticity/

New Zealand Qualifications Authority. (2002). *Biology, 2002 level 1: 1.6 Describe the functioning of human digestive and skeletomuscular systems* [Examination]. Wellington: Author. Retrieved from http://www.nzqa.govt.nz/nqfdocs/ncea-resource/exams/2002/90166-exm-02.pdf.

New Zealand Qualifications Authority. (2004). *The role of national qualifications systems in promoting lifelong learning: Background report for New Zealand*. [Report to OECD]. Wellington: Author. Retrieved from http://www.oecd.org/newzealand/33774156.pdf

New Zealand Qualifications Authority. (2006). *Secondary qualifications statistics 2005*. Wellington: Author.

New Zealand Qualifications Authority. (2007). Ongoing improvements to NCEA. Retrieved from https://web.archive.org/web/20081014100459/http://www.nzqa.govt.nz/news/info/ncea-improve-bkgrnder.pdf

New Zealand Qualifications Authority. (2010–2015). *Secondary school statistics*. Retrieved from http://www.nzqa.govt.nz/studying-in-new-zealand/secondary-school-and-ncea/find-information-about-a-school/secondary-school-statistics/

New Zealand Qualifications Authority. (2014). *Annual report on NCEA and New Zealand scholarship data and statistics 2013*. Wellington: Author. Retrieved from http://www.nzqa.govt.nz/assets/About-us/Publications/stats-reports/ncea-annualreport-2013.pdf

New Zealand Qualifications Authority. (2015a). *External moderation*. Retrieved from http://web.archive.org/web/20150317135513/http://www.nzqa.govt.nz/providers-partners/assessment-and-moderation/managing-national-assessment-in-schools/secondary-moderation/external-moderation/

New Zealand Qualifications Authority. (2015b). *Assessment (including examination) rules for schools with consent to assess 2015*. Retrieved from https://web.archive.org/web/20150421130338/http://www.nzqa.govt.nz/about-us/our-role/legislation/nzqa-rules/assessment-including-examination-rules-2015/6/5/

New Zealand Qualifications Authority. (2015c). *Annual report on NCEA and New Zealand Scholarship data and statistics (2014)*. Retrieved from http://www.nzqa.govt.nz/studying-in-new-zealand/secondary-school-and-ncea/find-information-about-a-school/secondary-school-statistics/

New Zealand Transport Agency. (n.d.). *Education portal*. Retrieved from http://education.nzta.govt.nz/

OECD. (2005). *The definition and selection of key competencies: Executive summary*. Retrieved from www.pisa.oecd.org/dataoecd/47/61/35070367.pdf

O'Neill, A., Clark, J., & Openshaw, R. (2004). Mapping the field: An introduction to curriculum politics on Aotearoa/New Zealand. In A. O'Neill, J. Clark, and R. Openshaw (Eds), *Reshaping culture, knowledge and learning? Policy and content in the New Zealand curriculum framework* (pp. 25–45). Palmerston North: Dunmore Press.

Openshaw, R. (2003). Preparing for Picot: Revisiting the "neoliberal" educational reforms. *New Zealand Journal of Educational Studies*, *38*(2), 135–150.

Openshaw, R. (2009). *Reforming New Zealand secondary education: The Picot report and the road to radical reform*. New York, NY: Palgrave Macmillan. http://dx.doi.org/10.1057/9780230100701

Osborne, J. (2014). Teaching scientific practices: Meeting the challenge of change. *Journal of Science Teacher Education, 25*, 177–196. http://dx.doi.org/10.1007/s10972-014-9384-1

Perkins, D. (2014). *Future wise: Educating our children for a changing world.* San Francisco, CA: Jossey-Bass.

Post Primary Teachers' Association (PPTA). (2007). *The NCEA: Nothing endures but change…* Retrieved from http://www.ppta.org.nz/membershipforms/doc_view/134-the-ncea-nothing-endures-but-change

Rennie, L., & Parker, L. (1996). Placing physics problems in real-life contexts: Students' reactions and performance. *The Australian Science Teachers' Journal, 41*(1), 55–59.

Scholarship Reference Group. (2005). *Report of the Scholarship Reference Group: A report prepared for the Associate Minister of Education.* Wellington: Ministry of Education.

Scott, A., & East, M. (2009). The standards review for learning languages: How come and where to? *The New Zealand Language Teacher, 35*, 28–32.

Sheehan, M. (2011). A question of bias? The Education and Science Select Committee inquiry into the setting of the 2004 New Zealand history examination. *History of Education Review, 40*(2), 176–188. http://dx.doi.org/10.1108/08198691111177244

Sheehan, M. (2013). *"Better to do than receive": Learning to think historically through internally assessed course work.* Retrieved from http://www.tlri.org.nz/sites/default/files/projects/Sheehan_Summary%20web%20ready%20%28v6%29.pdf

Sheehan, M. (2014). "A degree of latitude": Thinking historically and making historical judgements about internally assessed NCEA course work. *set: Research Information for Teachers, 2*, 18–23.

Shute, V., & Ventura, M. (2013). *Stealth assessment: Measuring and supporting learning in video games.* Cambridge, MA: The MIT Press.

Sinnema, C. (2011). *Monitoring and evaluating curriculum implementation: Final evaluation report on the implementation of the New Zealand curriculum 2008–2009.* Wellington: Ministry of Education. Retrieved from https://www.educationcounts.govt.nz/publications/curriculum/monitoring-and-evaluating-curriculum-implementation-final-evaluation-report-on-the-implementation-of-the-new-zealand-curriculum-20082009/executive-summary

Statement of Hon M L Wellington for the New Zealand Times. (1984, March 18). *New Zealand Times.*

Thomas, G., Johnston, M., & Ward, J. (2015). *Aligning measures of adult literacy and numeracy*. Wellington: Tertiary Education Commission. Retrieved from http://www.tec.govt.nz/Tertiary-Sector/Tertiary-Education-Strategy/TEC-commissioned-research-on-Tertiary-Education-Strategy-priorities/

Vaughan, K., & Cameron, M. (2011). *A guide to good practice in ITO structures and systems for on-job assessment*. Wellington: Industry Training Federation. Retrieved from http://www.nzcer.org.nz/research/publications/guide-good-practice-ito-structures-and-systems-job-assessment

Ward, J., & Thomas, G. (2015). *National standards: School sample monitoring and evaluation project, 2010–2013*. Retrieved from https://www.educationcounts.govt.nz/__data/assets/pdf_file/0018/161433/NSSSME-2010-2013.pdf

Wilson, A., & McNaughton, S. (2014). Using selected NCEA standards to profile senior students' subject-area literacy. *set: Research Information for Teachers, 2*, 61–68.

Wood, B., & Sheehan, M. (2012). Dislodging knowledge? The New Zealand curriculum in the 21st century. *Pacific-Asian Education, 24*(1), 17–30.

Wylie, C. (2012). *Vital connections*. Wellington: NZCER Press.

Wylie, C., & Bonne, L. (2016). *Secondary schools in 2015*. Wellington: New Zealand Council for Education Research. http://dx.doi.org/10.18296/rep.0001

Wylie, C., & Hodgen, E. (2011). *Forming adulthood: Past, present and future in the experiences and views of the competent learners @ 20*. Wellington: Ministry of Education. Retrieved from http://thehub.superu.govt.nz/publication/forming-adulthood-past-present-and-future-experience-and-views-competent-learners-20-pdf

Wylie, C., Hodgen, E., Hipkins, R., & Vaughan, K. (2008). *Competent learners on the edge of adulthood: A summary of key findings from the Competent Learners @ 16 project*. Wellington: Ministry of Education. Retrieved from https://www.educationcounts.govt.nz/publications/ECE/2567/35076/35079

Young, M. (2008). *Bringing knowledge back in*. London, United Kingdom: Routledge.

Young, M., & Lambert, D. (Eds). (2014). *Knowledge and the future school: Curriculum and social justice*. London, United Kingdom: Bloomsbury.

Zohar, A., & Ben David, A. (2008). Explicit teaching of meta-strategic knowledge in authentic classroom contexts. *Metacognition & Learning, 3*, 59–82. http://dx.doi.org/10.1007/s11409-007-9019-4

The authors

Dr Rosemary Hipkins is a chief researcher at the New Zealand Council for Educational Research. She began her career as a science and biology teacher and worked for some years in teacher education before moving to NZCER. Rose has led research projects related to both curriculum and assessment innovation in New Zealand and has a specific interest in dynamic interrelationships between curriculum and assessment. She has been tracking the implementation of NCEA since its inception and has published a number of research reports on this topic.

Dr Michael Johnston is a senior lecturer in the School of Education at Victoria University of Wellington. His principal expertise is in cognitive psychology and educational assessment. Previously, he worked at the New Zealand Qualifications Authority where he led psychometric and statistical work informing policy reforms to NCEA, and at the Ministry of Education, developing a tool to assist primary teachers to make valid and reliable judgements against the National Standards in reading, writing, and mathematics. He is a current member of technical advisory groups for both agencies.

Dr Mark Sheehan is the Secondary Programme Director in the Victoria University of New Zealand Faculty of Education. He has been involved in education matters for over 40 years as a teacher, lecturer, textbook writer, researcher, museum educator, and curriculum designer. Mark's research interests include the place of knowledge/assessment in the secondary curriculum, the development of threshold experiences in teacher education, critical/historical thinking, and the role of history in reconciliation (especially in regards to memory, remembrance, and indigenous epistemologies).

Index

academic subjects *see* disciplinary (traditional) subjects
accountability of teachers 39, 123, 125, 126–27, 130, 131, 132, 133
achievement-based assessment
    differences from unit standards 55–56
    dual nature of tasks assessed 53
    as learning for standards-based assessment 51–54
    quantitative *versus* qualitative achievement differences 52–53, 54, 55, 60
    teachers' personal recollections 49–51, 135
achievement criteria 8, 50–51, 112
    examples 52–53, 73
achievement objectives, New Zealand Curriculum 26, 28, 29
achievement standards, NCEA 7, 8, 26
    see also profiles of expected performance (PEPs)
    aligning with *New Zealand Curriculum* 151–63, 165, 167, 168
    comparison of pass rates for internal and external assessment 44–45
    curriculum concerns 75–77
    curriculum integration 151–53
    as curriculum units 46, 144, 147, 153, 182, 197
    development 61, 66, 67, 69–75, 109, 110, 183
    differences from unit standards 68, 77, 78–79, 111
    disciplinary elements of curriculum 71, 75–77, 80, 154
    double dipping, unit and achievement standards 79–80
    example 75–77
    external assessment 7, 41, 68, 70, 77–78, 87, 114–16, 159, 196–97, 206
    internal assessment 7, 33–34, 41–43, 65, 70, 75–77, 196, 206
    moderation 131–32
    national consistency 33, 44, 48, 52, 65, 106, 110, 124, 132
    national expectation of skills and knowledge 65
    percentages of students' results 41, 42
    as positive change influence 165–68
    response to concerns of progressive educators 77–80
    teachers' personal recollections 68–72
Alison, Judie 31
ART (Achievement, Retention, Transition) initiative 175–76
assessment
    see also achievement standards, NCEA; external assessment; internal assessment; norm-referenced assessment model; standards-referenced assessment model; variability in assessment and curriculum 5, 15, 18, 21–30, 46–47, 151–63, 165, 167, 168, 182, 194–98, 205–07
    essential elements 102–07
    integrated with coursework 206
    over-assessment 183, 184, 186, 206
    post-war years 12

PPTA views 16–17
pressures in lead-up to NCEA 18–20
reforms of 1980s 17, 19–20
skipping of assessments by students 181, 189, 194, 206
small components 4
assessment contexts 134–35, 145
external assessment 138–39
integration of assessments in rich contexts 143–44
internal assessment 140–41
tasks that engage students emotionally 141–43
teachers' personal recollections 135
variable impacts on different groups of students 135–37, 138
assessment judgements of teachers 48, 61, 84, 86, 110
see also variability in assessment
achievement standards 73–75, 123–24
achievement-based assessment 50, 51–52, 54
best-practice workshops 129
literacy and numeracy standards 174
low-decile versus high-decile schools 44–45
moderation 42, 122, 123–26, 127, 130–32
reliability 42, 122
unit standards 55, 61
attitudes to learning needed for success 175
Auckland Grammar 39, 97
authenticity challenges during assessment 168–71

Better Public Service targets 211, 212
boys' schools, high-decile 28, 38–39, 69, 78, 97, 98, 102–03, 106–07
Brash, Don 95
Burrell, Terry 138–39
Bursary 12, 22, 23, 66, 79, 82, 87, 90, 112, 113, 117, 118, 208
internal assessment 110
recollections of marking panel member and assessor 85–86, 94–95

Cambridge High School 43
Cambridge International Examinations 97, 98, 103n.1
check marking 125, 126, 132
check moderation 125, 126–27
citizenship capabilities 158–59, 167
Coddington, Deborah 99
Colbert, Kate 49–50, 55
Committee of Inquiry into Curriculum, Assessment and Qualifications (CICAQ) 17, 54, 64
Learning and Achieving report 49
communicative approach to teaching and learning 165–66, 167
community engagement 28
competencies, *New Zealand Curriculum* 27, 145, 152
Competent Learners study 175, 176, 184–85, 187
competition
global marketplace 11, 14, 15
between schools 18
between students 39, 40, 78–79, 102, 103–05, 106, 107
complex systems 201–03, 207–09, 210, 214

comprehensive understanding 157
constructivism 134
contexts *see* assessment contexts;
    learning contexts
course design 46, 65, 199
    assessment integrated with
    coursework 206–07
    bringing NCEA and *New Zealand
    Curriculum* together 153–54,
    162–63, 165, 168
    coherence and building capabilities
    for the future 157–60, 177
    coherent courses 154–57, 186
    combinations of learning
    needs 178, 179
    contextual and conceptual
    integration 160–62, 171–72
    Hobsonville Point secondary
    school 194–98
    science subjects 155–60
credits, NCEA 7, 21, 43, 45, 78,
    79–80, 110–11, 112, 194, 196,
    206, 213
    combination of standards 8–9,
    187–88, 209
    credit-farming and harvesting 43,
    184–86, 215
Creech, Wyatt 67, 68
critical thinking 6, 29, 53, 174, 178
Crooks, Terry 100
curriculum
    see also course design; *New Zealand
    Curriculum (NZC)*
    and assessment 5, 15, 18, 21–30,
    46–47, 151–63, 165, 167, 168, 182,
    194–98, 205–07
    design 26–27, 28, 152, 163, 186,
    194–98
    outcomes-based 22–23, 24, 25,
    28, 29, 56, 57–61, 75–76, 134,
    155, 183–84

planned review, 1987 17
reforms of 1990s 22–23, 46,
    54–55
responses to social changes 26–28
senior secondary curriculum before
    NZC 22–25, 183
senior secondary curriculum in
    NZC 25–26
whare tapa whā metaphor 24
cut scores 116–17

decile system 39
    achievement differential 40,
    44–45, 113
    high-decile schools 28, 38–39, 69,
    78, 97, 98, 102–03, 106–07, 123
    research on literacy in low-decile
    schools 174
    standards used at high- and low-
    decile schools 78–79
*Delivering Better Public Services:
    Boosting Skills and Employment
    …* 175
Department of Education 16, 18, 19,
    48, 49, 54, 69
    see also Ministry of Education
deregulation 14
design, as curriculum subject 24, 25
differential item functioning
    (DIF) 138
disciplinary (traditional) subjects 71,
    75–77, 118, 119–20, 147–48, 160,
    199
    coherence within 154–56
    labelling of students 121, 191, 192
    theoretical learning 191
    unsuitability of unit
    standards 58–62, 64, 67, 77–78
    value and status 80, 99, 121, 189,
    190

washback effect of approved UE subjects 171–73
distributed nature of thinking 170
diversity
    cultural 26, 28
    in New Zealand society 11, 14, 16, 28

East, Martin 167–68
economy, New Zealand
    change as context for educational change 13–15
    education policy responses to changes 16–18, 63
post-war years 12
Education and Science Select Committee, 2005 95, 96
Education Review Office (ERO) 43, 96, 196, 214
"elite" schools 28, 38–39, 69, 78, 97, 98, 102–03, 106–07
Elley, Warwick 64–65, 87–88
Emerson, Lisa 177–79
employment-based (vocational) education
    employment-oriented learning 6, 12, 21, 22, 57, 191
    labelling of students 121, 191–92
    unit standard assessment 57–58, 61, 65, 77, 80, 188, 192
endorsement of certificates and courses 6, 8, 9, 110–13, 121, 185, 187, 196
environmental education (education for sustainability) 14, 24, 25
epistemology 10, 63, 76, 79, 92, 104, 105–06, 113, 154, 192, 206–07, 209, 212, 213
equity 106

and assessment contexts 136–37, 138, 139, 140
and internal assessment 37–41
ethical thinking 192
evidence of achievement
    authenticity 168–71
    everyday work as evidence 206, 207
    evidence statements, NCEA 73–74
    innovative tasks 34
    naturally occurring evidence 70, 174
    Scholarship 37, 105
    unit standards 59
    variety of tasks and activities 209
external assessment 4, 42–43
    see also variability in assessment
    achievement standards, NCEA 7, 41, 68, 70, 78, 87, 114–16, 159, 196–97, 206
    ad course endorsement 9
    comparison of pass rates for internal and external assessment 44–45
    quasi-norms 64
    return of marked examination scripts to students 83, 85–86
    use of contexts 138–39
external assessment: examinations 4, 19, 39, 40, 41–42, 45, 69–70, 82–83
    see also School Certificate; individual examinations, e.g. Bursary
    cut scores 116–17
    examination prescriptions as de facto curriculum 22, 183
    grade-score marking 114, 116, 117, 121
    scaling 12, 38, 82–83, 89–91, 117

students' perspective 36–38
sufficiency marking 114–16

Farrant, Kirsty 158–60
feminism 16
Fitzpatrick, Katie 191, 192
Fountain, Gregor 70–71, 89–90, 97–98, 111
fragmentation problem 46–47, 63, 144, 153, 206, 208

gender impacts of science examination question contexts 136–37
Gilman, Shelley 160–62
girls' schools, high-decile 123
global marketplace 11, 14, 26
grades
    see also endorsement of certificates and courses; moderation; profiles of expected performance (PEPs); variability in assessment
    achievement standards, NCEA 8, 67, 68, 72–77, 78, 110, 114–17
    differentiation as student motivator 77–78, 104–05, 113
    examination results moderating next year's allocations 38
    and learning 48
    School Certificate 35, 36, 37, 113
    Sixth Form Certificate 19, 20, 35–36, 39
grade-score marking 114, 116, 117, 121
grain size of assessments 87, 209
group-assessment standards 170

Hall, Cedric 61–62, 84–85, 90, 91, 98–99
Haque, Bali 88, 97, 109–10

Hart, Sally 190
Hattie, John 100
Hawke, Gary 100
Health and Physical Education learning area 160, 189–93
history teaching 71, 187, 213
    achievement standard example 75–77
Hobsonville Point secondary school 194–98
Home economics course, example 160–62
Hood, David 62, 169, 170

industry training organisations (ITOs) 57, 65
information technologies, authenticity challenges 169, 170–71
interact achievement standards 166, 168
internal assessment 33, 67
    see also variability in assessment
    comparison of pass rates for internal and external assessment 44–45
    liberating potential 46–47
    moderation 7–8, 33–34, 40, 42, 45, 48, 82, 105, 110, 125, 126–33
    NCEA 7, 33–34, 41–43, 65, 70, 75–77, 196, 206
    opportunities 37–41, 133
    PPTA views 17, 18, 62, 63
    press report of poor practice in high decile school 123
    School Certificate 18
    Sixth Form Certificate 19–20
    student workload and experiences 36–37, 181, 196
    teachers' personal

recollections 34–37, 40–41
use of contexts 140–41
International Baccalaureate 98, 103n.1
internet 169

Kear, Andrew 86, 96
knowledge 9–10
   see also learning
   and achievement standards 65
   achievement-based assessment 54
   comparative status of different types 21–22, 29, 106, 189, 190, 192, 215–16
   everyday or prior knowledge 29
   lifeworthy knowledge 29–30, 39–40, 148–49, 154, 163, 177, 186, 191, 192, 193, 198–99, 206, 212
   mixed messages in New Zealand Curriculum 29–30
   recall *versus* ability to link ideas 95
   unit standards assessment 60, 64
knowledge society 15

Labour government policies 13–14, 17–18, 54, 68, 78, 99–100
Lange, David 17
language curriculum 25, 165–68
leadership at policy–practice intersection 213–16
learning
   see also knowledge
   academic 6
   and assessment judgements 48, 49–50
   attitudes needed for success 175
   egalitarian approach to valuing 21–22, 106
   employment-oriented 6, 12, 21, 22, 57, 191
   for gaining of qualifications 5–6, 20, 24–25, 43, 95, 153, 176–77, 182, 183–88, 194, 215
   lifeworthy learning 29–30, 39–40, 148–49, 154, 163, 177, 186, 191, 192, 193, 198–99, 206, 212
   purposes 24–25, 26, 27, 28, 39, 153–54, 183, 186
learning areas 22–24, 25, 27, 28, 29, 160, 183
   Health and Physical Education 160, 189–93
   Learning Languages 165–68, 179–80, 183, 191
learning contexts 134, 135–37, 138–39, 143–45
   contextual and conceptual integration within a course 160–62
   emotional engagement of students 141–43
   language teaching and learning 165–68, 179–80, 183, 191
   opportunities to display deeper learning 139
Learning Curves research project 78–79, 185–86, 188, 192
liberal-arts education 104
lifeworthy knowledge and learning 29–30, 39–40, 148–49, 154, 163, 177, 186, 191, 192, 193, 198–99, 206, 212
literacy-related standards 8, 78, 119, 120–21, 173–74, 177
Lowther, Helen 142–43

MacManus, Gerard 141–42
Mallard, Trevor 68, 78
managing-national-assessment (MNA) visits 128–29
Mandelbrot set 203
Māori
    see also Treaty of Waitangi
    activism 16
    students 79, 191–92, 193, 194
market-oriented policy 13–14, 15, 17, 18
marking
    check marking 125, 126, 132
    grade-score marking 114, 116, 117, 121
    marking by error 50
    sufficiency marking 114–16
Marshall, Russell 17, 64, 65
media studies 24, 25
Ministry of Education 18, 54, 72, 118, 124, 151, 169, 211, 213, 214, 216
    see also Department of Education
    ART (Achievement, Retention, Transition) initiative 175–76
moderation 122, 215
    annual analysis by NZQA 129
    best-practice workshops 129, 132
    for internal assessment 7–8, 33–34, 40, 42, 45, 48, 82, 105, 110, 122, 125, 126–33
    managing-national-assessment (MNA) visits 128–29
    shifting emphasis 129–33
    Sixth Form Certificate 19
    teachers' personal recollections 122–24
    three ways of carrying out 124–26
    validity 131

Monitoring and Evaluating Curriculum Implementation (MECI) project 152
Moses, Roger 98, 99, 103–04, 106–07, 111, 113
motivation of students 77–78, 104–05, 111, 113, 135, 184, 187–88, 196–97
"sporty" kids 191–93

National Certificate in Employment Skills 153
National Certificate of Educational Achievement see NCEA
National government policies 13, 14, 15, 18, 54–55, 95–96, 100, 174–75
National Standards School Sample Monitoring and Evaluation Project 128
naturally occurring evidence 70, 174
Nature of Science (NOS) strand 157–58, 160
NCEA
    see also achievement standards, NCEA; student experiences of NCEA; and other topics, e.g. credits, NCEA
    assessment pressures in lead-up 18–20
    complex intersection between curriculum and assessment 205–07
    core aims 21
    as diverse and resilient system 209–10
    earlier qualification with same name (1990s) 69
    flexibility 5, 18, 78, 153, 154, 168, 176, 177–79, 194–98, 205, 206, 208, 215–16

impact of system-wide influences 168–74
implementation 68, 78–79, 88, 97, 106, 109, 151, 183
influence on *New Zealand Curriculum* 164–68
levels 7, 8–9, 68, 72–75, 195, 196, 197
modular structure 78, 149, 153, 154, 193
overview 6–9
post-2007 reforms 97, 109–21
reimagining through complexity thinking 207–09
success 5, 174–77, 198, 199
as system that can learn 210–13
teachers' personal recollections 68–72
teachers' workloads 31, 167, 181, 210, 217
toleration of failure 211–12
washback to teaching and learning 164–80
neoliberalism 13–14
New Zealand Association for Science Education 167
New Zealand Association of Languages Teachers 167
New Zealand Curriculum (*NZC*) 4, 21, 22, 147, 170, 177
see also course design
achievement standards written to same achievement objectives 118–19
aligning with assessment 151–63, 165, 167, 168
competencies 27, 145, 152
framework for curriculum design 26–27, 149, 152, 153, 154, 182

Hobsonville Point secondary school 194–98
influence of NCEA 164–68
and knowledge 29–30, 147–49
selecting content for teaching 147–49
senior secondary curriculum 25–26
senior secondary years 182
vision statement 27, 28, 29, 217
New Zealand Qualifications Authority (NZQA) 9, 18, 42, 43, 54, 55, 57, 62, 69, 72, 211, 213
annual analysis of internal assessment performance 129
authenticity management 168–71
best-practice workshops 129, 132
Education and Science Select Committee report, 2005 96
management of variability 82, 84–85, 86, 87, 88, 89, 96–97, 109, 123, 127–33
managing-national-assessment (MNA) visits 128–29
NCEA post-2007 reforms 97, 109–21
restructuring 97, 109
and Scholarship examination 97, 98–99, 100, 104
New Zealand Qualifications Framework (NZQF) 7, 69, 153, 182
New Zealand Scholarship *see* Scholarship crisis, 2005; Scholarship syllabus and examination
New Zealand Transport Agency (NZTA) 141–42
New Zealand Vice Chancellors' Committee 62, 87–88, 118

235

Newlands College, Wellington 158–60
norm-referenced assessment model 3, 12, 16, 20, 38, 40, 63, 82–84, 90–91, 100, 101, 102, 103
Scholarship 104–06
numeracy-related standards 8, 78, 119, 120–21, 173–74
NZCER National Survey of Secondary Schools 103, 152, 164, 165, 176, 187

on-balance judgements 61
Organisation for Economic Co-operation and Development (OECD) 27
outcomes-based curriculum 22–23, 24, 25, 28, 29, 56, 57–61, 75–76, 134, 155, 183–84
over-assessment 183, 184, 186, 206

parents and families
 expectations 4–5, 70
 Hobsonville Point secondary school 197
 understanding of NCEA 193
parity of esteem 21, 29, 78, 79, 80, 106, 111, 112, 189, 215–16
Pasifika
 activism 16
 students 79, 191–92, 193, 194
PEPs *see* profiles of expected performance (PEPs)
Perkins, David 29–30, 148, 154, 192, 199
physical development of young children learning task 142–43
Physical World strand 156
plagiarism 168, 169, 170–71
Planet Earth and Beyond strand 155–56

policy
 Labour government policies 13–14, 17–18, 54, 68, 78, 99–100
 leadership at policy–practice intersection 213–16
 market-oriented policy 13–14, 15, 17, 18
 National government policies 13, 14, 15, 18, 54–55, 95–96, 100, 174–75
 ongoing work 211–13
 responses to economic and social changes 16–18, 26–28, 63
Post Primary Teachers' Association (PPTA) 16–17, 18, 62, 63, 88, 111–12, 175
Poutasi, Karen 97
powerful knowledge 9–10
Principals' Lead Group 69–70, 103
principles, *New Zealand Curriculum* 27
professional learning 216–17
 from moderation 45, 122, 123, 124, 125, 126, 128–29, 132, 133, 174
 NCEA standards and practices 206
profiles of expected performance (PEPs) 88–91, 96, 102, 115–16, 117, 126
provider qualifications 62

qualifications
 achievement of students 5, 198
 growing demand 14, 15
 as measurement of success 213
 NCEA core aim 21, 153
 post-war years 12
 as primary purpose for learning 5–6, 20, 24–25, 43, 95,

153, 176–77, 182, 183–88, 194, 215
    provider qualifications 62
    school leavers without qualifications 12, 14, 16, 106, 175, 193, 198
quality assurance *see* moderation
quasi-norms for external assessment 64
Queen's High School, Dunedin 142–43

recall *versus* ability to link ideas 95
Renwick, Bill 18
retention, secondary school 5, 14, 15, 16, 18, 38, 183, 198
Rhoades, David 131
Ross, Jim 64

safe driving learning and assessment task 141–42
safe-to-fail experiments 210
scaling, normative 12, 38, 82–83, 89, 90, 117
    PEPs compared to scaling 89–91
Scholarship crisis, 2005 69, 93, 98–99, 130, 212
    new examination process 100–02, 107, 114
    political fallout 99–100
    teachers' personal recollections 94–97
Scholarship Processes Advisory Group (SPAG) 100–01, 103
Scholarship syllabus and examination 9, 22, 37, 67
    comparison with NCEA processes 102
    Outstanding Scholarship award 100, 101, 102

Scholarship Technical Advisory Group (STAG) 100–01
School Certificate 19, 22, 34, 35, 40, 55, 66, 79, 112, 136, 208
    content coverage emphasis 71–72, 73
    grades based on previous year's School Certificate marks 36
    grain size of assessment 87
    internal assessment 18, 110
    major school exit-examination 12, 38
    norm-referencing of Sixth Form Certificate 83
    ranking 113, 117
    scaling 12, 38, 82, 89, 90, 117
    students' recollections 36–37
    as teacher qualification 15
science
    coherent course design 155–57
    curriculum 23, 25, 27, 71–72
    gender impacts of science examination question contexts 136–37
    prerequisites for specialist subjects 193
    reason for including science in *New Zealand Curriculum* 157
    science practices 170
Science in the New Zealand Curriculum 71, 155
Scottish Vocational Educational Council 61
secondary education
    assessment results as indicator of school quality 43–44
    autonomy of schools in curriculum-building 213–14
    economic change as context for educational change 13–15

NZCER National Survey of Secondary Schools 103, 152
post-war years 11–12
retention 5, 14, 15, 16, 18, 38, 183, 198
senior secondary curriculum before *NZC* 22–25, 183
senior secondary curriculum in *NZC* 25–26
transition to university study 6, 13, 51, 172, 177–80
Secondary Principals Association of New Zealand 88
semiskilled labour 12, 14
Sewell, Karen 96, 97, 109
Sixth Form Certificate 17, 19–20, 22, 35–36, 37, 39, 55, 66, 82, 83
skills
and achievement standards 65, 77, 80
semiskilled labour 12, 14
unskilled labour 12, 13, 14
Smith, Lockwood 15, 22, 63, 70, 89
Snelling, Bill 104
social conservatives 16
social justice 79, 106, 112–13
see also equity; parity of esteem
social moderation 124, 126, 127, 128, 129
social sciences curriculum 23, 25, 27
society, New Zealand
diversity 11, 14, 16, 28
education policy responses to changes 16–18, 26–28
specialisation in workplace 26
Sport in Education initiative 144
"sporty" students 191–92
St Matthews Collegiate, Masterton 160–62

standards 7
see also achievement standards, NCEA; unit standards
ABA as learning for standards-based assessment 51–54
combination 8–9, 187–88, 196, 209
standards-referenced assessment model 3–4, 17, 24, 65, 84–85, 90–91, 97–98, 100, 101, 102, 103
and endorsements 111, 112–13
and grade-score marking 117, 121
Scholarship 105, 106
Starpath research team, Auckland University 193–94
State Services Commission 88, 96, 97, 130, 131, 132, 211
statistical moderation 125–26, 129, 131–32
Strachan, Jim 49, 69–70, 86, 90, 96, 102, 110
streamed classes 12
structured observations of learning outcomes (SOLO) taxonomy 53
student experiences of NCEA 4–5, 181–88, 198–99
academic students 121, 190–91, 192
Hobsonville Point secondary school 194–98
labelling 121, 191–92, 193
making choices 181, 189, 193–94, 198
skipping assessments 181, 189, 194, 206
"sporty" students 191–92
tracking of progress 194
vocational students 121, 191–92
workload 181, 196

subject associations 214, 215
sufficiency marking 114–16

teachers
    see also assessment judgements of teachers; professional learning
    accountability 39, 123, 125, 126–27, 130, 131, 132, 133
    curriculum choices and perceptions of student options 189–93
    education and qualifications 15, 216
    manipulation of assessment results 43–44, 176
    support 180
    workloads 31, 63, 167, 181, 210, 217
teachers' personal recollections
    achievement-based assessment 49–51
    assessment contexts 135
    internal assessment 34–37, 40–41
    moderation 122–24
    NCEA development 68–72
    NZQA reforms 109–10
    Scholarship crisis, 2005 94–97
    unit standards 55–56
    variability in assessment 85–87
technological change 26
technology curriculum 23, 27, 192
Tertiary Education Commission (TEC) 173
tertiary sector, NZQA administration of assessment 57
tertiary study 7, 13, 14–15, 19, 39
    see also university study
thinking
    complexity thinking 201–03, 207–09, 214
    critical thinking 6, 29, 53, 174, 178
    ethical thinking 192
    higher order capabilities 192
    independent thinking 199
Tomorrow's Schools 17–18, 48, 54
Treaty of Waitangi 14, 28, 95

unemployment 12, 13, 14, 175, 198
unit standards 7–8, 54–55, 65–66
    differences from achievement standards 68, 76, 77–79, 111
    double dipping, unit and achievement standards 78–80
    earlier NCEA qualification (1990s) 69, 110
    in employment-based learning 57–58, 61, 65, 77, 80, 188, 192
    examples 57–58, 59
    how they work 56–57
    and idea of endorsements 111, 112–13
    moderation 132
    percentages of results by standard types 42
    phasing out 41, 80
    politics 62, 67
    qualitative and quantitative definitions of achievement 60
    resistance from universities 57, 61–62
    seen as being of low educational worth 78–79, 80, 111, 192
    teachers' personal recollections 55–56
    unsuitability for traditional (disciplinary) subjects 58–62, 64, 67, 78–79

universities
- NZQA administration of assessment 57
- resistance to unit standards 57, 61–62

University Entrance (UE) 9, 12, 16, 17, 19, 38, 55, 82, 108, 118, 121
- accreditation 19, 37, 118
- current requirements 119
- determining literacy and numeracy 120–21
- differentiating from Level 3 NCEA 118–20
- washback effect of approved subjects 171–73
- washback effect of literacy and numeracy requirements 173–74

University Entrance Board (UEB) 19, 39

university study 12, 15, 38, 39, 51
- determining eligibility 118–21
- expectations of first-year students 177–78, 179
- transition from secondary school 6, 13, 51, 172, 177–80

unskilled labour 12, 13, 14

values, *New Zealand Curriculum* 27
Van Rooyen, Karen 100
variability in assessment 81–82, 109
see also Scholarship crisis, 2005
- comparison of Scholarship and NCEA processes 102
- early years of NCEA 84–85, 96
- evolving management processes 88–92, 96–97
- management before NCEA 82–84, 85–86
- masking of pre-NCEA reliability problems 83–84
- predictable challenges of NCEA 87–88
- teachers' personal recollections 85–87

visual communication, as curriculum subject 24, 25

vocational education *see* employment-based (vocational) education

Waihi College 104
Wellington College 98, 99, 103
Wellington, Merv 39
whare tapa whā metaphor 24
work, changing nature 11, 26
writing skills 179

www.ingramcontent.com/pod-product-compliance
Lightning Source LLC
Chambersburg PA
CBHW080803300426
44114CB00020B/2809